IN SEARCH OF
ISAIAH BERLIN

A Literary Adventure

Henry Hardy

I.B. TAURIS

LONDON · NEW YORK

Published in 2018 by
I.B.Tauris & Co. Ltd
London · New York
www.ibtauris.com

Copyright © 2018 Henry Hardy

References to websites were correct at the time of writing.

ISBN: 978 1 78831 244 8
eISBN: 978 1 78672 490 8
ePDF   978 1 78673 490 7

A full CIP record for this book is available from the British Library
A full CIP record is available from the Library of Congress

Library of Congress Catalog Card Number: available

Text designed and set in Garamond Premier by Tetragon, London
Printed and bound by CPI Group (UK) Ltd, Croydon CR0 4YY

For Mary

Well, poor man, he obviously did think of himself as a biographer, but he won't do. He could help: he's been through my works a million times and performs wonderful services – if I don't know where a text is, he takes ten hours and finds it, finds the place.

Berlin in conversation with Michael Ignatieff,
18 June 1989 (MI Tape 11)

Contents

The cellar steps at Headington House: entrance to my Tutankhamun's tomb

List of Illustrations

TEXT IMAGES

CREDITS: © The Trustees of the Isaiah Berlin Literary Trust and Henry Hardy, except 122, 136, 229 Oxford, Bodleian Library, MS. Berlin 545 fo. 399, 570 fo. 59, 562 fo. 424, scans © Bodleian Library, Oxford; 150 © University of Kent; 152 Richard Willson / Guardian News & Media

PLATES

1. With most of the contributors to Berlin's first Festschrift
2. Headington House
3. Berlin's study at Headington House
4. Berlin's heroes and villains on his study door
5. At the BBC, London, 1964, for an episode of *Conversations for Tomorrow*
6. Supporting Wolfson College during Eights Week with Aline
7. In his room in All Souls
8. With Imogen Cooper
9. With the Israeli novelist Amos Oz
10. During his 1995 BBC TV interview with Michael Ignatieff

CREDITS: 1 Sandra Burman; 2 family of Isaiah Berlin; 3 Andrew Strauss; 4 Serena Moore; 5 copyright © BBC Photo Library; 6 Alice Kelikian; 7 John Crossley; 8 <www.johnbatten photography.co.uk>; 9 Heritage Image Partnership Ltd / Alamy Stock Photo; 10 BBC Motion Gallery / Getty Images, copyright © BBC (camera: Steve Plant)

Preface

> The last part of the Epilogue is full of good ideas the johnny can't work
> out. And of course, in the phrase of critics, would have been better left
> out. So it would; only Tolstoy couldn't leave it out. It was what he wrote
> the book for.
>
> *Arnold Bennett on* War and Peace [1]

This book combines two rather different narratives, both based on my extensive
correspondence with Isaiah Berlin. The first is the story of my work as Berlin's
editor. The second relates our philosophical exchanges about pluralism, religious
belief and human nature. Either part can be read without the other if the interests of the reader so dictate. The philosophy is almost entirely self-contained
in chapters 9–11. I could have followed Tolstoy's example and made these
chapters an Epilogue, but the two threads are intertwined, because it was my
response to Berlin's ideas that motivated my work on his writings. I didn't
want to conceal this fact, but I did fillet out the philosophical discussions from
their chronological positions in the editorial story so that they could be read
separately or simply skipped.

Berlin used to describe the way the nineteenth-century Russian intelligentsia
processed Western ideas as the 'boomerang effect':

> Transformed and vitalised by contact with the unexhausted Russian
> imagination – by being taken seriously by men resolved to practise what
> they believed – some of these ideas returned to the West, and made a
> vast impact upon it. They left it as secular, theoretical, abstract doctrines;
> they returned as fiery, sectarian, quasi-religious faiths. (SR 195)

It would be hubris to compare my obsessive worrying away at Berlin's ideas with
this phenomenon, or with Tolstoy's epilogue, but it is true that I took Berlin's
ideas seriously and tried to show that they had implications he had neglected;
and recording these investigations, for all that they report ideas this johnny
can't work out, was a primary motive for writing the book.

*

If any readers are curious about the personal background of the author, they may like to read the brief autobiographical sketch at http://bit.ly/2L9tWtb.

The acronyms used to refer to Berlin's books are listed on pages xiii–xiv. The selective biographical glossary on pages 285–6 comprises what were originally footnotes on selected persons mentioned in the text.

I should like to thank those who read drafts of the book and suggested improvements, which I have plagiarised at will: George Crowder, Kei Hiruta, Esther Johnson,* Ana Martins (who also suggested the book's main title), Beata Polanowska-Sygulska, Tatiana Wilde, my editor at I.B.Tauris (who also suggested the subtitle), and my copy-editor Sarah Terry. For help on particular points I am indebted to John Barnard, Angie Goodgame, Samuel Guttenplan, Nicholas Hall, Deborah Laidlaw and Mary Hardy. I also wish to take this opportunity to thank a number of colleagues who, in various roles, have given me vital editorial, archival, administrative or secretarial help in my work on Berlin's texts over nearly fifty years: Brigid Allen, Victoria Benner, the late Betty Colquhoun, James Chappel, Georgina Edwards, Hugh Eveleigh, Jason Ferrell, Steffen Groß, Nicholas Hall again, Roger Hausheer, Jennifer Holmes, Michael Hughes, Esther Johnson again, Aileen Kelly, Serena Moore, Derek Offord, Eleonora Paganini, Kate Payne, Mark Pottle, Tatiana Pozdnyakova, Kim Reynolds, Teisha Ruggiero, Natalya Sarana, Norman Solomon, Josephine von Zitzewitz.

Acknowledgement is due to Laurie Taylor and *Times Higher Education* for permission to quote the passage on p. 94.

My fellow trustees of the Isaiah Berlin Literary Trust have asked me to state that I wrote this book in my personal capacity, not as a trustee, and that all the views I express are therefore offered as mine alone.

HENRY HARDY
Heswall, July 2018

* For Esther's own encounters with Berlin, see her late husband Michael Johnson's essay 'Meeting Isaiah Berlin', available at http://bit.ly/2zE4kAd.

Abbreviations

All books are by Berlin unless otherwise indicated. Second and later editions are distinguished by adding the relevant Arabic numeral to the abbreviation for the title, so that RT2 is the second edition of RT. Page references are given by plain number, followed after an oblique stroke by the note number if relevant (so 10 = p. 10 of this book; AC2 138/1 = *Against the Current*, 2nd ed., p. 138, note 1). Full details of the items listed are available in the IBVL (see below).

A biographical glossary of some of the persons mentioned in the book follows the text.

A	*Affirming: Letters 1975–1997*
AC	*Against the Current: Essays in the History of Ideas*
AE	*The Age of Enlightenment: The Eighteenth-Century Philosophers*
B	*Building: Letters 1960–1975*
BI	*The Book of Isaiah: Personal Impressions of Isaiah Berlin*, ed. Henry Hardy
CC	*Concepts and Categories: Philosophical Essays*
CIB	*Conversations with Isaiah Berlin* by Ramin Jahanbegloo
CTH	*The Crooked Timber of Humanity: Chapters in the History of Ideas*
E	*Enlightening: Letters 1946–1960*
F	*Flourishing: Letters 1928–1946* (hardback US edition published as *Letters 1928–1946*)
FE	'Isaiah Berlin: 2 Freedom and Its Enemies', the second of two programmes about IB's life and times, consisting in large part of interviews of IB by Michael Ignatieff, recorded 15–17 May 1995, produced by David Herman, and first broadcast 15 November 1997 on BBC2 TV
FEL	*Four Essays on Liberty* (superseded by L)
FIB	*Freedom and its Betrayal: Six Enemies of Human Freedom*
FL	*The First and the Last*
HF	*The Hedgehog and the Fox: An Essay on Tolstoy's View of History*
HH	Henry Hardy

IB   Isaiah Berlin

IBVL   The Isaiah Berlin Virtual Library, http://bit.ly/2JoYMJo

KM   *Karl Marx: His Life and Environment* (subtitle dropped in KM5)

L   *Liberty*

LL   'I'm Going To Tamper with Your Beliefs A Little', dialogue between IB and Stuart Hampshire (the 2nd of 6 films on Oxford philosophy collectively known as *Logic Lane*, directed by Michael Chanan and produced by Noel Chanan), transcript at http://bit.ly/2JmO7it

MI   Michael Ignatieff

MIIB   MI, *Isaiah Berlin: A Life*

MI Tape   tape-recorded conversation with MI

MSB   Oxford, Bodleian Library, MS. Berlin (by shelfmark/folio, e.g. MSB 325/56)

NYRB   the *New York Review of Books*

ODQ   *The Oxford Dictionary of Quotations*

OED   *Oxford English Dictionary*

OM   *The One and the Many: Reading Isaiah Berlin*, ed. George Crowder and Henry Hardy

OUP   Oxford University Press

PI   *Personal Impressions*

PIRA   *Political Ideas in the Romantic Age: Their Rise and Influence on Modern Thought*

POI   *The Power of Ideas*

PSM   *The Proper Study of Mankind: An Anthology of Essays*

PU   Pat(ricia) Utechin

R   rushes for FE

RR   *The Roots of Romanticism*

RT   *Russian Thinkers*

SM   *The Soviet Mind: Russian Culture under Communism*

SR   *The Sense of Reality: Studies in Ideas and Their History*

TCE   *Three Critics of the Enlightenment: Vico, Hamann, Herder*

TCL   'Two Concepts of Liberty'

THES   *The Times Higher Education Supplement*

TLS   *The Times Literary Supplement*

UD   *Unfinished Dialogue* (with Beata Polanowska-Sygulska)

VH   *Vico and Herder* (superseded by TCE)

Introduction

THE GENIUS AND THE PEDANT

There is something to be said occasionally for bringing a young man forward.[1]

H. A. L. Fisher to Tresham Lever, 22 February 1932

I

This book tells the story of a serendipitous relationship between a thinker, writer and talker of genius and an editor with a strong liability to obsessive pedantry. Serendipitous, because neither participant planned that the encounter between them should occur, let alone have the outcome that it did.

The genius did not plan at all. 'What is the plan for today?' his mother used to ask him when she brought him breakfast in bed in their large house at 33 Upper Addison Gardens in Kensington. 'That used to madden me,' he told his biographer. '"I have no plan. I don't intend to have a plan." At the age of thirteen I said that. "Plan?"'[2]

The pedant planned too much, worrying about what to do with his life, and ended up spending most of it on a project that he could never even have conceived of if his path had not chanced to cross with that of the genius. He has never regretted the consequences of this happenstance.

Editorial work is thought of – if it is thought of at all – as a kind of low-grade literary drudgery best kept behind the scenes. It has been well said that the best editorial work is the least visible. But the form of intellectual midwifery practised by editors in their best moments can prove surprisingly exhilarating, both as an experience and in its results. To be sure, there are large tracts of drudgery to navigate. But the vision that informs the drudgery can infuse it with life and make it the instrument of a higher creative purpose.

There are many different kinds of editor, from the grand panjandrum editors of journalism and broadcasting to the humble publishers' copy-editors who ensure consistency and accuracy in a printed text. In the middle ground between these extremes we find the editor who sees a possible book or books in a dispersed collection of material, perceiving that this material can be structured to form a whole greater than the sum of its parts. Here too we find the editor who works on an unpolished, unpublished text – perhaps an abandoned rough draft, or a transcript of extempore spoken remarks – in order to bring it to publishable form. This is the territory where the present story unfolds, and here, as always, the editorial task is to enable readers to hear the author's voice as directly as possible, to prevent their being distracted, least of all by 'the trail of the passing editor'.[3]

The editor's role in the present case was more challenging, and proportionately more satisfying, than he could have dreamt. The genius was prolific, but had no desire to publish his work. He said that he wrote only on commission, like a taxi that does not move unless it is hailed. He was content that his addresses and lectures, once delivered, should waste their sweetness on the desert air, and that his occasional publications, often extracted from him with considerable reluctance, should languish in the pages of institutional pamphlets or esoteric journals. He admitted to no conception of having produced a large body of work of permanent value to a wide readership, work that could be coherently assembled in a series of thematic volumes. He did not see himself as having any kind of simple resonant message to deliver (except, perhaps, a warning against simple resonant messages), and did not seek disciples.

Those who knew his writings took a different view, and were concerned that his work was not being given its due. It ought to be salvaged from its piecemeal dispersal, organised, and rescued for posterity. There was a large editorial job here that badly needed doing. It was an exciting but daunting job that took forty years to complete. It transformed the editor's life, as well as the author's reputation.

The man of genius was a Russian Jew from the city of Riga named Isaiah Berlin, a philosopher, historian of ideas and public moralist who was born in 1909 and died in 1997. The pedantic editor is the Englishman who is writing these words, and who will now move to the first person.

I both loved and feared Berlin. The love is easier to understand. He was lovable in so many ways: brilliant, ebullient, engaged, positive, generous, inspired; delighted with the kaleidoscope of life almost like a child; overflowing with intellectual and moral charm; intensely interested in people and their ideas, and able to bring both to vivid life in speech and on paper to a magical degree, unparalleled in my experience.

The fear stemmed from his power over me. For the last twenty-five years of his life I worked with him as the main editor of his collected essays, always subject to his revocable acquiescence. He systematically underestimated the worth of his writings (while maintaining that he was systematically overestimated by others), and was liable to change his mind capriciously about what to include, even if I had already done the relevant work on the basis of an earlier assurance. He was almost pathologically indecisive. In one case, as will be seen, he even tried to withdraw a whole volume that I had readied for publication.

I should not have wished him to be bound by a decision that no longer seemed right to him. But it was frustrating that he was not more constant, careful and considerate, and I was continuously apprehensive that the rug would be pulled from under my feet. No matter how many volumes were published to enthusiastic critical acclaim, he was no more amenable to a proposal from me to publish another, and the case always had to be made again from scratch. The same happened after his death in 1997, when some of the literary trustees appointed by his widow Aline proved just as resistant to further publications. The *coup de grâce* came in 2017, when an offer from the publisher of this book to reissue Berlin's *The Age of Enlightenment* in a new edition was rejected, in the teeth of the trust's basic duty of keeping Berlin's work in print.

By the time of Berlin's death I had published eight new volumes. Seven more, and three new editions of works he had published before my involvement, appeared posthumously. A four-volume edition of his letters was completed in 2015. Now at last the main task is finished, and it is time to look back and tell the pedant's tale.

II

Question 34: What natural talent would you like to have?
Isaiah Berlin: Genius.[4]

What *is* a genius? I find the official definition seriously wanting. The OED defines a genius as 'an exceptionally intelligent or talented person'. In other words, genius is an ordinary ability possessed to an extraordinary degree. But this isn't right. A genius can do something quite different from ordinary mortals – different in kind, not just in degree.

3

I have no doubt that Berlin was a genius. Before I explain why, let me quote what he himself had to say about genius – a category that fascinated him, like intellectual depth.

A favourite definition drew on a remark by the ballet dancer Vatslav Nijinsky, a figure of legendary genius:

> I am sometimes asked what I mean by this highly evocative but imprecise term. In answer I can say only this. The dancer Nijinsky was once asked how he managed to leap so high. He is reported to have answered that he saw no great problem in this. Most people, when they leapt in the air, came down at once. 'Why should you come down immediately? Stay in the air a little before you return, why not?' he is reported to have said. One of the criteria of genius seems to me to be the power to do something perfectly simple and visible which ordinary people cannot, and know that they cannot, do – nor do they know how it is done, or why they cannot begin to do it. (PI3 380)

Defying gravity is not leaping higher than the rest of us: it is doing something the rest of us cannot do at all. Of course Nijinsky could not actually defy gravity: but he seemed to, and thereby displayed his genius.

Berlin also used to say that genius created new possibilities. Of the great Russian poet Anna Akhmatova, whom he first met in Leningrad in 1945, he said:

> I was suddenly in the presence of a poet of genius who revealed feelings, thoughts, forms of life which I never would have understood if they hadn't been [revealed]: [...] one's imagination was enormously widened by the mere fact that this person existed. (FE)

So it was by his own existence.

Berlin also gave us some clues to the presence of genius, some symptoms in oneself of encountering it. In particular, talking to a person of genius makes one's mind race. For him, Boris Pasternak and Virginia Woolf showed genius of this kind:

> Pasternak was a poet of genius in all that he did and was; his ordinary conversation displayed it as his writings do. I cannot begin to describe its quality. The only other person who seems to me to have talked as he

talked was Virginia Woolf, who, to judge from the few occasions on which I met her, made one's mind race as he did, and obliterated one's normal vision of reality in the same exhilarating and, at times, terrifying way. (PI3 380)

He used to say something similar about Ludwig Wittgenstein: 'Wittgenstein was a man of genius and he really did excite people immoderately' (LL 11); and again, 'I felt I was in the presence of a very demanding genius: [...] the examples were wonderful – "Half a mo', half a mo', I will think of an example"' (R). And about another philosophical genius, his friend John Austin, he said:

> He was certainly the ablest person I ever knew intimately among philosophers. When he was alone with one he was marvellous to talk with, because he didn't insist on one's translating one's own language into his language or some particular official language into which everything had to be translated. He understood what one said perfectly, talked about it with extreme acuteness and lucidity, and made one's thoughts race. (LL 8)

Talking to Berlin made one's thoughts race too, and made one feel briefly more intelligent than one knew oneself to be. With his rapid-fire bass delivery, the syllables tripping over themselves as his thoughts rushed ahead of his voice, he was a catalyst of intellectual vivacity – another criterion of genius. He made you feel larger than life, raised to a higher level; he trained his eye on you and you felt that at that moment you were the centre of his attention, the only person who mattered. He made the world of the mind intensely alive, personal, important, exhilarating – and fun – in a way that was quite new to me when I first met him. He liked to define an intellectual as someone who wants ideas to be as interesting as possible, and that definition provides part of the answer to those who ask why he was, and is, so celebrated. He perfectly exemplified what Germaine de Staël said of her contemporary Jean Jacques Rousseau: he 'set everything on fire' (FIB2 28).

One last definition of genius that Berlin offered is that it turns a paradox into a platitude. That too is a test Berlin himself passes, if only with his celebrated deployment of 'pluralism' – the recognition that ultimate human values, and the cultures they compose, are irreducibly plural, sometimes incompatible, and often incommensurable. Even if he did not originate this insight, he placed it front and centre and inaugurated the pluralist movement in contemporary moral philosophy, and a wider general awareness of pluralism, to which we shall return.

The personalities of most geniuses of the past are preserved only on paper, which makes it hard to convey the nature of their genius vividly. Fortunately, numerous recordings of Berlin, both audio and video, have been preserved, and one can cull from them suggestive evidence of his own particular genius. Before I try to convey further what this was, let me quote Berlin in full flow from one of these recordings. In a 1976 interview with Bryan Magee, he agrees with Magee's suggestion that philosophical questions are like questions asked by children:

> Children ask these questions of their elders. They don't say, 'What is time?' [...] What they say is, 'Why can't I meet Napoleon?' Supposing a child said that – it seems a quite natural thing for a child to do – and you say, 'You can't. He's dead.' And then [the child asks], 'Why is this? Why does this prevent one?' And then, if the father is sophisticated enough, he has to explain that death means the body becomes dissolved in the ground, he can't be resurrected, it happened a long time ago. And then [...] a sophisticated child will say, 'Well, can't all the bits be brought together again?' And then the father says, 'No, they can't.' What kind of 'can't'? And then a lesson in physics follows.
>
> And the child says, 'No, I don't really want that. I don't want Napoleon now. I want to go back to see him as he was at the Battle of Austerlitz. That's what I'd like.' 'Well, you can't,' says the father. 'Why not?' 'Because you can't move back in time.' 'Why can't I?' Then we have a philosophical problem. What is meant by 'can't'? Is not being able to move back in time the same sort of 'can't' as when you say 'Twice two can't be seven', or the same sort of 'can't' as when you say 'You can't buy cigarettes at two o'clock in the morning, because there's a law against it'? Or 'I can't remember'? Or 'I can't make myself nine foot tall by merely wishing it'? What sort of 'can't'? [...] And then we are plunged into philosophy straightaway.
>
> And then you have to say, 'Well, the nature of time.' And then some people would say, 'No, no, there isn't such a thing as time. "Time" is just a word for "before" and "after" and "simultaneously with". To talk about time as if it was a kind of *thing* is a metaphysical trap.' And we're launched.
>
> Well, most fathers don't want to answer the questions of their children in that way. They just tell them to shut up, not to ask silly questions: 'Go

and climb a tree.' But these are the questions which constantly recur; and philosophers are the people who are not terrified of them, and are prepared to deal with them. Children, of course, are ultimately conditioned into not asking these questions, more's the pity. The children who are not so conditioned turn into philosophers.[5]

What, then, *was* Berlin's genius? In a phrase, I should say that it was a genius for being human. A human of a certain kind, naturally: no one can be all things to all men. He was centrally concerned with people, and with their ideas – the life of the mind – but not only that. His genius was an accumulation of separate strands, none decisive by itself, but all simultaneously present in all that he did and was, especially in the way he thought and talked, creating a coherent personality that was arresting in the requisite way. Among these strands were incisive intelligence; intense engagement with the topic at hand; unflaggingly benign good humour and accentuation of the positive, seeing the point of people (mostly) rather than cutting them down to size; effortless wideness of reference over a huge range; extraordinary fluency in conversation and writing, with a nineteenth-century command of language, free from all empty critical jargon (no talk of *narrative* or *discourse*); sharp perceptiveness about human nature in general, and the particular nature of specific individuals; and utter lack of self-importance – 'I may be wrong; these are my views, for what they are worth'; 'I don't see myself as a person of much importance – and this is not false modesty, this is sheer realism' (R).

The final component of his genius that I want to mention is first-handedness, by which I mean the absence, as he used to put it of others, of anything between him and the object. He saw directly – not through a theoretical glass, darkly. He said this about the Russian critic Vissarion Belinsky, about Lord David Cecil, about Stephen Spender, about Wittgenstein. This unmediated contact with his subject matter brings to mind Schiller's distinction between the two types of poets that he called 'naive' and 'sentimental' – in Berlin's paraphrase, 'those who are not conscious of any rift between themselves and their milieu, or within themselves; and those who are so conscious' (AC2 361).

Berlin's directness of vision and comparative lack of self-consciousness makes him, for me, more naive than sentimental. This is paradoxical, given that he deploys the distinction himself in a celebrated essay of 1968 entitled 'The Naivety of Verdi', where the passage I have just quoted is to be found. Paradoxical, because the ability to distinguish the naive from the sentimental might be thought possible only for the sentimental, just as people with mono-chrome vision might be thought to be unable to contrast their own way of seeing with the usual polychrome version. Nevertheless, my placing of Berlin in the naive camp, in this special sense, seems to me to be right, far from naive as he was in the ordinary sense. He was not an ironic spectator.

Let me return to the first quality I listed, Berlin's intelligence, and make it more specific. I should not claim that Berlin was the most intelligent person I have ever met, but he had a special intellectual ability that he himself described in a letter of 11 December 1944 to his wartime colleague Donald Hall: 'I see a pattern on the carpet' (MSB 255/10). George Kennan captured this ability in a letter to Berlin of 16 June 1958:

> You have unquestionably the greatest critical mind of this generation – warmed with a charity that might well be the envy of 99 out of 100 Christians, and enriched with an ordering power so extraordinary that its mere operation is itself a creative act, affecting that which it touches & even changing it – just as scientific experimentation is said to alter, by its own action, the substance it is supposed to illuminate.

I cannot explain this power, but I can confirm that Berlin had it. One way in which it operated was that he grasped what you were going to say as soon as you began saying it, and what the next several conversational moves were going to be. As so often, he recognised his own qualities (if not *as* his own) in others, in this case in Maynard Keynes: 'He was the cleverest man I ever met. He knew what the end of your sentence was going to be almost before you began it' (R). In his written work, too, Berlin saw straight to the heart of a mass of distracting detail with a preternatural acuteness.

There is another paradox here, because Berlin was also fascinated by incon-sequential detail for its own sake, especially the idiosyncratic detail of people's lives and characters:

> When I walk in the street I like looking at people's faces: too much so – sometimes I start staring and they don't like it. But I like the shape of their heads, the expression on their faces [...]. There was a German poet in New Zealand during the war who was asked, 'What kind of landscapes do you like best?' He said, 'Human beings are my landscape.'[6] Entirely true of me. (R)

The poet was the German Jew Karl Wolfskehl. Berlin often quoted this phrase, for example in a letter to Marietta Tree of 16 August 1968, in which he also wrote: 'Like a bad encyclopaedia I am always trying to pepper people with a mass of trivial & obscure small facts which merely clutter up the memory gratuitously' (B 359). And to Denis Noël, a young admirer who wrote to him out of the blue on 14 October 1996, just over a year before Berlin died: 'I am fascinated by the vagaries of your life' (A 359).

This propensity helps to explain Berlin's taste for gossip, though it should be added that in his case the gossip was (usually) benign. But it was not only people who caught his attention: he loved gadgets and bric-a-brac too, and was often seduced by junk-shop windows into stepping inside and making bizarre purchases. Here is James Douglas, husband of the anthropologist Mary Douglas, remembering tutorials with him at New College before the war:

> He kept an odd collection of things which he had bought off the street traders who in those days sold things from the pavement in Regent Street, and also a magnificent gramophone with a handmade papier mâché trumpet, the then current equivalent of today's high fidelity equipment. As I would read my essay to him, he would wander round the room toying with his collection: a toy cow would fall off an inclined plane – 'I am so sorry! Please continue'; a blast of Verdi would emerge from the gramophone's trumpet as he accidentally dropped the needle on the disc – 'I am so sorry! Please continue.'[7]

Berlin's attraction to specific, unrepeatable detail is connected to his resistance to scientism, which is the assimilation of all disciplines to the model of the natural sciences: these he saw as predominantly concerned with what things and events have in common rather than with what makes them unique. But at the same time he was preoccupied with questions located at the other extreme of human affairs, especially the most general questions of morals and politics, which he often posed in resonant monosyllables: What is to be done? How should one live? Why are we here? What must we be and do?

Our answers to these questions are rooted in our conception of human nature, in our answer to the question 'What is man?', and all Berlin's work can be seen as an enquiry into this most fundamental of all human issues, however varied that work may seem. This was one reason why I called the last book by him published in his lifetime, an anthology of his best essays, *The Proper Study of Mankind*.

Oddly enough, there were gaps in his interest between the two extremes of personal specificities and human generalities, and one of these was day-to-day politics, curiosity about which he disclaimed:

> I was never interested in politics as such, in spite of being Professor of it. Politics were not at the centre of my thought. [...] I wasn't interested in day-to-day events; I was more interested in what might be called – it sounds a very conceited thing to say – in the more permanent aspects of the human world. (R)

That last phrase, 'the more permanent aspects of the human world', well describes the focus of his thought, even though his enquiries into these aspects were usually conducted in terms of the firework display of particularity that they generate. Indeed, his combination of eagle-eyed absorption in the absolutely specific and an exceptional instinct for the general truths that lie beneath is one of the main roots of his genius. There is depth in his concern with surfaces.

Into the life of this genius, in the summer of 1972, when the genius was sixty-three, entered, at the age of twenty-three, the wonderfully fortunate pedant who is now writing these words, five years older than his victim was when he first encountered him. In this case the dictionary definition is nearer the mark: a pedant is 'one who is excessively concerned with accuracy over trifling details of knowledge'. I use the term with some irony, of course – with British self-deprecation. Accuracy is quite rightly a key value in scholarly activity, whether scientific or humanistic, and accuracy about trifling details can be an indispensable foundation of accuracy about what is more important. What is more, Berlin himself strongly believed in even pedantic accuracy, though he was not notably good at achieving it. Once, when telling the story of Bertrand Russell's complaint to God, on arrival at the gates of heaven, that God hadn't provided better evidence of his existence, he observed: 'A very, very pedantic thing to say, but I think he was right' (R). And he wrote to me on 13 November 1975: 'I long for accuracy, even pedantry' (A 13). 'Facts are facts,' he would say when his mistakes were pointed out, or 'Truth is truth.' Maybe his tendency towards inaccuracy was a blessing in disguise, because an obsession with accuracy can act as a brake on creativity. In Berlin's case it also gave the pedant plenty of work to do.

This particular pedant, like many pedants, also exhibited a more general tendency to be obsessive. One form that his particular kind of obsessiveness took was a taste for detailed textual editing, for ensuring that a text was presented just so, so that all possible barriers were removed which might interfere with its impact on the reader: clumsy punctuation, unclarity of expression, distracting ugliness of typographical design. But there was also an echo in his temperament of Berlin's simultaneous interest in the particular and the universal. The particularities that engaged the pedant were the duller ones of scholarly accuracy and editorial precision, but the generalities were similar, since both genius and pedant had the childlike philosophical bent that longs to know the answers to the ultimate questions of human life, and both were dissatisfied with the tendency in some philosophical quarters to dismiss such questions as ill-conceived or even meaningless.

I have slipped back into the third person. It is time to revert, for good, to the first, and to go back to the beginning of the story.

[Tolstoy] was delighted by Belinsky's [...] idea that if one is to understand a writer, one must immerse oneself in him completely – and see only him and nothing else.

(SR 224)

I

THE BEGINNING

This brings the past to life.
Isaiah Berlin[1]

I first met Isaiah Berlin just before lunch on Saturday 24 June 1972, at an interview for admission to Wolfson College, Oxford, which was then not quite six years old, and occupied temporary addresses in North Oxford (47 and 60 Banbury Road) while its new buildings were being constructed on the banks of the river Cherwell at the end of Linton Road. I had driven down to Oxford that morning from Shrewsbury School (where I was working for a year between undergraduate and graduate work at Oxford), after giving my Latin A level set their last lesson on Book 3 of Lucretius' *De rerum natura* (*On the Nature of Things*), which argues against the immortality of the soul and teaches that death is not to be feared. Time was extremely tight, and I was worried about arriving behind schedule. I was indeed late, and flustered.

For many years I have been telling the story that I crashed my ancient Austin A40 just before arrival at my destination. My attention must have wandered for a second; my brakes were probably defective; and I ran into the back of the car in front of me when it stopped at a pedestrian crossing in the Woodstock Road, crushing my lights and bursting my radiator. I still have a clear memory of driving my car on to the pavement and sprinting to my interview. But a letter I wrote to my father at the time shows that this accident actually preceded an interview at Merton College nearly four months earlier. This is a sobering reminder that even the most vivid memories – perhaps especially those – are not to be trusted, a lesson that certainly applies to Berlin's own memory. But there is a link between the inaccurate memory and the true event. Merton did not give me the scholarship for which I had applied. If they had, I should never have met Berlin. I owe Merton a debt of gratitude.

The interview panel at Wolfson had assembled on a Saturday specially for my benefit. This made me even more self-conscious as I entered the first-floor front room of no. 60, which housed the College's then rudimentary library, to face my inquisitors. The panel comprised the President, Isaiah Berlin, the Vice President and Bursar, Michael Brock, and I think the social psychologist Michael Argyle, one of the College's original fellows. Berlin was immediately arresting and disconcerting with his trademark three-piece suit, his machine-gun verbal delivery and his obvious super-intelligence. He had no small talk, then or later, and went straight to the point. He had a lunch date elsewhere and was expecting a taxi. Every so often he would get up and go to the window to see if it had arrived, which added to my discomfiture. I did not yet know that there was an irony here, given his customary insistence that he was not self-starting as an author, but an intellectual taxi.

I cannot have given a very good account of myself. All I remember specifically is that Berlin asked me what I wished to study for the thesis that formed part of the degree course for which I was applying, the BPhil in philosophy. I told him that I wanted to rebut Ludwig Wittgenstein's so-called 'private language argument', in order to defend the possibility of interpersonal communication about the intrinsic quality of subjective experience, a possibility the argument appeared to rule out. 'Oh, are people still interested in that?' he asked in surprised tones. The topic had been much discussed in previous decades, and he seemed to think it by now obsolete. More unease on my part.

Nevertheless, I was for some reason accepted. Michael Brock had also interviewed me at Corpus Christi College (Berlin's own undergraduate college) in 1965 for admission as an undergraduate (though he had left Corpus for Wolfson by the time I came up in 1967), and would have known some of my Corpus referees, which may have helped. In any event, I gradually came to know Berlin well. He was astonishingly present and accessible as President of Wolfson, often sitting in the common room from lunch until dinner, talking to anyone who cared to listen, and sometimes listening to anyone who cared to talk. Unfortunately I can't remember many specific details of these remarkable conversations – or monologues – and regret not keeping a diary. But one or two particular occasions have lodged in my memory. Once a few students were discussing with him possible titles for a Wolfson College magazine that I planned to set up. I had suggested 'Lycidas', which is Greek for 'Wolfson', and which was eventually adopted.[2] Berlin launched into a recitation of Milton's *Lycidas*, much of which he had by heart, while his interlocutors' jaws dropped. He must have learnt the poem when he was a pupil at St Paul's School in London in the 1920s. On another occasion he walked the length and breadth of Oxford with me to meet my landlord, the wildly eccentric antiquarian, numismatist and Anglican vicar of St Frideswide's, Osney, Arnold Mallinson, with whom he hit it off marvellously, talking about the more obscure past members of the royal families of Europe. He also came to the vicarage when the Wolfson choir that I had formed and which I conducted combined forces with the St Frideswide's choir for a special evensong to mark St Frideswide's Day (19 October) in 1973, and premiered an anthem for St Frideswide (patron saint of Oxford)[3] that I had composed to words by my fellow Wolfsonian and fellow lodger Christopher Schenk.[4] Berlin told me, to my surprise, that the piece reminded him of Messiaen, and after the service he paid court to Mallinson in his parlour. Ten years later Berlin and I made the four-mile circuit of the University's Wytham Woods to discuss philosophy: his doctor had advised him to exercise more, but the walk was longer than he expected, and left him somewhat out of breath (even though our average speed was only 2.3 mph), and late for his next appointment.

Like so many others, I was mesmerised by his conversation, unlike any that I had previously encountered – and quickly came to believe that this was a rare human being with a rare understanding of his fellow creatures, and a rare ability to express it. It has often been observed that those who did not know Berlin personally cannot understand his impact on those who did. Berlin himself describes a related problem:

> It is always difficult to convey to others what it is about a particular occasion – particularly a private one – that makes it delightful or memorable. Nothing conveys less to the reader or (rightly) nauseates him more than such passages as 'How we laughed! Tears rolled down our cheeks', or 'His irresistible manner and his inimitable wit drew gusts of merry laughter from us all!' (PI3 105)

Berlin is writing here about a dinner given on a visit to Oxford in 1934 by the US judge Felix Frankfurter. Something similar might be said of any attempt to convey to those who did not meet Berlin what was remarkable about his person or his mind. Fortunately there are resources to draw on that can help circumvent this difficulty – two in particular.

First and foremost, Berlin's mind can be inspected through the medium of his writings and letters. Unlike some other famous conversationalists, for example his contemporary and friend the classicist Maurice Bowra, a celebrated wit in person but less compelling in print, Berlin wrote as he spoke – often literally, since in later life he dictated most of his first drafts, and most of his letters. To read his printed words is to be ushered into his presence at one not too distant remove. Recordings of him talking reinforce this process vividly, even if his sometimes poor articulation and rapid speech can pose problems: he was in this sense not a good lecturer. He was the natural master of long, complex but almost always well-formed sentences, an intuitive prose stylist with more affinities to the nineteenth century than to the twentieth. This was partly due, no doubt, to his Russian origins and his reading of the Russian classics when young. But his style was also very much his own, and readily recognisable, with its timeless vocabulary and plain prose, its unpretentious lucidity, its rushes of well-chosen adjectives. The latter exemplified one of the most marked features of his style: he would use a profuse descriptive verbal cascade to create a cumulative, pointillist picture of his subject. As his friend Noel Annan wrote, with some understatement, 'He will always use two words where one will not do' (PI3 451).

Secondly, Berlin's exceptional gift for viewing the world from the vantage point of another observer paid rich dividends when the person in whose shoes he placed himself partook of his own characteristics. In describing others, he often described himself, brilliantly, if unawares. There is a striking example of this phenomenon in the essay about Frankfurter from which I have just quoted, and the beginning of the passage also illustrates the Berlinian verbal cascade:

> Courage, candour, honesty, intelligence, love of intelligence in others, interest in ideas, lack of pretension, vitality, gaiety, a very sharp sense of the ridiculous, warmth of heart, generosity – intellectual as well as emotional – dislike for the pompous, the bogus, the self-important, the *bien pensant*, for conformity and cowardice, especially in high places, where it is perhaps inevitable – where was such another combination to be found? And then there was the touching and enjoyable Anglomania – the childlike passion for England, English institutions, Englishmen – for all that was sane, refined, not shoddy, civilised, moderate, peaceful, the opposite of brutal, decent – for the liberal and constitutional traditions that before 1914 were so dear to the hearts and imaginations especially of those brought up in Eastern or Central Europe, more particularly to members of oppressed minorities, who felt the lack of them to an

agonising degree, and looked to England and sometimes to America –
those great citadels of the opposite qualities – for all that ensured the
dignity and liberty of human beings. (PI₃ 106)

Hardly any adjustment is needed if this is to stand as a piece of inadvertent
autobiography, answering the rhetorical question about where another such
combination of qualities was to be found. Admittedly, there is a case for not
placing courage in the foreground of an account of Berlin's character, as he himself was aware – though it would be a mistake to exclude it entirely. Maybe, too,
his Anglomania was less childlike than Frankfurter's: more -philia than -mania.
But the rest fits the bill. More generally, it is not hard to elicit from Berlin's
writings a sense of what mattered to him, what personality traits he admired,
what manner of man he himself was. Of course, it is possible to admire people
for possessing qualities one lacks oneself, sometimes the more so just because
one lacks them; but in Berlin's case those who knew him can tell these qualities
apart from those that he shared with the objects of his penetrating gaze.

Three other essays by Berlin, in particular, contain similarly self-descriptive
passages, which I reproduce here because they convey his living personality
far better than I could in my own words. The first is the opening paragraph of
his introduction to Alexander Herzen's autobiography, *My Past and Thoughts*:

> Alexander Herzen, like Diderot, was an amateur of genius whose opinions
> and activities changed the direction of social thought in his country. Like
> Diderot, too, he was a brilliant and irrepressible talker [...] – always in
> an overwhelming flow of ideas and images; the waste, from the point
> of view of posterity (just as with Diderot), is probably immense: he
> had no Boswell and no Eckermann to record his conversation, nor
> was he a man who would have suffered such a relationship. His prose
> is essentially a form of talk, with the vices and virtues of talk: eloquent,
> spontaneous, liable to the heightened tones and exaggerations of the
> born storyteller, unable to resist long digressions which themselves
> carry him into a network of intersecting tributaries of memory or
> speculation, but always returning to the main stream of the story or
> the argument; [...] above all, his prose has the vitality of spoken words
> [...]; we hear his voice almost too much – in the essays, the pamphlets,
> the autobiography, as much as in the letters and scraps of notes to his
> friends. (AC₂ 236)

In the next paragraph he adds:

> Tolstoy [...] said towards the end of his life that he had never met anyone with 'so rare a combination of scintillating depths and brilliance'.⁵ These gifts make a good many of Herzen's essays, political articles, day-to-day journalism, casual notes and reviews, and especially letters written to intimates or to political correspondents, irresistibly readable even today, when the issues with which they were concerned are for the most part dead and of interest mainly to historians. (AC2 237)

A little later in the same piece, he writes of Herzen's early works that they

> possess qualities which became characteristic of all his writings: a rapid torrent of descriptive sentences, fresh, lucid, direct, interspersed with vivid and never irrelevant digressions, variations on the same theme in many keys, [...] quotations real and imaginary [...], mordant personal observations and cascades of vivid images [...]. The effect is one of spontaneous improvisation: exhilarating conversation by an intellectually gay and exceptionally clever and honest man endowed with singular powers of observation and expression. (AC2 245)

In another essay on Herzen he translates a passage from Pavel Annenkov's 'A Remarkable Decade' in which the author characterises Herzen in terms very similar to those deployed by Berlin himself – terms that again apply well to Berlin too:

> I must own that I was puzzled and overwhelmed, when I first came to know Herzen – by this extraordinary mind which darted from one topic to another with unbelievable swiftness, with inexhaustible wit and brilliance; which could see in the turn of somebody's talk, in some simple incident, in some abstract idea, that vivid feature which gives expression and life. He had a most astonishing capacity for instantaneous, unexpected juxtaposition of quite dissimilar things, and this gift he had in a very high degree, fed as it was by the powers of the most subtle observation and a very solid fund of encyclopedic knowledge. He had it to such a degree that, in the end, his listeners were sometimes exhausted by the inextinguishable fireworks of his speech, the inexhaustible fantasy

and invention, a kind of prodigal opulence of intellect which astonished his audience. After the always ardent but remorselessly severe Belinsky, the glancing, gleaming, perpetually changing and often paradoxical and irritating, always wonderfully clever, talk of Herzen demanded of those who were with him not only intense concentration, but also perpetual alertness, because you had always to be prepared to respond instantly. On the other hand, nothing cheap or tawdry could stand even half an hour of contact with him. All pretentiousness, all pompousness, all pedantic self-importance, simply fled from him or melted like wax before a fire. I knew people, many of them what are called serious and practical men, who could not bear Herzen's presence. On the other hand, there were others [...] who gave him the most blind and passionate adoration. (RT2 216)[6]

Berlin himself almost idolised Herzen, writing 'There is no writer, & indeed no man I shd like to be like, & to write like, more' (F 279). But I don't believe he consciously tried to imitate him, or saw himself as like him: that would have been alien to his unselfconscious nature.

Finally, in his essay on Georges Sorel, Berlin again scores a near bullseye:

Sorel's writings have no shape or system, and he was not impressed by it in those of others. He was a compulsive and passionate talker, and, as is at times the case with famous talkers – Diderot, Coleridge, Herzen, Bakunin – his writings remained episodic, unorganised, unfinished, fragmentary, at best sharp, polemical essays or pamphlets provoked by some immediate occasion, not intended to be fitted into a body of coherent, developed doctrine, and not capable of it. Nevertheless, there is a central thread that connects everything that Sorel wrote and said: if not a doctrine, then an attitude, a position, the expression of a singular temperament, of an unaltering view of life. His ideas, which beat like hailstones against all accepted doctrines and institutions, fascinated both his friends and his opponents, and do so still, not only because of their intrinsic quality and power, but because what in his day was confined to small coteries of intellectuals has now grown to world-wide proportions. In his lifetime Sorel was looked on as, at best, a polemical journalist, an autodidact with a powerful pen and occasional flashes of extraordinary insight, too wayward and perverse to claim for long the attention of

serious and busy men. In the event, he has proved more formidable than
many of the respected social thinkers of his day, most of whom he ignored
or else regarded with unconcealed disdain. (AC2 375–6)

Berlin's writings were not so unsystematic or polemical; nor was he so disdained
or disdainful. But the sentence about a central thread is spot on. If anyone exem-
plifies a singular temperament and an unaltering view of life, it is Berlin. It is
part of my purpose to elicit and exhibit aspects of that thread, that temperament
and view of life, in the course of telling my story, which starts in earnest with
a conversation in late 1974 in the upper common room of Wolfson College's
new buildings in Oxford.

MAKING BOOKS

Herbert Hart says that you have transformed my reputation for ever, and had a more decisive effect on it and indirectly me than anyone has ever had. It may well be so. What a charge to labour under!

IB to HH, 2 October 1979 (90)

2

A PROJECT IS BORN

I had no idea, when I joined Wolfson in September 1972, before Michaelmas Term began, that I was about to discover my vocation. I had never read any of Berlin's work, and knew next to nothing about him. But among my Wolfson contemporaries, soon to become a friend, was the philosopher Samuel Guttenplan, who had worked as Berlin's research assistant in New York in 1966 and had come to Wolfson in 1971 as a doctoral student at Berlin's suggestion. Sam knew Berlin and his work well, and I asked him where I should start. He directed me to *Four Essays on Liberty*, published three years earlier. This is the book that Berlin regarded, surely rightly, as his most important (in 2002 I incorporated it into *Liberty*). I took it with me on a visit with friends during a university vacation to a remote cottage on Exmoor called 'Greenlands', near Exford, then owned by relations of mine, afterwards the home of Ranulph and Virginia Fiennes. I devoured the book, and was transfixed. Berlin liked to refer to the unmistakable sensation, when reading, of encountering unusual excellence, writing, for instance, of an essay by L. B. Namier: 'This essay was of an altogether higher quality. In reading it one had the sensation – for which there is no substitute – of suddenly sailing in first-class waters' (PI3 123). This was the sensation I experienced on first looking into Berlin.

The book's author was obviously a man of rare insight, a man plentifully endowed with that 'sense of reality' that he welcomed when he found it in others. There was room for disagreement on this or that point, but on the large human issues one felt in safe hands. Here, I realised, was a writer and thinker of – yes – genius, whose work ought to be as widely available and as widely read as possible. He addressed the same fundamental questions that had long absorbed me, and his conception of our predicament struck me as 'truer and more humane' (L 216) than anything I had come across before. His key values were freedom and variety, a pairing which included irresponsibility and frivolity as well as more serious components, and he linked the two in convincingly important ways. As Noel Annan later put it: 'he

seems to me to have written the truest and the most moving of all the interpretations of life that my own generation made' (PSM2 xxxi). In particular,
I saw in his work, rightly or wrongly, an escape route from the suffocating
religious indoctrination of my youth, which gave me a powerful personal
reason to welcome and champion his ideas, and loomed large in our later
correspondence.

Sam knew too of my long-standing editorial bent. At school I had pointlessly and laboriously typed out a handwritten play on the Irish potato famine
by my then best friend Stephen Green (now Lord Green of Hurstpierpoint).
I had produced magazines both as a schoolboy and as an undergraduate, and, as
recounted earlier, was planning one at Wolfson, which had previously had none.
I was editing a miscellany of writings by my bizarre landlord, which I published
under my own imprint, created for the purpose, in December 1974, with a
somewhat arcane title suggested by Berlin.[1] Evidently the process of gathering
together a jumble of material and turning it into a presentable form appealed
to my somewhat obsessive organising nature.

Sam saw that Berlin, misleadingly famous for non-publication, was a suitable case for treatment, an editorial project waiting to happen, and felt that
such a project was altogether more worthy of pursuit than my other ventures
thus far. He knew that Berlin had published a number of essays and lectures in
obscure places; and he shared my high opinion of Berlin's work. Sometime in
1974, when I had completed my BPhil in philosophy and allegedly embarked
on the conversion of my BPhil thesis into a longer DPhil version, and Wolfson
had decamped to its new buildings in Linton Road, he suggested to me that
I should ask Berlin if I might act as his editor, and publish a collected edition
of his fugitive writings.

I felt extremely diffident about this idea, which seemed (and indeed was)
somewhat above my pay grade, but I was immediately and strongly attracted –
indeed excited – by it. I believed that Berlin had important things to say about
topics central to human self-understanding, and I knew that he said them
with infectious eloquence. He was already widely regarded as one of the most
important contemporary thinkers. There was no one remotely like him. Much
of his work was comparatively unknown. What more attractive editorial project
could possibly be imagined? How could I resist the chance to work closely with
him, and incidentally get to know him even better? For someone of my odd
disposition this was an extraordinarily fortunate opportunity, and I wished
to grasp it. So I boldly asked Berlin what he thought. I must have done this

in person, as there is no correspondence about my initial approach, and I am
unlikely to have discarded it if it had occurred.

It emerged that he had received a number of similar proposals beforehand,
but had turned most of them down, partly on the grounds that he wanted to
publish one or two 'proper books' before authorising collection of his existing
pieces – an activity he thought of (wrongly, it seems to me) as more naturally
occurring posthumously. But one earlier applicant for the role of Berlin's editor,
the late political analyst Robert G. Hazo of Chicago, had previously secured
Berlin's agreement that he should act as his editor in the fullness of time. He had
compiled a bibliography of Berlin's work (though it ran to only 42 items),[2] and
had sent him the result on 26 January 1970, suggesting that he might edit *The
Collected Essays of Isaiah Berlin*, which he saw as a single volume comprising all
Berlin's previously published essays, including those in FEL and those assigned
to *Russian Thinkers*, which had been under contract to Penguin since 1968
with David Shapiro as editor. This would have been an impractically enormous
volume, even if it had contained only those essays that Hazo was aware of.

Berlin replied that such a collection was premature, but he gave Hazo what
he regarded, surely reasonably, as a firm undertaking – oddly, since he hardly
knew him:

> I am most grateful to you for all this devoted labour, by which I am indeed
> also deeply touched. I think the idea of a single volume had better wait
> a little until the other 'works' have appeared, otherwise it will pre-empt
> them too far. *Essays and Addresses* are usually published posthumously.
> I have no objection to a single volume containing all this, but I honestly
> think it ought to wait for three or four years. The time for it is not quite
> yet, but when the time arrives I should be only too grateful if you would
> undertake this task.[3]

The 'other "works"' he had in mind were RT and what after numerous vicissitudes[4] became *Vico and Herder*, which had by then been under contract to the
Hogarth Press, under a succession of different titles, for a decade. Only once
these volumes, at least, had been published was he ready to approve a collection
of other material.

There is a certain oddity about this position, given that both these books
were also collections of essays; but Berlin seems to have regarded them as more
solid and coherent than the other collections that had been mooted. In my

own discussions with him, it also became clear that a book on the origins of Romanticism, with its own origins in lectures delivered in Washington in 1965, was also in his mind, but in the end he seemed to accept that the prospect of such a work was sufficiently distant and uncertain not to constitute an insurmountable barrier to other plans. Indeed, he never wrote a word of it.

Once he had decided to agree to my proposal, Berlin had to extricate himself from his commitment to Hazo. He wrote to him on 6 February 1975, saying that Oxford University Press had suggested a collection of his essays and approached 'a member of my college'[5] to help edit it. There was a modicum of truth in this. OUP did from time to time suggest that Berlin publish with them, and my friend Nicholas Wilson, then their philosophy editor, had indeed asked me if I might edit his work for them. But Sam Guttenplan had already lit the fuse, and OUP were only one of the publishers I had in mind for the new project. Perhaps Berlin believed that an OUP connection helped his case. 'I am writing this to you', he told Hazo, 'in order to remove any possible sense of obligation which you may still feel in regard to these writings.'

This tactic failed. Hazo protested on 18 February, citing Berlin's 1970 letter. Berlin's reply of 27 February displays some embarrassment, but argues the transatlantic divide as a fatal barrier to the necessary collaboration between author and editor, and offers compensation.[6] To a suggestion from me that we should print a fulsome acknowledgement to Hazo, Berlin replied on 5 March:

> I am waiting for Hazo's reply to my somewhat tortured letter. If he answers more in sorrow than in anger, I shd certainly *beg* you to exaggerate his help with the bibliography: it can only give pleasure & cannot do harm to anyone.[7]

Hazo's reply of 31 March reported that he did not feel he could resist Berlin's decision, but expressed 'consternation', and asked for an acknowledgement of his research, and financial compensation for his time and expenses, to the tune of $1,330. He thought Berlin had behaved poorly, and he felt 'used'.

In his reply of 24 April Berlin denied that he was under any 'legal or semi-legal'[8] obligation to Hazo, and observed of the sum asked for in compensation: 'by English standards this figure seems astounding'. But he would settle a formal account. He added that their exchanges showed that the relationship 'could not have ended happily', and that 'divorce is preferable to an unhappy relationship'. He was sorry to have caused Hazo pain, but felt no guilt. On the same day, with hardened heart, he wrote to me: 'As for Mr Hazo, I have written him a moderately unfriendly letter – an acknowledgement to him should, no doubt, be made, but not in excessively warm terms, as his letter was really rather nasty.'

Hazo replied on 12 May, observing reasonably enough that the difficulties of 'trans-oceanic collaboration'[9] were just as great in 1970 as they were in 1975. He defended his bill, which he enclosed, and which Berlin paid on 2 June, bringing this unsatisfactory episode to a close.

I felt bad about supplanting Hazo, even though there was no realistic prospect of his scheme coming to fruition. Berlin had undeniably treated him shabbily, even if this was the result only of thoughtlessness, and he ought to have felt guilty. He had even flirted unfaithfully (perhaps in a moment of forgetfulness) with a publisher in 1972 before he broke with Hazo, in terms that would have alarmed Hazo had he known of the exchange:

> I had better be allowed to publish some solider works first [...] before this flotilla of tiny coracles and collapsible eggshells is launched upon some not too smooth waves – I seem to stir up polemics by my mildest utterance. Do you not think so? It would, I think, be best to postpone the matter for two or three years, but in the meanwhile, if you are kind enough to do it, to produce some alternative schemes for a collection of this sort for the mid-1970s.[10]

Berlin's withdrawal from his agreement with Hazo was just the kind of blow I continuously feared would fall on myself, and the fact that it had fallen on Hazo gave me good reason, I believed, to entertain such a fear. On 4 May 1975 I wrote to Andrew Best, then Berlin's and my literary agent at Curtis Brown, 'I do not want to become another Mr Hazo.' If Berlin did not want to do something, even a clear earlier commitment would not stand in his way. Not for nothing was he the over-indulged only surviving child of doting parents. He was almost always charming and generous, but there was a ruthless streak too, which also surfaced if one challenged him too persistently about something on which he had firm views that he did not wish to reconsider. In the event I emerged comparatively unscathed, despite occasional setbacks, but I was never able to relax, and daily anticipated disaster.

At this point I ought to deflect a possible misunderstanding. I am not in the least seeking to undermine or controvert Berlin's reputation as a good and wise man. I believe he was both. I would go further and call him a great man, and, as I have already said, a genius. But he did elicit uncritical admiration in some quarters, and this has tended to alienate those who cannot quite believe the hype. More personally, it has often been assumed that I myself am one of his most uncritical admirers, but this is not right, just as the widespread belief that I was his student is not right. My admittedly deep admiration for him is tempered by the awareness that he had his own share of human imperfections. This is no bad thing: turning a human being into a saint is a failure of the 'sense of reality' that Berlin valued so highly. He did not himself sanctify even his heroes, for all that he admitted to being a natural hero-worshipper. Nor should we sanctify him.

Once there was agreement in principle, my first task was to establish what Berlin had written. All this was happening in the pre-internet era, when such things took more time. He had kept no systematic records, and had only a patchy memory of what he had published. He was present-oriented, and tended to dismiss his publications from his mind once they had appeared. As I recall, my main initial sources were a cupboard of offprints at his Oxford home, the splendid Georgian mansion known as Headington House, and a drawer of clippings there from the press-cutting agency Durrant's, kept by his private secretary, Patricia ('Pat') Utechin, who became my companion-in-arms and in due course close friend. From these sources, plus various library catalogues, an article by the political theorist Alan Ryan in *Encounter*,[11] Hazo's list and no doubt many other now forgotten places, I compiled an initial bibliography of Berlin's publications, writing to him on 16 February 1975 to ask what he could add to the list. Even those who knew his work best were surprised by the amount of material this exercise uncovered.

This was the first (or first surviving) letter generated by the project, the first of embarrassingly many. But Berlin was not good at sticking to the point in conversation – a very attractive quality unless one wanted to make practical progress – and I almost always wrote him a letter when I wanted to do business. This one begins: 'I fear the time has come to ask you some questions.' How many hundreds of questions did I ask between then and Berlin's death more than twenty years later? I shudder now at the relentless fusillade of enquiries I lobbed in his direction. But however many there were, it was not enough. Since his death I have repeatedly thought of questions I ought to have put to him while he was alive, since only he (if anyone) knew the answers. But it is now too late, so there is no use repining. However, even as things are, his replies to the questions I did ask are well worth having. He was an exceptionally scrupulous correspondent, and usually replied fully and patiently, point by point, to my many enquiries. I did not reread our correspondence until a decade after his death. There is so much more in them than I remembered: more matter, and more evidence of his personality. I was not conscious of building up a resource for clarifying some aspects of his mental world, but I now see that that was what I was in fact doing.

To start with, our discussions were largely bibliographical and editorial, and do not provide appetising fare for general consumption, though there are some interesting sidelights. There were seventeen questions in the initial batch, in addition to the general request to tell me what works of his I had overlooked. During 1975, by steps that it would be as tedious to relate as it was time-consuming to undertake, the bibliography grew to 137 items, and was published in the autumn of that year in *Lycidas*.[12]

Berlin's answer, in a letter of 20 February 1975, to the seventeenth and last question is worth preserving. He had mentioned in conversation some radio talks that he had given in 1952 on the enemies of freedom. I asked him for details, and he replied:

> I delivered six talks, no less, on 'Freedom and Its Betrayal', on the BBC – each an hour long – to which I suspect I owe my chair; none of them published in the *Listener* or anywhere else. Transcripts exist, but are full of errors (theirs and mine), exaggerations, and things I would rather not have said. They dealt with the Encyclopedians, Rousseau, Fichte, Saint-Simon and de Maistre (the last is one of my longest unpublished works, which is due to appear in a book, if I write it, called *Two Enemies of the Enlightenment*, promised to Columbia University, where they were delivered as lectures in, I think, 1964 or '65, called after a Columbian professor of philosophy, whose name I simply cannot remember).

They were the Woodbridge Lectures (so named in memory of Frederick James Eugene Woodbridge, 1867–1940), delivered at Columbia University in New York on 25–8 October 1965. Annotating a note of mine dated 4 December 1979 asking again – the repetition was inadvertent – whether the BBC talks had been published, he wrote:

> *Not* published because hour-long (nothing so long, I am bound to admit, was *ever* permitted by [the] BBC before): the then editor, my

schoolfellow Maurice Ashley, still extant [1907–94], wrote me & said that they were simply far too long. So they were never published in any form anywhere. Better so.

Berlin's 1975 description is characteristically approximate. He omits specific mention of two of his six subjects, Helvétius (not an *Encyclopédiste*) and Hegel, and fails to make clear that the last lecture, on Joseph de Maistre, is not 'one of my longest unpublished works', but a much abbreviated version of it. The long version was probably first drafted in the 1940s,[13] and was revised many times over before being rejected by the *Journal of the History of Ideas* in 1960 as too long, too repetitious and covering too much familiar ground. This must rank as one of the most obtuse publishing decisions of the twentieth century. Berlin did not want to cut his text, and since the Columbia volume never materialised, the essay finally appeared in print only in 1990, as 'Joseph de Maistre and the Origins of Fascism', in *The Crooked Timber of Humanity*. Berlin is quite right, though, about the errors in the transcripts, of which my favourite among those committed by the BBC typists as they tried to make sense of his gabble is the consistent appearance of Saint-Simon as 'Sir Seymour'.

In parallel with the preparation of this bibliography, I read all the essays by Berlin that I could find, some of which he initially denied having written.[14] They fell naturally into six categories. As I wrote to Nicholas Wilson on 7 February 1975: 'There is philosophy, politics, history of ideas, Russian literature and thought, Jewish studies, and portraits of men of action and men of letters.'[15] The first two categories I proposed to combine, since they were comparatively sparsely populated; the fourth was already spoken for as RT (not at this point part of my scheme). This left me with four thematically organised volumes in all, to be introduced by experts in the relevant fields.[16] I produced a list.

There followed a good deal of discussion of exactly which pieces should be included, and in which volumes: in a letter to Michael Brock of 15 July 1975 I wrote that my initial scheme 'had to be revised several times in the light of Isaiah's and publishers' comments'. The details of this discussion I shall omit, as they are not too arresting. But some important issues did crop up. Even the organising categories I proposed were open to question. In early May 1975 Berlin wrote: 'I don't think I want a separate Jewish volume at all'; moreover 'I do not want "Jewish Slavery and Emancipation" to be reprinted at all, because it would be bound to cause a lot of controversy even now.' I replied on 15 May:

I am sorry you don't want a Jewish volume. If you don't, you don't, but I was surprised, in view of the existence of *Trois essais sur la condition juive* [French translations (published in 1973) of 'Jewish Slavery and Emancipation', 'The Life and Opinions of Moses Hess' and 'Benjamin Disraeli, Karl Marx, and the Search for Identity']. If you allowed that, I reasoned with myself, you would allow my proposed volume of Jewish Studies. Is it that, although you are prepared to publish pieces about Jews and Jewish problems one at a time, you feel that to gather them all together is too solid and explicit an avowal of loyalty? From my point of view the only problem is that, although it is possible to redistribute the Jewish pieces among the other categories, there is a sense in which they sit unhappily in other company: the Jewish predicament is unique in a specially strong way – it is not simply one parochial manifestation of a human problem which all individuals and nations have to relive in their own historical and cultural context. To this extent Jewish studies differ from other studies in the history of ideas, or in contemporary politics, where the limitations of time and place seem a thinner veneer over universal preoccupations and dilemmas. I do not say that this provides irresistibly strong grounds for grouping the Jewish pieces together, but it does explain why I preferred in the initial scheme to do this. I wonder how strong your opposition to a Jewish volume is? I am sure it would satisfy a demand, if that counts at all.

This was a rather cheeky response, but throughout our relationship I felt I had to push as hard as I dared, at every step, in order to secure the best outcome that I could in the face of Berlin's ingrained self-doubt, hesitancy and caution. More often than not my boldness paid dividends, where a more cautious, deferential, polite approach might have been rebuffed. I am astonished now, as I reread our letters, how accommodating he was in the face of my relentlessness. Despite the large difference in age and status between us, he never pulled rank, and mostly treated my enquiries and suggestions and disagreements as if they were those of an intellectual equal. But from time to time I went too far even for him, and was chastised accordingly. These indirectly self-inflicted wounds did cause me pain, though they were a necessary side-effect of the perpetual battle I fought to secure my objective of (re-)publishing as much of Berlin's work as I felt deserved it, in the most effective possible way. But Berlin never allowed my errant behaviour to rankle for long, always returning to a generous – perhaps too generous – appreciation of what I was doing. For example:

> My heart is genuinely a little too full for decent expression of what I owe to you – now & for years. Gradually, it will, no doubt, be articulated. As always with me, you must wait, be patient, & it will come with time.[17]

A humorous twist to this appreciation occurs in a letter of 8 January 1980:

> Since my debt to you is so large, it is clear that you are now free to diminish it by some piece of independent enterprise that is sure to cause me acute embarrassment some time – not too many such acts, perhaps, but to some you are now entitled, especially as I see no way of diminishing the debt at my end – for what can I possibly do towards this?

The first definite offence I can recall was not to do with my publishing project. The Wolfson College Music Society had been inaugurated in December 1974 in the College Hall with a recital of three of Bach's solo cello sonatas by Mstislav Rostropovich, who gave his services free as a personal favour to Berlin, even buying his own ticket. The proceeds were used to endow the society, which I ran in its early days. I arranged a second concert for 1 March 1975, given by two Russians, the violinist Alla Sharova and the pianist Hilda Sachs. In the flyer advertising the concert I wrote: 'Hilda Sachs was born in Riga like Sir Isaiah Berlin (this will be the last concert before his retirement as President of Wolfson).' Berlin regarded this, I think, as irrelevant and embarrassingly vulgar, and objected. I revised the flyer accordingly. This is one of a series of occasions on which I misjudged his reaction, sometimes more seriously than in this instance. It reminds me of when Berlin and I were among those watching the Wolfson crews rowing on the river Isis (Thames), and an American commentator atop the Oxford University boathouse observed through his loudhailer that the assembled company was honoured by the presence of – and here he named two or three titled heads of houses, mentioning their handles. An Englishman promptly seized the implement and announced: 'I should like to apologise for that last remark, which was extremely vulgar and somewhat colonial.' Berlin did not notice these remarks himself, but laughed when I reported them to him. He was not one of those named.

At about the same time I made another mistake. Because of the *Encounter* article by Alan Ryan in which he had suggested the compilation of a bibliography, as well as because of Berlin's many publications in its pages, I asked *Encounter* if they would be interested in publishing my bibliography. I was then ignorant of the row that had erupted in 1967 about the CIA's covert funding of the magazine via the Congress for Cultural Freedom: the CCF had concealed the source of the funds from one of the editors, Berlin's close friend Stephen Spender, leaving him embarrassed when the truth emerged. Berlin said he was equally unaware. Spender resigned. Berlin cancelled his subscription, strenuously objecting not to the funding itself but to the concealment of its origins. I had to withdraw my suggestion in confusion, only to be told by an *Encounter* staff member that my second letter gave me even more cause for embarrassment than my first.

Perhaps the most serious misjudgement occurred in April 1975. Let me set the scene. When Berlin retired from the Presidency of Wolfson the previous month, I had written him a letter in which I tried to say what I and others felt about having been there with him:

> It is said that you dislike sentiment. Nevertheless you will allow me to voice briefly and unsentimentally what has been on numerous lips recently, and in numerous hearts, lest it should be thought unfelt because unsaid. To have been at Wolfson under your presidency has been a happy and unforgettable experience, and to see your period of office coming to an end fills us all with gloom. Even if All Souls reclaims you after your period in the wilderness, we hope that you will venture forth occasionally into the snowy wastes of North Oxford and visit us. For various reasons my own time at Wolfson has I think been overall the happiest of my life: without Wolfson, I think graduate life in Oxford would have been miserable. (13 March 1975)

That evening a dinner was held in Wolfson to mark Berlin's retirement. His official portrait, by Derek Hill (now in the college library), was unveiled, speeches were given, and a musical *jeu d'esprit* was performed: Ruth Padel, a junior research fellow, and I sang parts of Berlin's entry in *Who's Who* to the music of the Papageno–Papagena duet from Mozart's opera *The Magic Flute*, accompanied by Berlin's successor, Sir Henry ('Harry') Fisher, at the piano.[18] Two days later, soon after the moment of retirement (midnight), Berlin wrote me the moving reply included at the end of the third volume of his letters (B 597–8).

So far, so good. However, dismayed by the first impressions I had formed (rightly or wrongly) of his successor, I idiotically expressed this dismay in a letter. Hearing from Pat Utechin that this communication was not well received, and belatedly understanding why, I wrote again to apologise for my faux pas. Berlin replied to both letters together:

> Do not, I beg you, take anything to heart. Of course you should not over-react, or say such things to me about my successor. I must not, for obvious reasons, either listen or indeed overhear them. The least I can do is avert my gaze and know nothing while he is assuming his office. Everyone has his own style – I must be the last person to be invited to take up a critical attitude. However, I need not go on about this. You understand it perfectly well, and I am only sorry that it has caused you anguish: sorry not about anything I have done, as it were, but by existing and becoming the occasion. Let us call it a mildly tactless swerve. (24 April 1975)

It was not the only such swerve by any means, but it is the one most seared into my memory.

I return, after this Berlinesque digression, to the issue of a Jewish volume. Pat Utechin reported within a fortnight of my plea, making clear that the Jewish essays were non-negotiable:

> He will *not* have the Jewish pieces publ. during lifetime – as he admits himself, for fear of hornets – he's fearfully sensitive about being thought (by Jews, by Israelis) to be not-Jewish-enough – even anti-Jewish. You'll have to swallow this, I think he's immovable.[19]

I understand his reasons better now than I did then. He did not wish to sequester these essays in a separate corral, but preferred to regard some of them as contributions to the general history of ideas, others as addressed to a Jewish readership – to the family, as it were – and therefore unsuitable for inclusion in my edition. Some of the former group were reassigned to other volumes, others dropped from the scheme, to my regret (though I rescued them later).

Nor did he wish his book reviews (with one or two exceptions) to be preserved in my selection, writing in the same letter in which he declined a Jewish

volume: 'I remember looking at Rowse's collected book reviews, which did
appear in one of his volumes, and thinking how trivial it was, how conceited
and irritating – a handful of dust.' I remonstrated gently about this, while not
disputing the general principle:

> I don't think the fact that Rowse's reviews were not worth reprinting can
> be taken as sufficient grounds for allowing all book reviews to perish!
> Something like Chomsky's review of B. F. Skinner's *Verbal Behavior* can
> become a minor classic in its own right. (15 May 1975)

The same, I might have observed, could be said of Berlin's 'Winston Churchill
in 1940', which began life as a review of *Their Finest Hour* (1949), the second
volume of Churchill's war memoirs.

Otherwise my broad plan, once it had been revised to take account of our
extensive discussions, was accepted. David Shapiro graciously allowed us to
absorb the volume on Russian thought into the series, with the Russianist
Aileen Kelly, also from Wolfson College, acting as co-editor with me (indis-
pensably, since my O level Russian was rusty and rudimentary), though the
paperback would remain with Penguin. There would be three further volumes:
on philosophy, on the history of ideas, and on twentieth-century figures. The
contents of the published volumes differ at many points from my initial list, for
example by the exclusion of essays on Soviet Russia from the Russian volume
(these had to wait another three decades to be collected as *The Soviet Mind*),
but the relationship between starting and finishing points is perfectly visible.
The series as a whole was rather boringly dubbed *Selected Writings*, I think by
Andrew Best. Not that I can think of a better portmanteau title, if indeed one
was required at all.

Naturally I wondered why Berlin accepted my own proposal when he had
rejected or postponed its predecessors. A note I wrote to myself at the time listing the arguments in favour of the scheme begins with the donation of Berlin's
royalties to Wolfson (I cannot remember whether this was my idea, though it
may well have been), and this certainly helped to persuade him. I also listed
the beneficial effect on the publishing career I had embarked on (he was always
supportive of Wolfsonians in their undertakings); the opportunity the project
afforded Berlin to determine his own canon rather than leaving this task to the
vagaries of his literary executor(s); the rebuttal of the popular image of him
as a non-writer; and the fact that my participation would free him from the

editorial work on his own past writings that he so recoiled from, while leaving him in control of the contents of the selection. I also suspected a secret hope that the essays were better than he would admit to himself. He later gave his own account of his motives, as we shall see.

I began editorial work in the summer of 1975 alongside continuing work on my DPhil, which suffered as a result, though I didn't mind this in the least. A letter of 18 August shows the first evidence of what later became a consuming preoccupation with clarifying Berlin's ideas, and I return to this issue in later chapters. I wrote:

> Since we last met I have been on holiday (to Exmoor), and among other things I had a chance to read a great deal of your work, much of it for the first time. This was a source of great fascination, and numerous questions and comments occurred to me which I hope I may perhaps write down some day when the dust has settled after the publication of the *Selected Writings*. But for the time being the editor must stick to his appointed task, and confine himself to practical matters.

By the autumn I had developed a sense of how much amendment would be needed to Berlin's quotations and references if they were to pass scholarly scrutiny. Although he was entirely in favour of accuracy, his enthusiastic disposition, and his gift for improving quotations – making the unmemorable memorable – made him unreliable, and I had to try to make the necessary corrections without spoiling the fun. I mentioned my predicament in a letter of 2 November 1975, in order to ensure that he supported what I proposed to do:

> I have just finished the most formidable task, perhaps, of all – your Machiavelli article. I feel I ought to tell you – I hope I can say this without a trace of self-congratulation: none is felt – that a very high proportion of the footnotes were inaccurate. I expect you know this – I don't think you corrected proofs of this article. Anyway, all is now in order, and it has been very absorbing making it so: not least, I have learnt a lot about Machiavelli!

The remark about proof-correction, if well meant, was an unconvincing rationale for the errors. I knew, and he knew that I knew, that these had very little to do with proofreading. He replied on 13 November:

As to my bits and pieces – I am not at all surprised that my footnotes are inaccurate. I am wildly unscholarly and I am sure the book on Vico will be exposed mercilessly by some pundit. Yet I long for accuracy, even pedantry. It would be nice to think that my confusions are the vice of some mysterious virtue, but I fear this is not so.[20]

This stimulated me to attempt, on 6 December, a long and rambling defence of Berlin's exceptional gifts against his lack of self-confidence. I argued that the talents of pedantic accuracy and imaginative insight can exclude one another, and that the latter is far more important:

> What does seem absolutely clear to me is that the capacities with which you are endowed are infinitely preferable, and it has always surprised – I would even say saddened – me that you yearn for inferior virtues which to some degree you may lack.

I appealed to an article by him on 'General Education', in which he argues that it is the ratio of ideas to facts that counts – the more ideas, the more worthy of respect:

> The academic value of a subject seems to me to depend largely on the ratio of ideas to facts in it. [...] our respect for the specialist on cheeses is not high: we value his work but not him; and the sole reason for this is the low content of ideas – hypotheses, powers of reasoning, capacity for general ideas, awareness of the relationship of elements in a total pattern – in such painstaking but intellectually undemanding work. (POI2 270)

No one is less cheesy, in this sense, than Berlin.
   Without denigrating the pursuit of accuracy, I urged that

> one must not be crippled by a phobia about being discovered in error. There is a whole psychological syndrome connected with having one's work published which seems to me to rest on something of a misconception: that the act of publication involves a claim that what is published is the final word, immune from criticism, to be defended to the last unless one's name and honour are to be lost. Rather, surely, publication is a means of disseminating ideas for discussion and improvement.

(I expand on this point in an article in the TLS.)[21] I hope that my letter was not an indefensible manifesto for an irresponsible intellectual swashbuckler. Berlin did not reply, perhaps because my remarks were (it now seems to me) a string of platitudes, and not even particularly convincing ones at that.

The next step was to approach potential publishers. Andrew Best sounded out several possibilities, including OUP and the Hogarth Press (both of whom had works by Berlin on their past or future lists), and also Duckworth and Heinemann Educational. OUP wanted to exclude much of the philosophy volume, and to rearrange the remaining material according to a two-volume proposal of their own, which effectively scuppered their prospects, since the scheme offered to them was the result of extensive consultation between myself and Berlin, and my work was already well advanced on that basis. Colin Haycraft of Duckworth sent me two astonishing letters whose lofty tone ensured that we would not choose his firm. On 26 November 1975 he wrote:

> I have written to Andrew Best making our 'offer'. I don't quite understand what you mean by the 'difficult task' of choosing a publisher. It is only difficult, I imagine, if you conduct an auction. You talk also about 'best terms': in fact terms are more or less standard. We certainly do not feel 'unjustly dealt with' – merely that the whole matter seems to have been rather ineptly handled!

I replied on 1 December:

> The task of choosing a publisher is difficult because a number of excellent publishers have expressed an interest in publishing Sir Isaiah's writings, and it is difficult both to choose one from among their number to do the job, and to disappoint the others. What you call the 'auction' has nothing to do with it – indeed if it were merely a matter of an auction, the choice would be the easiest thing in the world: we would simply take the highest bidder. As for terms, I agree that royalties are more or less standard (though even here there proves to be a not negligible discrepancy): but advances are clearly not so norm-bound.
>
> I do not see where the ineptitude comes in – at any rate as far as we are concerned.

Haycraft's second letter is dated 22 December 1975:

I see that you now admit or realise that to all intents and purposes 'best terms' just means the highest advance. Agents of course like advances because they contribute to their immediate turnover, and for this reason they will always try to persuade the publisher that the author needs one. In this case the only question at issue is whether the publisher who expressed the first and strongest interest will do the job well. You will understand now, I imagine, why I feel that the matter has been ineptly handled. If you are too inexperienced or the agent too dim to see that we are the right publisher there is nothing more I can say.

His last sentence is a strong contender for the title of 'shortest suicide note in publishing history'. I replied on 30 December, meeting all his points, and concluding:

How do you know whether the interest you expressed was either the first or the strongest? You cannot possibly know this. Even if it was both of these, there might be another 'question at issue': whether another publisher might do the job better.

Berlin's mild preference was for the Hogarth Press, whose former co-proprietor Leonard Woolf had commissioned VH, and whose sales director, Hugo Brunner, who had worked with him on that volume, he liked a good deal personally. It was Hogarth who prevailed, in February 1976 (the month in which VH appeared) – despite the agent's initial preference for Heinemann, in the person of Alan Hill. An announcement appeared in the *Bookseller* of 6 March, though the contract was not finalised until 9 July.

Selected writings of Isaiah Berlin, edited by Henry Hardy: contents

(Volume A)   Concepts and Categories: Philosophical Essays

1   The Purpose of Philosophy
2   ~~Induction and Hypothesis~~   I.B. now
3   Verification
4   Empirical Propositions and Hypothetical Statements
5   Logical Translation
6   Equality
7   The Concept of Scientific History
8   Does Political Theory Still Exist?
9   'From Hope and Fear Set Free'   (c. 250 pages)

(Volume B)   Against the Current: Essays in the History of Ideas

1   Montesquieu
2   The Life and Opinions of Moses Hess
3   Benjamin Disraeli, Karl Marx and the Search for Identity
4   Georges Sorel
5   The Originality of Machiavelli
6   The Bent Twig: A Note on Nationalism
7   The Counter-Enlightenment
8   The Divorce Between the Sciences and the Humanities
9   A Note on Vico's Concept of Knowledge
10   "Alexander Herzen" (introduction to My Past and Thoughts)

     Bibliography of Isaiah Berlin's published writings   (c.300 pages)

(Volume C)   Memoirs and Tributes

1   Mr. Churchill in 1940
2   Hubert Henderson at All Souls
3   President Franklin Delano Roosevelt
4   Chaim Weizmann
5   Richard Pares
6   Felix Frankfurter at Oxford
7   Aldous Huxley
8   L.B. Namier – A Personal Impression
9   Maurice Bowra
10   Jacob Herzog – A Tribute
11   ~~Zionist Politics in Wartime Washington: a Fragment of Personal Reminiscence~~ I.B.
12   J.L. Austin and the Early Beginnings of Oxford Philosophy
13   John Petrov Plamenatz
14   Edmund Wilson (if written in time)   (c.210 pages)

(Volume D)   Russian Thinkers

1   Russia and 1848
2   The Hedgehog and the Fox
3   Herzen and Bakunin on Individual Liberty
4   A Remarkable Decade
5   Russian Populism
6   Tolstoy and Enlightenment
7   Fathers and Children   (c.300 pages)

                                                          H.R,D.H.
                                                          12 March, 1976

The contents list appended to the agreement with the Hogarth Press for *Selected Writings*;
Berlin has replaced item C11 with 'Auberon Herbert'; the volumes were published in the order
D, A, B, C in 1978–80; the title of Volume A is mine, that of Volume B a response by IB to
my characterisation of its contents (see p. 273, note 12); Volume C was published as *Personal
Impressions* (IB's title: see p. 79); I do not remember who replaced Volume D's contractual title,
Russian Essays, with the one listed here.

3

PHILOSOPHICAL LETTERS, OR, COLD FEET

Some time after I had completed work on the philosophy volume, I received a letter from Berlin, dated 6 April 1976, which was the worst example of his infirmity of purpose that I ever experienced. After casting doubt on the need for the introductions we had already agreed on, he continued:

> What I am more dubious about – suddenly, but deeply – is the need for one of the four volumes – namely, that that includes the philosophical essays. These really do seem to me pretty dead by now; whatever their merits, they will be rightly regarded as dated, if not actually obsolete, by philosophers, and no one else could possibly take any interest in them. One or two of the more popular ones could perhaps be included in the other three volumes. The idea that a totally representative selection of 'my works' should appear entails a degree of importance, and therefore legitimate interest in my person or my works, which, without any false modesty, seems to me totally unjustified by the facts – as any honest reviewer would be bound to recognise, even if some of them might be too kind to say so. The Russian essays have a certain unity and perhaps some value in themselves; so do the memoirs, eulogies etc.; and there may be something to be said for a volume of miscellaneous pieces; but that should be all.
>
> Come and argue about this with me if you would like to, but I feel fairly convinced on this issue. I really do not think that Verification, Reductionism, the Logic of History from A to Z,[1] etc. are good enough to reprint, and they would merely lower the value of the rest. Three volumes are surely enough? [...] Do not be too stern with me: I think that your appreciation of my works is too generous.

Berlin dictated a second letter (dated 10 April) covering the same ground, evidently having forgotten the first one. In the course of this he writes:

All those papers in *Mind*, the *Proceedings of the Aristotelian Society* etc., or almost all, are perhaps not much worse than the average contents of philosophical periodicals of the time, but not much better: and looked at now seem pretty dead stuff to me. A valuable philosophical essay really does have to be capable of making some impact – representing some, if not boldly original, then at least sharply ice-cutting historically important point of view. This these essays do not convey. 'The Purpose of Philosophy' may just be rescuable; so may 'Does Political Theory Still Exist?', and even 'From Hope and Fear Set Free'; but all that stuff on deduction, verification, hypotheticals, reductionism and even equality belongs to its time and place and nothing beyond that.

Dismayed, not only because the editorial work was done, I fought back, and the following exchange ensued, beginning with a letter from me dated 18 April:

I am of course distressed that you are having cold feet at this late stage over the publication of the philosophy volume. Let me put the case for it once again, perhaps in a little more detail than heretofore. Forgive me if you find me long-winded, but I must do my best to persuade you. I daresay nothing I can say will reassure you, given your deep-seated insecurity about appearing in print, but it is worth a try.

You began your professional life as a first-order philosopher, and it is still primarily as a philosopher that you are known. You may think this inappropriate, now that you have moved into the second-order field of intellectual history, but the fact remains that the label seems to have stuck – and not entirely inappropriately, since it is mostly philosophers whose ideas you chronicle. In addition to the two best-known of your philosophical essays, reprinted in *Four Essays on Liberty* ['Historical Inevitability' and 'Two Concepts of Liberty'], you have written and published the nine essays that constitute the agreed contents of *Concepts and Categories* [...]. These essays form a natural unity – an introductory portrait of philosophy's nature followed by a variety of case studies – and (in my view) form an essential part of the collection of your writings which I am editing, if this collection is to be at all representative. The essays are of considerable interest in themselves, and their interest is crucially added to by the fact that you wrote them:

anyone who knows anything about you, and is thus a potential purchaser and reader of your published writings, would expect to find them in any collection of your papers that laid any claim to cover the range of your output.

That is the broad picture. I think I can best fill in some of the detail by picking up the various points you make in your two letters. First, you say that some of the essays are dated. In one way there may be some truth in this: viz., one can tell from the kind of topic with which they are preoccupied, from the type of opponent they attack, at what stage in the development of English philosophy they were written. But neither is this surprising, nor, surely, does it constitute (at any rate by itself) an argument against publication. The first of the three volumes of Ryle's *Collected Papers* (for example) contains a lot of material that is strongly dated in this sense, but its being so dated neither prevents it being of intrinsic philosophical interest, nor prevents it being of interest as written by Ryle, as showing part of the intellectual route he followed on his way to *The Concept of Mind* and so forth. The same might be said of some of Austin's *Philosophical Papers*.

The fact that philosophy has moved on to other concerns does not mean that what was said earlier can no longer be true, or that it is not part of the foundation on which latter thought is built, or that it is no longer interesting in itself. It does not mean that it is not informative (not necessarily damagingly so!) about its author. *These* are the counts on which early material is worth reviving. Goodness, if one never published anything that was not bang up to the minute, what a mass of invaluable material would never see the light! It has always annoyed me that both reviewers and historians of ideas often glibly assign writers they are discussing to this or that period or school, in a dismissive way, as if the fact that they are obviously a natural part of their contemporary intellectual environment somehow devalues or even invalidates what they had to say. You know the approach: 'So-and-so, writing when he did, and under the influence of such-and-such a circle, could hardly help espousing the views so characteristic of ...' and so forth. It seems to me perfectly certain that the fact that a piece of work bears the marks of the temporal or other context in which it was produced constitutes absolutely no part of a reasonable case against its being judged of value or interest. I am sure you will agree.

43

You say that reprintable philosophy should be, if not boldly original, then at least sharply ice-cutting, embodying a historically important viewpoint. This is an exorbitantly high standard to apply! How much philosophy meets it? One per cent at the very most. A higher percentage of what gets reprinted, perhaps, but not much higher. In any case, you are perhaps over-modest about your essays. I am not going to maintain (I don't think it's true, and even if it were you would never admit it) that you are in the foremost rank of creative pure philosophers, but you are, and showed in those papers that you are, remarkably good at philosophy: you must at least admit that, and it is enough [cf. 265–6]. Besides, there are other qualities in these essays which make them (as well as characteristic of you) other than run-of-the-mill – the status to which you seem determined to relegate them.

If you wanted detailed chapter and verse I would have to go through them again and try to pick out paradigm cases of what I have in mind. But I can give you some general impressions from memory. You are not swamped by the prevailing orthodoxy, as so many are; you have a refreshing candidness and directness about dissenting from received opinion; both in content and in style your philosophical writing is highly individual and characteristic; you have an often exhilarating command of your material, and a discrimination and felicity in presenting it that is by no means shared by other philosophers; you do not make issues seem more complex or obscure than they really are, because you have yourself perceived them clearly, and have no need to cloak confusion with verbiage; your philosophical essays show your skill in sustained minute argument in a way not matched anywhere else in your work.

I hope I am not embarrassing you. On top of all this is the fact that the issues about which you wrote were, and still are, of the first importance in philosophy: the distinguishing features of philosophy; the nature of inductive belief; the role of verifiability; the possibility of phenomenalism; objections to reductivism; what kind of equality we should have as a political ideal; whether history is a science; the status of political theory; whether knowledge liberates (I pick only a selection of the salient issues you discuss). These are none of them dead issues. If any of them are out of fashion at present, they will come back into fashion again. Think of the unutterably trivial subject matter of much of the philosophy in periodicals! This is not a charge that can be levelled against your essays, whatever other weaknesses you may imagine they possess.

Add to this that some of the papers you are worried about have already been in demand for reprinting,[2] and recent reprinting at that. If you suspect me of an undiscriminating and automatic approval of everything you write (a charge to which I plead not guilty – my appreciation of your work, as of your person, is of a warts-and-all variety, not of a can-do-no-wrong kind: admiration is well laced with frustration), then I appeal to the judgement of other philosophers more distinguished than myself, more qualified to judge your work, and more likely to do so in a detached way. 'Verification' was reprinted in 1968 in Parkinson's *Oxford Readings in Philosophy* volume, and 'Empirical Propositions and Hypothetical Statements' in an American collection on the philosophy of perception in 1965; 'The Concept of Scientific History' has been reprinted twice, in 1963 and 1966, and indeed I understand that you yourself until recently planned to include it with the essays on Vico and Herder as part of a three-essay volume which has now appeared in pruned form as *Vico and Herder* – which makes me particularly surprised that this is one of the essays you are hesitating about.

Do not these reprintings show anything? I think they do. Of course, there are some [essays] that have not been reprinted: but of what worthwhile collection is this not true – and usually to a greater extent than in this case? And even if one or two of the essays are of comparatively less interest than the others, they should be included if only for completeness's sake. This volume is after all not independently conceived, but part of a collection of your writings.

This brings me to what may be our most significant disagreement. As I see it, we are publishing a collection of all your major papers in four areas, with certain individual exceptions certainly (the two pieces on Romanticism which you don't want to reprint in case they steal the thunder of the [book based on the] Mellon Lectures; the political Jewish pieces; the pseudonymous/contentious Russian political pieces),[3] but with no generic lacunae. Anyone who owns all the volumes, together with your previously published books, will possess your main oeuvre to date. [...]

Would I be right in thinking that this picture worries you somewhat? I fancy you may think of the project rather more as four independent books, each to be justified on its own merits (and three of them, in your view, so justifiable), books which happen to be written by I. Berlin, though this forms no part, or only a small part, of the reason for publishing them. You say 'The idea that a totally representative selection of "my works" should appear entails a degree of importance, and therefore legitimate interest in my person or my works, which, without any false modesty, seem to me totally unjustified by the facts': I wonder if you really believe this?

I do not know how you feel about your reputation, and I do not pretend to understand why it has the precise nature it has, but surely you must know (even if you don't wholeheartedly welcome it) that – how to put this? – your reputation is such that the fact that you are the author of a book is for many a sufficient reason for reading it, and enjoying the experience. You have said all along that few will read your selected works, but, *pace* your disclaimer, this *is* surely false modesty. Chatto & Windus were not relieved, as you guessed they might be, that you thought the philosophy volume not worth including: when I last spoke to Hugo Brunner he confirmed (what I suspected) that as a publishing proposition the philosophy volume is thought to be perfectly sound, and would be bound to sell profitably. Donald MacRae at Heinemann Educational thought the same, with some force. Naturally this isn't in itself a sufficient reason for publishing a book, but it does go some way to meeting your particular hesitations.

You are, as always, thinking of what reviewers will say. I think you are unduly pessimistic, for the reasons given. But in any case your reputation is so firmly established that it could not conceivably be significantly affected by a hostile reception of the philosophy volume, even if this occurred, which it won't. Forgive me for saying that the spectacle of someone of a distinction as established as your own believing that his reputation is at risk from the publication of a volume of essays not all of which may be of the very highest rank is worrying. In any case it is I who am to blame if the volume is a mistake – the selection appears as mine, even if it has your passive *imprimatur*, and it is I who should receive the critics' castigations for mis-selection, if any were forthcoming. Maybe it is just that you hate unfavourable reviews – as indeed you do. But (again forgive me) is this really something that should be allowed to decide the issue? I can imagine, I think, how you feel about this:

but does the detached part of you think that adverse criticism really matters? [...]

To omit [this volume] would be to emasculate the whole scheme as I see it. I have a particular interest in this volume, as a philosopher (albeit a lapsed one like yourself), and that is one reason why I did the work on it first, and enjoyed doing it, and am looking forward especially keenly to its appearance. I even used a quotation from one of the papers you want to throw out as an epigraph for a chapter of my DPhil thesis![4] Forgive me, please, if anything I have said in this letter seems to you in any way impertinent: I have tried to give my reasons for thinking the volume worth publishing as fully and as honestly as possible. I hope your cold feet will be a little warmed, at least.

Berlin replied on 3 May 1976:

I am moved by your letter, but not to the extent of changing my mind. I think we have somewhat different views about the qualifications, as it were, of these – as I call them – posthumous volumes of mine. I do not believe that mere interest in what I am, the particular directions in which I have moved, etc. is a sufficient reason, by itself, for supplying evidence for this in a convenient form for the curious. Anything I am prepared to put my name to must, in my opinion, however fallible, be of sufficient intrinsic value to deserve publication in a collected form. This seems to me tenable in the case of the Russian essays, the obituaries, and some of the general essays as well. It does not seem to me, at any rate, tenable in the case of the purely philosophical pieces.

Despite the anthologisers, at least three of these essays – induction, phenomenalism, verifiability – have had their day: the issues are not dead, but the points I have used and the objections I have urged have been absorbed into the general body of belief on the subject. Doubtless you could ask some just judge, like David Pears, or Urmson, and they would surely corroborate this. It is very well for Ryle's or Austin's papers to be published, but they are major influences on British philosophy; this, for a variety of reasons, could also be thought to hold of Freddie Ayer; but do you really think that a volume of, say, Urmson's essays or Kneale's – very respectable philosophers both, and of influence in their day – could be justified? And more so in my case? I do not, however, deny that some of these essays, say, on political topics, and maybe one essay on pure philosophy, could be sandwiched in (or, as the late Crossman used to say, 'spatchcocked') with the rest. So let us discuss it.

I really do feel grateful to you, not merely for everything you have done, are doing, are likely to do, but for the sincere compliments you pay me, which I am trying not to inhale. I think I have enough scepticism of my own powers, and, indeed, lack of intellectual confidence, not to have my head turned, or begin saying to myself that perhaps, after all, I am a better man than I have all these years supposed myself to be.[5] My sensitiveness to reviews is due not so much to general hatred of self-exposure and the uncertainties of criticism as to a perfectly proper (it seems to me) fear that the critics may tell the truth as I see it myself, and perhaps go a little too far in that direction – but the direction itself is one that if I were writing about my own works I should inevitably take myself. Hence all this fuss. Every time I have received honours of any kind, I have always felt that if anyone took such things seriously they might easily feel just indignation: I began feeling it myself, and was astonished at the standards evidently used by those who are so foolish as to honour me in such fashion. [...]

I wrote again on 5 May 1976:

I can see you are going to be obdurate. I am sad about this, but, I fear, powerless to persuade you that you are mistaken in your modesty. I was talking to Chris Schenk the weekend before last, and the subject of your philosophical papers came up: I was reassured when he volunteered the information (before I had said anything about my opinions) that he had read some of your pieces when he was an undergraduate, and had felt that they stood out among the general run of the material he was recommended to read, as being unusually free from irrelevant convention-observing or pedantic-objection-anticipating clutter – as getting straight to the point, and confronting it incisively, in its essentials, and constructively. He did not find in your work the fruitless, highly localised point-scoring that characterises so much of the material in philosophy periodicals. What is more, he actually used (unprompted!) the words 'They seemed to cut a great deal of ice' of the essays: I find this peculiarly telling, since you yourself used the epithet 'ice-cutting' in an earlier letter to describe what you thought your essays did *not* achieve! Is the author the best judge of his own work? I know this isn't true of me.

I shall conclude my catalogue of the merits of your philosophical writings by saying that I concur with Chris Schenk, and would add that these writings also manifest a width of reference, a readiness to risk large, enlightening and suggestive generalisations and speculations, rare in professional philosophical circles. I am only sorry you never applied these talents more positively to the problems of free will versus determinism: the remarks you have made to me in conversation on this topic suggest that you might write something addressed specifically to the solution of this problem which, if not amounting to the stroke of genius which you believe is needed, yet would set the ball rolling in that direction. Maybe you will still do this one day.

I am perhaps more sensible of what you see as the shortcomings of your work than I may convey – but it is in spite of these (not in ignorance of them) that my judgements about publishability are formed. It is interesting that you mention Urmson as a possible parallel. I do indeed think that a volume of Urmson's papers would be worth publishing, and I have often thought of suggesting this to him! [I made this suggestion to OUP, unsuccessfully, after Urmson's death.] This will only confirm your poor opinion of my judgement! I will ask him when I next see him what he thinks of your papers – and I will ask David Pears too, whom I am to see shortly.

If I cannot persuade you to adhere to the original agreement, can I ask you at least to grant stay of execution? I mean that, if you cannot bear to have the philosophy volume published as planned, as one of the first two to appear, then let us publish the other three volumes first, and see how you feel thereafter. Perhaps in the light of the excellent reviews the other volumes are bound to receive you will be feeling less apprehensive about the reception the philosophy volume might receive. Perhaps, indeed, you may simply change your mind again. These are other reasons (in addition to the point about mismatchedness) why I should prefer not to move any of the philosophical material to the other volumes.

I wonder if there is any parallel in the annals of publishing to the situation we find ourselves in. I mean, a volume is ready in all respects for the press, editor and publishers wish to publish it, the public wishes to purchase and read it, and yet the author decides to withhold it. This provides an interesting piece of publishing history if nothing else! The more usual predicament, I take it, is for authors to thirst for publication, and yet fail to produce acceptable material.

There is one last point I must make before I rest my case, if you will forgive it. I would prefer, so far as is possible, not to find myself again in the situation of undertaking work on an agreed programme, afterwards to find that it is not to bear fruit. You and I and Andrew Best had a formal meeting last summer specifically to determine the contents of your *Selected Writings*, and one of the main purposes of this meeting was to give me a secure basis on which to undertake detailed editorial work. This I accordingly did, and I had finished the work on the philosophy volume by the time you let me know of your change of heart: I will not embarrass you further by estimating how long the work took. I mention this entirely without bitterness, and I would not for a moment use it as an argument for publication: it would be intolerable for me to think that any kind of moral duress formed part of your reason for agreeing to publish. I bring this point up at all only as a preliminary to asking you to produce any further second thoughts (of which I dearly hope there will be none) now rather than later. Obviously neither you nor I can intervene in your inscrutable psychological processes effectively enough to ensure that you will not at a later stage be disposed to change your mind (!), on a large or small issue, but would it be presumptuous to ask whether you would be prepared to commit yourself with some degree of firmness – after due consideration and further painful brooding if you feel it is required – to the publication of the remaining material in the scheme? The work entailed in checking your references etc. is as you know not negligible, and I think I must know, as far as concerns what still remains to be done, where I stand. [...]

I am grateful to you for your forbearance in the face of my onslaughts: I know that I sometimes express myself with a directness to which it would be easy to take exception. You are magnanimous in choosing rather to be touched by my compliments, which, as you perceive, are indeed sincere.

Berlin returned to the fray on 18 May 1976, introducing the welcome participation as referee of Bernard Williams:

Apart from the question of the philosophical essays, I shall *not*, all things considered, ask for any significant modifications in the plan for my post-humous works, as I think of them. As for philosophy, the view that what I am mainly concerned with is the reaction of reviewers is not correct: it derives, I suspect, from a hypothesis of the Warden of Wadham [Stuart Hampshire] about my reasons for doubt on this matter, but this hypoth-esis is ill-founded. My reason for hesitation is not the probable reaction of reviewers, but my estimate of the worth of these works themselves: I think it is right to publish old pieces in a collected form if, and only if, the essays are either (1) of sufficient value in themselves, or (2) are of obvious contemporary interest, or (3) throw light on the intellectual development or attitudes of someone of sufficient originality and eminence to be worth studying for his own sake. I am clear that I do not belong to the last group; I am dubious about the first, and somewhat dubious about the second. Bernard Williams has promised to try and convince me that my doubts on 1 and 2 are not sufficiently well grounded. If this generous offer succeeds, and he and/or Pears are good enough to take the trouble of trying to persuade me that these works are worth collect-ing, I may – I won't go further at present – yield to such argument. [...] Sorry to give such trouble – but you must always have anticipated this. My permanently self-critical attitude can, I fear, be a source of annoyance to those who think it merely tiresome, not to say neurotic.

Williams recorded his verdict in a letter to Berlin of 27 May 1976:

I have been rereading your earlier philosophical works and have arrived at some judicious conclusions.

Negatively, first. The first half of 'Induction and Hypothesis' is too inextricably rooted in the reflections of Miss MacDonald [to whose paper it was a response] to make it to posterity, I think. The second half is more independent of her paper, and I also think it interesting, but it would probably make a rather anomalous fragment by itself. 'Logical Translation' I am doubtful about, on the grounds of its having been overtaken by events: the current Davidsonian types of interest in analysis, canonical forms of statement, etc. have different enough motivations from what you were attacking, but sufficient contrast with what you were advocating, for there to be a rather laborious problem about what exactly you were and were not attacking (more precisely, to what your attack would or would not extend). On the other hand, it is a rather splendid affirmation of pluralism, and very interesting in relation to its time; it will also look different again on the next swing of this particularly tireless pendulum. I think that this piece could possibly reappear but I would not press for it.

'Verification', however, is clearly worth reprinting. It not only occupies a significant historical place, but has excellent arguments which are relevant to ongoing discussions about constructivist theories of meaning etc.: NB your device of understanding a conditional via a conditional *bet* is important in Dummett's discussions of these matters. 'Empirical Propositions and Hypothetical Statements' should certainly reappear. I confess I have always been extremely attached to it personally. Phenomenalism, like the belief in immortality, is something which I have never *for ten seconds* been disposed to accept, and the first good philosophical argument I can recall inventing as an undergraduate was against it: I recall reading your piece with great enthusiasm and sense of well-being as a clear affirmation of evident but perversely neglected truth. But apart from these autobiographical enthusiasms, it is my belief that it is very good, stands up very well, and indeed has more to say now than the demure paraphrases in the manner of the time which e.g. Warnock followed it up with: for a firm, if less Verdian, affirmation of the (real) non-existence of the (merely) hypothetical, see Dummett in the trendiest of all current philosophical collections, Evans & McDowell, *Truth and Meaning*.[6]

So I very much hope that you will agree to at least the latter two pieces going in. If that leaves Mr Hardy too short, I don't think 'Logical Translation' would do any harm at all. [...]

Berlin wrote to thank Williams on 31 May 1976:

Thank you ever so much for your most welcome letter about my posthumous *Selected Writings*. It was very good of you to look at them all again – whatever you may say, it must have been something of a nuisance and a bore – no, no, don't reassure me, it must, it must. However, I am quite sure that you are right: 'Verification' has some historical justification, and I am glad you liked the piece on hypothetical propositions etc. – I remember how stern Stuart was with me for ignoring the formal and material modes, and how Strawson quite correctly pointed out various obvious objections which phenomenalists could make – which I still think not worth bothering about, since all that matters is the central issue. All I write is by nature dishevelled – the well-combed and neatly fitting wigs of Warnock and other Wykehamists are not for me – if this sounds like making a romantic virtue out of irremediable mental disorder ('the chaos of the papers on your table doubtless represents equal chaos in your mind', said the eminent Irish scholar Myles Dillon to me once), it is just that. Anyway, thank you very much indeed – I shall act according to your advice and report to Henry Hardy, who will be much relieved. My contempt for my own works cannot really be assuaged; nevertheless, I am of course delighted to hear from someone as critical and as truthful as you undoubtedly are that they may not be quite as worthless as in some sense I shall continue to think them to be.

He wrote to me on the same day:

[...] I have now had a very full and, it seems to me, objective letter from Bernard Williams, which I enclose. [...] I trust Bernard sufficiently not really to need an opinion from David Pears [whom I did not consult, so far as I remember], but if you have it already I should be extremely interested to learn it, whatever it may be. I am sure that Bernard is right about 'Induction and Hypothesis'. If you are very keen on 'Logical Translation', let that go in too. So I suppose I am in effect won over to the original scheme, provided you leave out the piece on induction (which David Pears used to think quite well of), and possibly 'Logical Translation'. So I am made of wax after all.

The parenthesis about Pears in the last sentence about is a very characteristic instance of Berlinian cognitive dissonance: he didn't want the article included, but he didn't want it thought that this was because it was below par. Since it begins with a summary by Berlin of MacDonald's article, it does not depend on prior acquaintance with her arguments, and could well have gone in, but I did not want to risk pressing my advantage too far.

The reprieve was naturally an enormous relief, and the book is still in print (now in a second, expanded, edition, to which I stupidly failed to add the excluded essay) forty years afterwards.

4

SELECTED WRITINGS

I think these subversive writings which everybody attacks – that's what really gave me such reputation as I have. All these little paper volumes which Henry Hardy has kindly collected from all kinds of obscure articles published in pretty unknown periodicals – that's what created a certain outlook, gave me a position.[1]

To be well thought of by people one greatly admires is a source of great satisfaction.[2]

Such fame at my age![3]

I

Despite Berlin's promise not to make further changes to our plan, he did, almost immediately. He told me that his 1972 Jacob Herzog Memorial Lecture, 'Zionist Politics in Wartime Washington', which was accompanied by a short memoir of Herzog, should not after all appear in the volume of memoirs and tributes (not yet called *Personal Impressions*), as had been agreed, and crossed it out in the list of contents appended to the contract for *Selected Writings* (see 40). The lecture had been serialised in Hebrew in the Israeli newspaper *Ha'aretz* in 1972, and had attracted a three-part hostile critique by Nathan Yellin-Mor in that organ.[4] Berlin was concerned about stimulating further adverse publicity, and also felt that the lecture was not really part of his general oeuvre. I disagreed:

> Your inclination to exclude the piece on Herzog and its companion 'Zionist Politics in Wartime Washington', it will come as no surprise to you, I greatly regret and wish to resist. The latter essay is in some ways the most interesting in the [...] volume, because it is the nearest thing you have written to a chapter of your autobiography – as well as being of great intrinsic interest. The Herzog piece belongs with it as a sort of

preface. We have discussed all this several times, and I thought come to an agreement that it could go in. It would perhaps be ungracious of me to point out that you did assure me recently that there would be no more substantial changes to the contents, and there is no doubt that the omission of the Zionist politics piece would represent a very substantial change: but as you know I am an ungracious being, and so I have done so. But as ever, naturally, you will do what you want – how strong are your feelings on this? By whom would you be persuaded? (1 August 1976)

He changed his mind again, whether or not because of my plea, and on 10 September I wrote: 'I am very pleased to hear from Pat that "Zionist Politics ..." and the Herzog tribute are definitely to stay in. I should have been extremely sad to have lost them.' But by the time I came to submit the volume to the publisher, he had reverted to his previous opinion, and the lecture had to wait to be republished posthumously, twenty-eight years later, as an appendix to the first volume of his letters. The tribute to Herzog remains uncollected.

By January 1977 work on RT, the volume due to be published first, was nearly complete, and I sent Berlin a final list of queries. On 31 January he replied: 'I'll try to look up the list of queries on the *Russian Thinkers* volume. You call these corrections "nearly final": make no haste! I am all in favour of procrastination. The whole prospect fills me with alarm.' Pat Utechin added a comment: 'The last three sentences are enough to make one go stark staring mad. Thank *heaven* the contract is signed, otherwise I'd not rate your chances of getting anything done at more than a farthing.' I wrote back to Berlin:

I am sorry you are still filled with alarm about the 'whole prospect' of your *Selected Writings*. I wish I could reassure you – I think the best medicine may be the reviews which, I am sure, *Russian Thinkers* will receive. This volume is delivered to the publishers now [...], so I fear the time for the procrastination you desire is past!

I enclose a draft of an Editorial Preface for *Russian Thinkers*. [...] I tried to say something [...] to convey the fact that editing your work has (forgive me) certain special problems attached to it – not least overcoming your self-critical attitude. But I failed to come up with anything that didn't sound either patronising or self-congratulatory, so must leave it to you to mention this, if you wish to. You may feel that even some

of what I have said is inappropriate, in which case let us discuss it [...].
Peter Carson of Penguin has read *Russian Thinkers* and is as enthusiastic
about it as the rest of us. But I know you will be unmoved by this, as by
all favourable evaluations of your work!

The following month I addressed the question of how to address Berlin:

Dear [Sir] Isaiah,
    Your having said to me in All Souls on Saturday that you hated being
called 'Sir' makes me rather uneasy about employing what is strictly the
correct form of address in writing to you. I would willingly write 'Dear
Isaiah' if you wished: but since the price of leaving you unbeknighted
seems to be what you might regard as an excessive degree of familiarity,
I must await your instructions! (7 February 1977)

Berlin replied:

You must call me Isaiah, and there's an end on't. [...] 'Sir Isaiah' grates
on my eyes and on my ears every time. As it was bound to be used constantly, you may well ask why did I not decline this honour when it was
offered to me: that story I shall tell you when next I see you, and you
will, I think, understand, and not condemn my motives. (14 February)

The story was that he accepted for the sake of his mother, who would have been
devastated had he refused. Of course, he need not have told her of the offer; but
it's true that the thought of her intense pleasure was a venial excuse.
    In late 1977, when RT was about to appear, *British Book News* asked me to
write something about the project of which this was the first instalment. I was
nervous about saying something that Berlin would disapprove of, so I wrote to
ask what he would like me to say:

I write to you with what feels like diffidence to ask a question which
I knew would come up sooner or later – and now has – though I have
not looked forward to dealing with it. I have been asked by [...] *British
Book News* [...] to write a short piece for their editorial page about
your *Selected Writings*. I suspect that there will be other such requests
too, from journalists et al., since the venture is, rightly, regarded by the

literary establishment as of some importance. As your editor, I am the natural person to be asked to give an account of the genesis and history of the project.

I don't want to say anything in response to such requests which you would disapprove of (though I reserve the right to express a good opinion of your work which modesty might forbid you to endorse!). So I am writing to ask what sort of line you would like me to take (what, indeed, is the true answer) when I am asked why you consented to the publication of this selection, having declined a number of previous invitations of a similar kind. You will understand why I would rather not ask this: but I must give some kind of answer, and it had better be one that you endorse.

For the rest, I can cope – I hope – on my own. That is to say, I can explain how the editorial bug I conceived by putting out Mallinson's book, combined with my regard for your work, made editing your essays seem an unbeatably worthwhile publishing undertaking to me. I must, I fear, remain silent about the emendation of footnotes, translations etc. – though I can say something general about checking all these things. This is all immensely trivial, of course, but *something* must be said!

If there is anything else you would like me to bear in mind, do let me know. I really have no clear idea of your own valuation of your own work, which makes it hard to be confident in explaining that the selection will appear in the face of a certain scepticism on your part. Do you *really* rate your essays as low as you sometimes affect to do? Do you feel that there is some great mine of potential talent in yourself that your temperament has not allowed you to exploit to the full? Do you truly believe that those – such as Aileen and Roger [Hausheer] [...] – who set great store by what you have written are in some way deluded? Perhaps in your heart you acknowledge merits in your work which you cannot assent to aloud. (14 November 1977)

Berlin replied on 21 November:

You can, of course, say anything you like about the works themselves, but there is, I think, no harm in telling the truth (I hope you will agree that it is the truth – things can look very different to different eyes, a platitude of some relevance to this case), namely:

1. That I have always adopted a somewhat critical attitude towards the value of my own published work, and had never suggested to any publisher that it be republished; but that since I was constantly criticised for spending most of my time on teaching and lecturing, and publishing too little, I thought I could meet some of these criticisms by agreeing to the republication of, for example, the *Four Essays on Liberty*; the fact that this collection was not widely reviewed⁵ convinced me further that the interest in my political essays, for example, was limited.

2. I also felt that, before republishing already existing essays and lectures, which might indicate that I had no more to say, I should first be permitted to write and publish one new book (do not, for God's sake, call it a major work) on a subject which has always interested me, namely, the intellectual sources of Romanticism, on which I had delivered Mellon Lectures, then broadcast by the BBC, which, indeed, reviewers and others had been urging me to publish as they stood. As I am a very slow worker, and doing far too many other things, this work, although I am currently engaged on it, will take some years to finish; perhaps the 'Essays and Addresses' should more properly follow that, rather than be my sole contribution to the history of ideas, which has always been my basic interest.

3. But when a group of graduates at Wolfson, headed by yourself, assured me that despite my still unwavering conviction that a good deal of my work was now obsolescent, or consisted of too many *pièces d'occasion*, whose value had diminished with the passing of the relevant occasions – and assured me that not only would they find a publisher ready to print selected pieces (some, even they agreed, had better be consigned to oblivion), but would edit them and provide them with introductions themselves – that I would not, in effect, be required to do anything to them *at all* – for they saw that I shrank from the thought of re-reading them and bringing them up to date, etc., as being likely to plunge me into self-critical gloom – and when the idea occurred that the proceeds, if any, might be devoted to the needs of Wolfson College, towards which my feelings were very strong and warm, and where I had been exceedingly happy⁶ – my resistance weakened, especially as I was realistic enough to realise that the book on Romanticism might yet take two or three years to complete. I had thought, moreover, that my essays on Russian topics were not too bad, especially considering the relative

dearth of anything on the subject in English. And you could perhaps (if you were willing) testify to the fact that my modesty in this matter was rooted in the belief that I had plenty to be modest about – and that the praise which kind friends were good enough occasionally to provide convinced me of the goodness of their hearts but not of the validity of their judgements.

All this seems to me mainly true. You ask me whether I really rate my essays as low as I sometimes affect to do – believe me, it is no affectation. I do not believe in any great mine of potential talent in myself still unexploited. I do, indeed, believe that Aileen and Roger and yourself overestimate my work: I think this must be because of the fervour with which I talk at times about things in which I am interested, rather more than the intrinsic value of the ideas themselves. I should like to think that I am wrong about this – nothing is nicer than praise by honest men – but I remain unshakeably convinced that I have all my life been overestimated.

So say what you will. I feel terrible about this: rather like the man who at some testimonial dinner was praised to the skies by the man who proposed his health. He gracefully acknowledged, with pleasure, all the handsome things that had been said about him, but said that there was perhaps one attribute of his which had not been mentioned by anyone and of which he felt proudest of all – his conspicuous modesty. I remember, too, although I was not present, that there was a famous Balliol dinner, at which praise was showered on the Master, Lord Lindsay, who, in reply, among other things, after thanking everybody for everything, said that there was one thing that he had missed – nobody had spoken of a nice, honest chap called Sandy Lindsay. I don't want to be like that! Is that vanity? Perhaps. All I really want said is that although even I recognise that some of my pieces are less good than others, I do not think any of them begin to reach the level of some of the writers I truly admire, e.g. Herzen, or Brandes or Edmund Wilson, to name only three men who had something new and important to say and knew how to say it. So there.[7]

I made some use of Berlin's suggestions, as can be seen from the article that appeared, as well as adding matter of my own.[8] It was preceded by a headnote written by *British Book News*, which began:

A fellow scholar at Oxford is reported to have said of Isaiah Berlin that 'He is the man who pronounces "epistemological" as one syllable.'⁹ Anyone who has ever heard this fascinating talker, whose ideas seem to tumble out even faster than his words, will know exactly what he means.

Here are the parts of what I wrote that do not duplicate Berlin's letter or my own narrative:

When Isaiah Berlin was awarded the Order of Merit, Maurice Bowra wrote in a letter to Noel Annan: 'I am delighted about Isaiah. He is much better than all alternatives [...] and very much deserves it. Though like Our Lord and Socrates he does not publish much, he thinks and says a great deal and has had an enormous influence on our times.'¹⁰

Bowra's belief that Isaiah Berlin rarely ventures into print has been widely held, but it does not fit the facts. He has published a great deal on a wide variety of subjects – principally philosophy, political theory, the Russian intelligentsia of the nineteenth century, and the history of ideas generally – but most of his work has appeared in (often obscure) periodicals and symposia, or as occasional pamphlets; much of it is out of print; and only half a dozen essays have hitherto been collected and reissued.¹¹ I have happily had the opportunity to help put this deficiency right, by editing a four-volume collection of his essays. This, I hope, will dispel once and for all the myth that he does not publish, as well as making more of his work as readily accessible as it has long deserved to be.

The first volume, *Russian Thinkers*, includes two of Berlin's most celebrated pieces, 'The Hedgehog and the Fox', on Tolstoy's view of history, and 'Fathers and Children', his Romanes Lecture on Turgenev and the liberal predicament. Bakunin, Belinsky and Herzen are the other protagonists. The gifted young Russian scholar Aileen Kelly has written a splendid introduction which sets the essays in the context of Berlin's work as a whole. The essays in the second volume, *Concepts and Categories*, are contributions to philosophy, and there is an introduction by Bernard Williams, one of the leading philosophers of our time. *Against the Current*¹² contains a dozen essays in the history of ideas [...]: the emphasis is on the originality of the intellectual contributions made by individuals, among them Moses Hess, Machiavelli, Montesquieu, Sorel and Vico. The introduction by the young historian of ideas Roger Hausheer reveals the originality of Berlin's own contribution to the study of ideas. Finally, *Tributes and Memoirs* [*sic*] is a collection of Berlin's *éloges* on the twentieth-century scholars and statesmen he has known and admired: J. L. Austin, Bowra, Churchill, Aldous Huxley, Namier, Plamenatz, Roosevelt, Weizmann and a number of others.[13]

I came to know Isaiah Berlin at Wolfson College in Oxford, a new college for dons and graduate students that began life in 1966 under his presidency, backed by funds from the Wolfson and Ford Foundations. I had come there to read for a postgraduate degree in philosophy. Until then, to my shame, I had only the vaguest idea of what he had been and done. He was born in Riga in 1909, but has spent his adult life, apart from the war, in Oxford – at Corpus Christi as an undergraduate, and thereafter at All Souls (where he now is again), New College and Wolfson. It was at All Souls in the 1930s that he wrote his brilliant book on Karl Marx. He was Professor of Social and Political Theory for a decade before moving to Wolfson, whose beautiful buildings by the Cherwell, and whose open and democratic organisation, unique in Oxford, are lasting reminders of the beneficent effectiveness of his period of office. To have been there during those years was an exceptionally happy experience.

Berlin's writing too, like the college he created, is imbued with his personality, his values and standards. Apart from the great intrinsic interest of what he has to say about ideas (and this alone would place his work in the very front rank), perhaps the most attractive feature of his writing, as of his lectures, is the degree of engagement, moral commitment, that he brings to the subjects that preoccupy him. This contrasts strikingly, and favourably, with the kind of detached academic pedantry so common among scholars – that obsession with purposeless detail of which Berlin is delightfully free. Add to that his genius for capturing the atmosphere of a cultural milieu separated from our own both in time and by many of its basic presuppositions, and his deftness at portraying an individual personality; add his sometimes breathtaking ability to cut through a mass of extraneous detail, and to express the underlying essence with a firmness and clarity that gives form to what previously seemed chaotic and unintelligible; add, in short, his usually penetrating and sympathetic powers of *understanding* – of people and their motives and hopes and fears as well as of ideas and movements and their origins and offspring – and it will be clear why his work is so valuable and important. His contribution to our intellectual life is both entirely *sui generis* – against the current of the times – and significantly richer and more humane than the background from which it stands out.

I first raised with him the question of reissuing his scattered essays early in 1974. I was then in the throes of editing a collection of writings by my octogenarian friend Arnold Mallinson, a totally charming but bizarre Anglican vicar with whom I was lodging. Mallinson says of himself: 'I never throw anything away, and I never organise anything.' This combination of traits allowed me to conduct a successful search of attics and cupboards, and to round up a weird and miscellaneous anthology which it would never have occurred to him to put in hand himself. As a result I acquired a strong taste for the kind of editorial work that makes possible the publication of a book which otherwise would not have appeared. It is largely a type of midwifery, doubtless, but has the added attraction of allowing a vicarious claim to a tiny fraction of the paternity.

This, together with my admiration for Berlin's work, made the prospect of collecting and editing his essays enormously appealing, as I knew that he was certain never to undertake this himself. [...] I realised that I might find it difficult to overcome his modesty, and his feeling that the time might not be ripe for what could seem like a kind of summing-up. Even now, he refers to my selection as his 'posthumous writings'. Nevertheless, he did allow me to persuade him that a collection of his essays might appear. [...]

Even had he wanted to undertake the editorial work himself, he was far too busy. He appears to live a permanently treble-booked life, as President of the British Academy, a trustee of the National Gallery, a director of Covent Garden, and under many other hats, quite apart from giving lectures around the world and talking to undergraduate societies (not only in Oxford), colleges of education, and sixth forms. His programme would reduce most people to a state of nervous exhaustion.

Indeed, it is remarkable that he has found time to write as much as he has. When I tentatively suggested to him that I might edit his work,

I had come across only his best-known writings, and so I enquired what else he had published. He mentioned a few things, but added that not only had he forgotten about many of his smaller pieces, but he had kept no record of them, so that the compilation of his bibliography would be a task beyond human capability. To my bullishly obsessional disposition this was a red rag, so I set out to discover for myself what he had written, using every device I could muster, and published the resulting list the following year. Even those who knew him and his work best were surprised at the number and range of items, and the editorial project I had undertaken became even more attractive. [...]

The rest is perspiration. The pursuit of elusive references in Oxford's Bodleian Library, the choice of publisher, the securing of introductions, would make dull reading. The first volume, *Russian Thinkers*, is published this month by the Hogarth Press, who also published *Vico and Herder*; the American publisher is Viking. The remaining volumes will follow during the course of the next two years. The project as a whole is the most worthwhile publishing venture with which I am ever likely to be associated.

Some eyebrows (including Berlin's) were raised at the first sentence of my last paragraph, but I had wanted to allude somehow to the prodigious amount of work involved. Even now some people think that all I had to do was to gather the essays and send them to the publisher.

Berlin must have seen, and perhaps even read, the published text of my piece. However, by the time it was reprinted in *Lycidas* the following year, it is clear that he had forgotten all about it, since he wrote to me on 8 January 1980 to thank me for my 'infinitely generous and charming article about the ghastly job of editing my works', as if he had no prior acquaintance with it.

Advance copies of RT arrived in early December 1977. On the very day when I received my first copy both Berlin and I were among those invited to dinner with Jerome ('Jerry') Bruner, then Watts Professor of Psychology and a Fellow of Wolfson, at his College house at the end of Garford Road. I took the book with me and laid it proudly on the coffee table while aperitifs were served. As soon as Berlin saw it, he turned it over so that his name, in elegant large lettering by Michael Harvey on the front of the jacket, could not be seen. This reaction typified his attitude to seeing his name in print, and to the volumes that I produced.

Reactions from readers began to arrive. Michael Brock observed that 'I never knew a writer whose voice can be heard more clearly in his prose.'[14] He was struck by the modesty of the author's preface, in which Berlin had written that Aileen Kelly's 'steady advocacy has almost persuaded me that the preparation of this volume may have been worthy of so much intelligent and devoted labour'. He told Berlin, in an allusion to his appointment to the Order of Merit in 1971, that he deserved the following note from Buckingham Palace: 'HM desires it to be known that she does not confer the OM on those academic persons whose works are unworthy of reproduction in collected form.'[15] The volume was published on 5 January 1978.

Before it appeared, I had written to Berlin to suggest that his long-cherished wish to write about his 'Meetings with Russian Writers in 1945 and 1956' (the title of his eventual account) might finally be fulfilled as part of the volume of memoirs we had agreed:

> [...] an idea has arisen which just might appeal to you. I know that one of the few things you really do want to get written is an account of what the OUP file calls 'The Russian Bloomsbury',[16] and I believe that you are unsure as to what would be the most appropriate context for it to appear in – partly perhaps because of what might be its intermediate length. It seems to me that it would be entirely appropriate for such an account to appear in *Memoirs and Tributes*: how does this idea strike you? It would add substantially to the interest of that already fascinating volume. It would mean, of course, your writing the account by the end of 1978 – but I daresay it is something you could dictate from memory comparatively quickly? Do give the suggestion serious consideration. (2 January 1978)

Berlin replied:

> I ought certainly to record all this – I don't know how long it will turn out to be, seven or eight thousand words or a little longer, perhaps. I think that if I do it at all it ought to appear first somewhere else, in some magazine of interest to people interested in Russian writers, and not solely tucked away in the volume of memoirs and tributes.[17]

He thought it would be too long for the TLS, and suggested a two-parter in the NYRB. In the end both these journals published the shortened version (with additions in the NYRB) that Berlin delivered in the Examination Schools in Oxford as a Bowra Lecture entitled 'Conversations with Russian Poets' on 13 May 1980 – his last ever full-dress public lecture, and the last in the series honouring his friend.

When RT finally appeared, most reviews were highly favourable. But no amount of acclaim shook Berlin's scepticism about the value of his work. A review of RT that bucked the trend – one of the first reviews I saw – was by the eighty-five-year-old Rebecca West.[18] At this earliest stage of public exposure I was wildly oversensitive to criticism, and minded terribly every word written against the project (by the end, anything was water off my back). Unfortunately West's review was one of the most negative we ever received, declaring Berlin to be (among other things) repetitive, uncritically over-enthusiastic, patronising and inaccurate. I wrote to Berlin on 15 January:

> I hope you weren't too upset by Rebecca West's spiteful review in the *Sunday Telegraph*. Has she some grudge against you, or is it just the bitchiness of old age? She so overdoes it. As for Keats, it does seem that your gloss on 'negative capability' gives it a sense Keats didn't intend (see ODQ), but this is not a matter of proof-reading; and I resent her unsubstantiated slur on this aspect of the book. At least Crankshaw in the *Observer* was enthusiastic. I wonder if any of us should write to Rebecca West. If you do, do send me a copy.

On Keats, West had written: 'The proof-readers have fallen by the wayside; and have passed a terrible bloomer in a misquotation from a letter of John Keats which is one of the key passages of Romantic criticism.' In a letter to George and Thomas Keats of 22 December 1817, Keats wrote:

> it struck me, what quality went to form a Man of Achievement especially in Literature & which Shakespeare possessed so enormously – I mean *Negative Capability*, that is when man is capable of being in uncertainties, Mysteries, doubts, without any irritable reaching after fact & reason.

In RT Berlin identified negative capability and empathy, but the empathiser must, as Berlin puts it in a letter to Lidiya Chukovskaya (B 541), 'transpose himself into others', surely a further step. Keats did write to Benjamin Bailey a month earlier (22 November 1817), 'if a Sparrow come before my Window I take part in its existince [*sic*] and pick about the Gravel', but this is a description of a different mental act, and not here called negative capability. The two mental acts are linked in a letter to Richard Woodhouse of 27 October 1817, where Keats says that a poet 'has no Identity – he is continually in for – and filling some other Body', but it still seems a stretch, at any rate on the basis of these passages, to take 'negative capability' to refer to the frequently but not universally conjoined acts.

Berlin replied:

> R. West: she *may* know in how little esteem I hold her: she is a rather *détraquée* ['deranged'] old lady, and when the new Herzen edition (in English) appeared, said H. was *wildly* overestimated: so it is nothing but blind prejudice. On *no* account is she to be written to: her views are worthless & don't annoy me – it is like being kicked by a super-annuated old cow. Anyway one shd never reply to reviewers unless there is a *blatant* misstatement of fact. As for negative capability: K. ascribes it to Shakespeare; perhaps Middleton Murry's book on Keats & Shakespeare explains his meaning: I wd rather not surrender without some resistance.[19]

Shortly afterwards a review by Nicholas Richardson spoke of 'a cumbrous editorial apparatus apparently, if hopelessly, designed to embalm the most effervescent of all contemporary historians'.[20] In my prickly state I bridled at this dig, which seemed wildly exaggerated at best, telling Berlin that I hadn't enjoyed it.[21] By this criterion the mere act of collecting scattered essays is a funerary activity, and the mere provision of an introduction must amount to the scattering of the author's ashes. It struck me as perverse to say that something we were doing in order to give the work of an author a longer life succeeded only in burying him.

Twenty years later Stefan Collini referred to 'a slightly bastardised state of [Berlin's] essays', observing that 'Henry Hardy has done his best to kit them out in full footnoted fig'; he added that 'this is no doubt helpful for those who wish to trace one of Berlin's references, but it does threaten to domesticate what had been personal and stylish into appearing merely conventional and industrious'.[22] I have quoted and responded to both barbs in RR and RT2, observing in the former case:

Stefan Collini is of course right that to add references in footnotes to a plain text is to commit an alteration of tone. However, it is an alteration of which Isaiah Berlin thoroughly approved; had it not been, I should not have undertaken it. When Collini's charge was put to him during his final illness, Berlin rejected it outright, observing that the provision of references 'has turned what were mere belles-lettres into scholarship'.[23] This remark displays Berlin's customary, and excessive, modesty and generosity, but it is answer enough, both to Collini and to Richardson, particularly if one adds that Berlin himself, when the necessary information was to hand, provided prodigious footnotes of his own.[24]

Another hostile review was published later in the year by Martin Green, who observed of the endorsements on the book's US jacket: 'Such a hush of awe is overblown and calls for deflation.' His notice ends by recognising that 'To make us see Tolstoy and others from an unexpected angle is the sort of thing that Berlin has done for us. But we need not fall at his feet to display our gratitude.'[25] About this Berlin seemed to mind more, writing on the back of the envelope containing a letter dated 4 April 1979:

> Mr Green is a horrible figure who suffers from envy (in all his works) rationalized as moral indignation. All his factual [assertions] (as opp to his poor view of me, to which he is presumably entitled) about Belinsky, Leavis, Tolstoy etc. happen to be false. I have so far *not* written him. I rather want to but, on the other hand, I feel like Froude on Freeman "I do not wish to enter into any relations with him, not even those of hostility".[26] Better left alone and yet .... I long to write a crushing private letter. Shd I resist this desire? On the one hand, he is an embittered hack; on the other, truth shd be defended ...

He also argued the toss (in a letter to me) with Mary-Barbara Zeldin, who had written a review accusing him of repetition, inconsistency, prolixity and stylistic and grammatical error, and raising a series of specific points of disagreement. Berlin demolished her points one by one, observing in midstream: 'God knows why I should list all her absurdities, but having begun I should like to go on.'[27]

11

οὔτοι συνέχθειν, ἀλλὰ συμφιλεῖν ἔφυν.
(My nature is to join not in hate, but in love.)

Sophocles[28]

By early 1978 introductions had been written or agreed to for the first three of the four volumes of *Selected Writings*: Aileen Kelly had introduced RT, Bernard Williams CC, and Roger Hausheer was working on what turned out to be a brilliant but very long introduction to *Against the Current*. This left me without an introducer for the volume still at that time called *Memoirs and Tributes*. Berlin and I had discussed the possibility of his introducing this volume himself, as I reminded him on 7 February:

> Are you prepared to make a decision now as to whether you will yourself undertake the introduction to vol. 4 – possibly a short Hume-like autobiographical sketch, as we discussed earlier? I very much hope you will do this. But if you won't, I think I should commission someone else to do it – who on earth? – now, or else I'd be cutting things too fine.

Pat Utechin conveyed Berlin's scepticism about any such introduction on 13 February:

> No, on no account he will [*sic*] write the intro to vol. 4 (and, he added, don't let him think he will persuade me on *this* one). And he, indeed, believes that any intro to this one is entirely unnecessary – what could anyone say (he asks) save 'Here are some splendid little pieces about splendid chaps'?

Her note was accompanied by the author's preface to CC, which gave what came to be Berlin's standard account of his conversion from philosophy to the history of ideas, though it omits the part about the transatlantic flight in a bomber in 1944, during which, according to Berlin, the die was finally cast (CC2 295–6).

I tried again on 14 February 1978:

I suppose there is no hope of my persuading you to write the introduction to volume 4? But will you also veto in advance any suggestions I may make about another introducer? If you would suggest someone yourself, that would be useful. You ask through Pat what anyone could say. Well, they could write a short account of your life showing where the characters about whom you write fit in. That's what I'd hoped you'd do yourself. Is there any point in my persisting?

Berlin's reply is dated 23 February:

As to the introduction to vol. 4, I really am not prepared to write a short account of my life with the various characters stuck in in appropriate places like currants in a cake. I think the result would be somewhat absurd. Nor can I think what anyone else could say about a collection of obituaries and fragmentary memoirs. In such cases, asymmetry seems to me preferable to absurdity. I cannot think of a single argument in favour of a special introduction. I feel sure that nobody will complain of its absence.

On 17 March 1978, in another of my more risky (and in hindsight shaming) boutades, I unilaterally asked Noel Annan – who had been invited to write IB's biography, but had declined – if he would, in principle, write the introduction, believing that Berlin would not have authorised such an approach if I had asked him to do so. Annan's reply of 21 March is interesting. He says that Stuart Hampshire would be a better choice, but doesn't rule himself out if I want him 'to write an introduction about Isaiah's view of human beings', which I did. His last paragraph introduces a reservation that was new to me at the time:

There is an awkward tombstone, however, in the middle of the garden. Isaiah's wonderful perception about human beings does not prevent him – indeed it probably compels him – to look for their feet of clay. He is the very reverse of the ordinary Englishman who is always said to have such [a] cold exterior beneath which beats a hidden warm heart. Isaiah's heart is enormously warm but within it is a lump of ice. Do you really want me to say that?

This thought was echoed twenty years later by Roger Hausheer in his introduction to PSM, where he speaks of Berlin's

> remarkable capacity to deploy a cool impersonality combined with
> a warm responsiveness, both towards the great, stable visions of the
> human condition, and to idiosyncrasies of feeling and temperament on
> the part of individuals. That is the secret of his mental constitution: the
> intellectual core has the hard clarity of a diamond, while the periphery
> flames and sparkles with that intense engagement that makes his essays
> on people so irresistible. (PSM2 xlv)

In my reply to Annan I encouraged him to be tactfully frank, and asked him
to explain what he meant by the 'lump of ice':

> Do you mean simply that, deep down, he is rather unforgivingly critical
> of almost everyone, despite the misleading surface gush? Or do you mean
> something quite different – perhaps to do with his obvious streak of
> egocentricity (is it more thoroughgoing than we suspected?), his failure,
> perhaps, to identify entirely with sufferings which he may outwardly
> describe and respond to with great virtuosity, his tendency to let people
> down at the last minute with anguished mien but unruffled spirit? Maybe
> I'm completely on the wrong track. Is his warmth a show, or genuine but
> superficial? What exactly did you have in mind?

Annan did not answer these questions.

It must have been conveyed to me that my approach to Annan was not a
kosher step to take, since I wrote as follows to Berlin on 5 April:

> Noel Annan – I'm sorry if it was unsettling of me to approach him
> without clearing this with you first. I agree that it was not entirely proper
> form to do so. Let me explain quite candidly why I did it. (By the way,
> I did *not* ask him to write your biography. Not that, if he did, it would
> necessarily be a bad book, would it?)
>   The explanation is this. You said in a letter to me that you didn't
> think vol. 4 needed an introduction at all, and you expressed this opinion
> quite strongly. But you didn't actually forbid me to approach a possible
> introducer, to see if, in principle, given your agreement of course, he

would be willing to write an introduction. I still believed (and believe) that the book would benefit greatly from a good introduction, and so I am doing my best to achieve one. Strictly, of course, I could have written to you and said 'I appreciate that you are dead against the idea, but may I write to Annan none the less and see if he'd do it in principle?' I felt I couldn't do this, because if you'd given the go-ahead to write to Annan, it would have amounted to your saying, in effect, 'I am against an introduction, whoever writes it, but you may nevertheless see if Annan will write one.' I judged that if I could persuade Annan in advance that, if you agreed, he would write an introduction, and then write to you saying that I had Annan's agreement in principle, you would be more likely to agree than if I'd gone to you in the first place. And indeed, I'm glad to hear from Pat that you're not necessarily against an introduction by Annan. I hope that when he's read the pieces he'll agree to do it: I should certainly be fascinated to read what he had to say about your view of people.

So I own up openly to unscrupulousness! My behaviour was based on a utilitarian calculation as to which course would be most likely to yield an introduction to vol. 4. It is good of you to overlook my skulduggery. I made quite clear to Lord Annan that your agreement would be necessary before I could commission him firmly.

This account makes me shiver today, because of my defiance of Berlin's clearly expressed view, but I should like to say in my defence that Berlin's self-effacing temperament did make his initial reaction to suggested courses of action unreliable guides to his settled response. He was the last person whose wishes one ought to have second-guessed, given his celebrated position on proponents of 'positive' liberty who believed they knew better what people's wishes were than the people themselves. But the whole enterprise on which I was engaged was based on a systematic refusal to accept his negative instincts at face value, and in the light of the upshot I do not repine.

Forced into a corner, Berlin did agree, on 18 April 1978, to an introduction by Annan: 'Very well. It is very good of Lord Annan to agree to do this, and I cannot do less than accept gratefully.' I missed the gritted teeth; and this was far from the end of the matter. The writing of the piece turned into a long and uncomfortable – not to say excruciating – saga in which draft succeeded draft, and Berlin tested Annan's friendship by repeatedly asking for revisions, not all of them obviously justified.[29] Annan was patient and painstaking in response, but showed anger with Berlin to me at times, as will emerge.

At one point Berlin and Annan met to discuss a draft text. With monumental tactlessness (given what I knew about Berlin's deep reservations) I wrote to Berlin shortly beforehand, on 30 September 1978: 'I hope your deliberations with Noel Annan next weekend have a mutually satisfactory outcome.' Berlin responded on 2 October:

> I shall be seeing Noel Annan soon, and hope that our old friendship will not crack under the strain of what I shall have to say to him. As for your hopes and fears in your relevant paragraph, it seems best to me to say nothing: it would put our friendship under too great a strain if I were to describe my reaction to your words. I shall confine myself to saying that the entire situation is painful to me, and could have been avoided: as for explaining this further, some things are better unsaid.

This stung badly, as it was doubtless meant to. But is the piece really so bad? I am not persuaded.

On 4 December Berlin wrote:

> Letter after letter! Noel Annan's piece is far better than it was, but there are still one or two 'bad' bits – not very important ones, but one in particular which would embarrass too many people without cause. I will write to him again. Sincere and laudatory as his introduction is, and now shorn of its direct errors of fact, especially about philosophy (for which we have to thank Stuart Hampshire), and warm-hearted as it plainly is, I shall, I am afraid, have gooseflesh whenever I think of it, for the rest of my life. Hubert Henderson once told me, about Sir Roy Harrod's life of Keynes, that everything in it was two or three degrees out, just wrong by a thin margin, and that this produced a continuous feeling of irritation, when things were nearly but never quite right about a man whom he knew – or thought he knew – far better than Harrod knew him, which caused him to refuse to review it. About pieces on oneself, one must speak with greater humility and caution: a man hears his own voice quite differently from the way others hear it; nevertheless, I shall never be quite reconciled to it. You will think that I am making far too much of all this. I expect I am. I shall not say a word about this to you again.

[He did.] All I ask is that people should not write or say to me anything about how well captured my views and personality [are], how exact, and yet generous, the vignette is. But they will. No more on that. (A 94)

The last flurry of this episode occurred when Berlin's friend Robert ('Bob') Silvers, then co-editor of the *New York Review of Books*, formed the impression that Berlin was not against his publishing the introduction when the time came. Annan had offered him the text and Silvers wanted to publish it. Silvers wrote to me that he had told Berlin this, and that Berlin had not objected. I told Silvers, in a letter I copied to Berlin, that I was glad to hear this. Berlin understood me to be saying that he was not against such a serialisation, which did indeed seem to be a reasonable conclusion to draw. He wrote:

> Am I not against it? I am very much against it. I should dislike that very much indeed. Would you please tell Bob Silvers that, and I will too, sometime. I can just live with the idea of that introduction as part of a volume, but the idea of detaching it and publishing it as a separate vignette is wholly intolerable to me. Why ever did you think that I was not against this prospect? I am greatly relieved that you have informed me of this – suicide might have followed if you had not. (5 March 1979)

My guess is that this is one of the many examples of Berlin saying one thing to one person, another to another, unless he was simply not thinking through the implications of what he said. He may not have been willing to tell Annan or Silvers in terms that he did not want the piece to appear in the NYRB, leaving them with the impression that the way ahead was clear. After receiving Berlin's rebuke, I wrote to Annan and Silvers conveying his unwillingness to see the piece published separately. Annan strongly believed serialisation to be his authorial right, and demurred forcefully. This shocked and surprised me, as I expected Annan to withdraw in the light of his friend's feelings, whatever he might think of his arguments. I wrote long, anguished letters to Annan on 21 March and to Berlin on 22 March, throwing myself on their respective mercies, and hoping that one of them would yield. I tried to persuade Annan not to insist:

> I wish Isaiah were less sensitive. He expends an enormous amount of emotional energy in unnecessarily (in my view) protecting himself from what he sees as over-exposure or adverse publicity. But he is what he is,

and my relationship with him is such that I could not possibly defy him in a matter of this kind, even though I agree with you entirely that it is your right to make what use you wish of what you have written, and to expect normal pre-publication serialisation from your editor and publisher. I suppose what I am asking you to do – if the worst comes to the worst, and I hope it won't – is to join me in making an exception to your expectations in Isaiah's case. I don't really understand why I am prepared to do this – you may think it craven of me – but I suppose at least in this instance it is because the *Selected Writings* is something I've cooked up very much in co-operation with him, and it would be against the spirit of the enterprise to handle any part of it in a way that to my knowledge displeased him. Does this make sense to you?

To Berlin I explained Annan's view in these terms:

Annan's line is that, when he is commissioned to write a piece, he expects his editor and publishers 'to do everything they can to give it publicity and to facilitate its publication elsewhere' [16 March]. In his view, this includes pre-publication serialisation. As a result, he comes close to saying, even if he does not quite say, that, if we will not allow pre-publication serialisation, he will not be willing for us to use the piece as an introduction to vol. 4. He writes:

If Isaiah is ashamed of my piece, by all means withdraw it. I would not for the world, even after all our efforts to write something which is truthful, offend him, and neither he nor you are under any obligation to accept what I have written and publish it as the introduction to this volume of essays. But if you do intend to publish it and you then refuse to give it legitimate publicity, that is nothing less than an insult. I am deeply offended.

I have of course assured Annan that you are not 'ashamed' of his piece – that that is not the issue at all. But I doubt if this will make much difference.

What is to be done? The Gordian knot would be cut, of course, if you were to allow pre-publication serialisation; but, given what you have said about your feelings on this score, I daren't hope for this. Maybe you will wish to speak to Annan yourself and find agreement that way? Strictly, of course, the copyright in the piece is Annan's, and he can publish it where and how he likes once it has appeared as the introduction to vol. 4. His publication rights are limited only before its publication in vol. 4 – quite properly, he leaves the arrangement of its pre-publication serialisation to me in consultation with Hogarth, though he is, I think, perfectly entitled to expect that we *will* arrange this, *ceteris paribus*.

But other things, of course, are not equal. You do not wish the piece publicised in that way, and for me that was enough – your wishes take precedence over normal expectations in this as in every case, as you know. But this does not appear to be the way Annan sees things, and this is what has caught me unawares. I am very sorry to land you with this problem – you will doubtless wish to remind me that it is ultimately of my own devising, but will graciously refrain from doing so.

Would you mind less if the serialisation occurred in, say, the TLS? Is it the NYRB in particular, for some reason, that seems to you a forum for over-exposure? If so, we could certainly arrange for the TLS to handle it. But I fear it is any sort of isolated airing that you resist – am I right?

I await your response in some trepidation. Above all, I beg you not to accept Annan's suggestion that we might drop the introduction altogether. I'm sure that would cause more pain on all sides than is necessary, as well as greatly impoverishing vol. 4.

Berlin wrote an equally anguished reply on 27 March 1979:

Whatever happens, this is bound to end badly. Whatever I say to Lord Annan about my feelings will not assuage his deep resentment. I fear he cannot understand that one may not want any personal publicity at all, however favourable – or, if he does, this is outweighed by the feelings of the insult to himself. On the other hand, if the thing does appear separately, whether in the TLS or the NYRB, it will cause me pain for the rest of my life. It leaves me in a ghastly dilemma. The TLS is anyway out, quite apart from anything else, because to print this encomium after the other – first Aileen,* then Noel – would involve both them and

---

* Aileen Kelly's introduction to RT had appeared in the TLS as 'A Complex Vision: Isaiah Berlin and Russian Thought' (30 December 1977, 1523–4).

me in a ridiculous situation, and provoke undesirable and not entirely undeserved sneers from various quarters, published and unpublished. The prospect fills me with such distress that I can scarcely continue this letter. I shall have to talk to Noel sometime, but the prospect is dreadful. Anyway, I will do what I can. Meanwhile, I will write to Bob Silvers.

PS (29 March): I suppose I'll have to capitulate [he didn't]. This really will remain a permanent wound; *how much* did you know about Lord A. when you wrote him?

At the end of the long process of repeated revision, on 8 May 1980, Annan wrote:

You may deliver the MS to the Hogarth Press as it stands. Isaiah has made it clear that he does not want any serialisation anywhere – although he allowed the introduction to the first volume to appear in the TLS.
    I spent more time & care on that piece than [on] almost anything I have ever written. I never want to see the bloody thing again. You can correct the proofs, I won't.

Berlin's final response to Annan, written five days later, can be read in part in the last volume of his letters (A 104–5). Here he tries to deny, for me unsuccessfully, that he is a public figure, 'a natural object of public interest'. In the unpublished part of the letter's first paragraph he writes:

the days I have spent on tenterhooks have been worth it, and I wish to say again that, quite apart from the immense relief (there is nothing like it, the thought of future misery averted, it is a truly golden feeling), I consider that you have acted with noble forbearance. It was a sacrifice I had no right to demand on the altar of friendship. In short, thank you very much indeed. I shall never forget this kindness – I really was agonised.

And at the end of the letter he returns to these sentiments:

let me say once again that, holding the views that you do, and the proper ambitions that you have, you have behaved wonderfully. How can I convey this in the brief note that I am expected to write for vol. 4, if only to thank you for writing the introduction? I shall not succeed.

Against this background the sentences about Annan in his author's preface to the book take on added force:

> I wish to record my deep gratitude to my friend Noel Annan for writing the introduction to this miscellany, and to tell him, and his readers, that I am only too well aware of what reserves of sensibility, conscience, time, sheer labour, capacity for resolving the conflicting claims of truth and friendship, knowledge and moral tact such a task unavoidably draws upon; and to thank him for his great goodwill in agreeing to perform it. (PI2 xxxii–xxxiii)

III

In mid 1978 a series of huge letters passed between Berlin and me in which I asked about the sources of a large number of unreferenced quotations in the essays destined to become AC, and Berlin did his best to supply answers. These exchanges are not without their comic moments, among which are vain attempts by Berlin to persuade me that sometimes no reference is required. For example, on 6 June:

> Again, you don't need a reference, it is a very famous formula [*la terre et les morts*: see e.g. PI3 144], always attributed to Barrès, nobody bothers about where it is to be found – like 'blood and soil' as a Nazi slogan (did Hitler use it in *Mein Kampf* or somewhere else? Who knows, who cares?)

For me the fact that nobody so bothers is an increased incentive to pin down the original source. *I* care.

I wanted Berlin to write a substantial preface to AC, explaining his view of the history of ideas. After all, he had written interesting prefaces to both previous volumes. But he was not to be persuaded, writing to Pat Utechin on 17 August 1978:

> [...] if it is necessary to thank Hausheer, I shall do so in a brief note: but perhaps you wd look at the preface by me to H. Schenk's book on Romanticism: there is a passage there on the need for the hist of ideas, which *may* be useful: I am *not* prepared to write a proper manifesto as

requested by Henry: the readers will have to remain in ignorance about what stimulated my interest in the history of ideas – I fear.

Of course, Berlin had said something about this stimulus in the preface to CC, but he was not willing to enlarge on this. What he wrote about the discipline in his preface to Schenk's book is indeed relevant, and may be read in that book as well as in *The Power of Ideas* (POI). All that eventually appeared in AC was a short but deservedly fulsome acknowledgement to Roger Hausheer. For the last volume, *Personal Impressions* (PI), he initially refused, perhaps understandably, to write any preface at all, though in the end he came round, thanking Annan handsomely in the words quoted above.

The publication of PI was delayed in order that it should contain Berlin's new piece on his meetings with Russian writers. I tried to persuade him to write this sooner rather than later, but he had postponed his Bowra Lecture on the topic in order to spread the burden of his commitments, and was not to be hurried. This exercise yielded a touching statement by him of our differing temperaments in a letter of 31 January 1979:

> [...] just as my extreme resistance to producing texts with rapid efficiency is part of my temperament (as opposed to that of, say, Lord Annan), hence my steady refusal to produce reviews, so your inclinations to the opposite are equally unalterable: in neither case are we compelled by the demands of the external world. To delay the publication of vol. 4 will not really decrease the momentum of the sales of this particular edition. Equally, I could produce my Russian piece – probably by June – but it would be even more imperfect than it will be anyway and I should suffer for ever from acute self-blame. 'Fear shame' is the motto on a large stone fragment of some fallen pilaster lying about in the All Souls portico – it must have been part of the coat of arms of some forgotten fellow – I think it is probably the governing motto of my life.

He went on to explain his reasons for the delay:

> My reasons are genuinely medical: I have to give a talk at St Antony's on the 15th of this [*sc.* next] month, and feel acutely nervous about that – not so much about the talk, though that, like every lecture I have delivered, worries me intensely, but for fear of the physical consequences.

My London doctor is very firm about that. If I had to deliver the Bowra Lecture in the summer, on top of my two visits to Israel (one in connection with Einstein, the other, the [Jerusalem] Prize), I really should be done for. So your stern admonitions to me are based, I think, on a slight misunderstanding about my physical condition. Having given you that degree of guilt, I stop. I think all will be well. Noel Annan's introduction is going to worry me a great deal more than the inclusion or exclusion of my Russian piece. This worry, like all things, will pass. Let me urge a larger perspective upon both yourself and myself, to allay our respective neuroses: ataraxia is no good to artists, but greatly to be desired by persons like us.

And in a handwritten PS about another query he wrote: 'Wait, I beg you! (my permanent cry to you – ripeness is all: [...] "festina lente" ['Hurry slowly'].'

I must have protested about the delay, and argued (idiotically) that it would be better to press on with vol. 4 and publish the essay on Akhmatova, Pasternak and others elsewhere, since on 13 February 1979 Berlin wrote:

> *Personal Impressions*: I think you are right. My fear is not of making a fool of myself – that I do not mind too much – but of being guilty of blunders, or superficiality. I am not a scholar by temperament, as you well know, but I do not want to go too far in generalising without evidence, referring to non-existent data, etc. I have the greatest respect for scrupulous accuracy and learning, and do not wish to fall too far below standards which I believe in even if I cannot attain to them. This is different from 'making a fool of oneself': I do not wish to be justifiably scorned – being laughed at I do not mind much. Very well. Let the Bowra Lecture be printed somewhere else.

Happily this plan was abandoned, and the final volume appeared in October 1980, not without further futile and ill-advised attempts on my part to accelerate matters. Its title was suggested by Berlin himself in a letter of 2 October 1978:

> I have thought of a better title for vol. 4 than any of the previous ones: *Personal Impressions* – less good, in my view, *Personal Sketches*. This would cover the projected piece on the Russian literary scene as well. [...] I have consulted the Warden of Wadham (I wish you had asked him to introduce vol. 4),[30] who thinks it a most adequate title.

IV

In May 1977 I had moved from my London publishing job to a position in the paperbacks department of OUP in Oxford (whose target market was the general reader), and I took the opportunity to publish paperback reprints of certain books that contained contributions by Berlin. This was part of my overall project of getting as much of Berlin's work back into print as I could, by one route or another. It has to be confessed that not all of these books were likely to meet the Press's normal sales criteria, but, in the spirit of OUP's more academic arm, then called the Clarendon Press, I believed that the publication of a few modestly selling reissues of good quality was a proper activity for an academic publisher. One of these was Hans Schenk's *The Mind of the European Romantics*, with a preface by Berlin; another was Herzen's *From the Other Shore* and *The Russian People and Socialism*, published in translation in Weidenfeld & Nicolson's series The Library of Ideas in 1956 with an introduction by Berlin (one of the series editors); both were republished by OUP in 1979.

Another regular tactic of mine was to secure serialisation of Berlin's work as often as I could. My first port of call was usually the NYRB. I sent Berlin's introduction to Bob Silvers to see if, in principle, he might be interested in publishing it. I did not mention to Berlin that I had put out this feeler, no doubt for reasons similar to those behind my initial approach to Annan. Silvers was willing, and when I reported this to Berlin he wrote:

> The Herzen introduction: oh dear! Quite right to doubt my enthusi-
> asm. It is marvellous of you to have suggested it, and of Silvers to have
> accepted it – but I do hope the original date will be stated somewhere:
> the reprinting of ancient works of this sort does not seem to me to be
> what contemporary journals should be doing, and I feel vaguely ashamed
> of having this foisted upon the public – it almost seems like promotional
> matter. Oh dear! You ask why Weidenfeld didn't serialise it – he paid no
> attention to that series at all, it made very little money and he quickly lost
> interest in it: it was an excellent series, like most of his books – but his
> motives are not totally, wholly and purely intellectual. (30 January 1979)

Later he changed his tune, writing: 'Bob Silvers assumes that I knew all about your offering it to him. I shall not expostulate, but there *is* a limit to forcing people to be free or acting as someone else's real or higher self' (4 April). I take his point, but as he wrote in a letter quoted below, it is perfectly acceptable for a publisher to 'investigate possibilities', if not to actualise them without consultation (though even that might be argued about, on Annanesque grounds).

When the proofs arrived, I did not show them to him. I knew that he would be bound to make changes, as he always did when a proof was supplied to him, and since the time had passed for making changes in the book, I didn't want to allow the creation of two versions of the same text – something that I had experienced at Berlin's hands before, to my discomfiture. Today I no longer suffer from this unsuitably monistic desire for textual consistency, and happily revise texts on each reappearance. But at that time I minded about such textual plurality a great deal, feeling that there should be one final definitive text: hence my behaviour in this instance. My attitude was justified, I thought, by the fact that many, or indeed most, of Berlin's changes were stylistic adjustments that often made no perceptible difference either to his meaning or to the quality of his prose. Pat Utechin used to speak through gritted teeth of having to retype something repeatedly in order to make substitutions such as 'lovely' for 'delightful'.[31] He couldn't leave his texts alone, and made numerous changes at every opportunity, to the despair of typesetters as well as secretaries and editors.

Berlin was not pleased by my conduct, writing on 8 February 1979:

> I have just had a conversation with Bob Silvers, who expressed astonishment and incredulity at the fact that you should not have shown the proofs of the introduction to *From the Other Shore* to me. I can understand your motives all too well, but he thought this was going a little too far. I cannot help agreeing.[32]

Five days later he returned to the fray, evidently in response to an attempt at self-exculpation from me:

> It certainly is not standard practice for an editor to arrange for the serialisation of his author's work without consulting him first – to investigate possibilities, yes, but to drive things to the proof stage, certainly not: most of the serialised authors I know – say, Arthur Schlesinger or Lady Donaldson or Freddie Ayer – would have been far more outraged than I seem to be if this had been done to them. Of course I am aware that your motives are perfectly pure and wholly benevolent, but too far is

too far, and can easily become counterproductive, personally and even intellectually. So do hold your hand, I beg you!

I had not in fact driven things to proof stage before informing him of my approach to Silvers, as can be seen from Berlin's letter of 30 January quoted above: he had forgotten that I had told him of my exchange with Silvers. But it was a mistake to withhold the proofs from him, for all that my motives were indeed as he said. It was also futile, since Silvers sent him a proof anyway, and Berlin wrote to me on 23 February:

> Leaving aside for private and personal discussion your rights and duties as editor and my rights and duties as your malleable material (given the close friendship between Bob Silvers and myself it really was not unreasonable of him to take it for granted that you would not have approached him without consulting me), let me report to you with some apprehension that Bob has sent me a proof of the introduction and wondered whether I would like to add something to it. I have made some small corrections in the proof, which I shall return to him: of course this creates minor discrepancies between the OUP text and the NYRB, but this was also the case with my Herder book version and that in *Encounter*, the Vico as printed in the Tagliacozzo symposium and the NYRB, the introduction to Venturi and NYRB, etc., and I glory in such things, however improper this may seem to you. It is no good trying to teach an old dog new tricks, and I do not propose to compromise on this point. If the OUP, in the circumstances, declined to reprint my introduction, I should even accept that. And you know perfectly well that no reader has ever paid the slightest attention to these minute differences. I propose to send Bob the attached piece, as an addition at the end.

Again, all I had in fact done was to 'investigate possibilities', which he had allowed to be proper. In any event, with his customary generosity he palliated his rebuke by signing off 'with unaltered love & devotion & gratitude'; the changes were made and the postscript added in the NYRB version, but not in the book, which had gone to press. Another victory for textual pluralism.

I was not unaware even at the time of my tendency to go too far, writing to him about another offence, in connection with his essay on Einstein, on 6 April:

I must apologise once more for overstepping the bounds of propriety. Am I fated to go on, till death us do part, intermittently offending in this manner? I would like to think that I might be slowly learning from experience. I too wish very much that you should not come to regret your candour to me in the past[33] – this is something I value very greatly indeed.

Given my repeated pushing of the boundaries, in however noble a cause, I am astonished that Berlin's general demeanour towards me, except for the brief moments when he was justifiably irritated, remained so calm, open and benign. Later in the same letter I returned to the subject:

Without watering down my apology in this particular instance (I see that I should have refrained entirely from moral innuendo),[34] perhaps I might say something briefly about my habit of plain speaking, in anticipation of the next time it runs away with me. From the age of seven I was brought up by a stepmother who required of her stepchildren that they should never disagree with her or criticise her in any way. At least, she required that they give no outward signs of any dissension. Whether she made any corresponding inward requirement I do not know – perhaps it never even occurred to her that there might be a mismatch between outer and inner. I remember once having the courage to say, mildly, that I disagreed with her about something comparatively unimportant, and she stormed out of the room in a temper. This fired me with a determination to say what I thought (as an antidote to years of pretending to think other than I really did), and – perhaps even more – not to reject plain speaking in others. My stepmother's attitude ensured that she could never know whether what I said to her was true or feigned. I would hate to be in that sort of uncertainty myself. I am sure that I overreacted to this experience, but perhaps my telling you of it will help you to forgive me for my future transgressions (which I shall nevertheless endeavour to avoid!).

I also believe, of course, on quite general grounds, in freedom of speech, as I take it you do, and that if one is ever going to do or say anything interesting in life, one is bound to take risks which will on occasion lead to marks being overstepped (perhaps this is a philosophy for someone lacking in finer sensibilities?). But I hasten to add that I quite see that none of this has anything to do with the kind of misjudgement for which you quite rightly reprimand me.

As the years have gone by I have become much more cautious, though I still believe that it is sometimes necessary to stick one's neck out in order to achieve a desirable result not approved in advance by comfortable *bien-pensant* opinion. Berlin himself, despite his protestations to the contrary, was too worried about what the fashionable academic establishment might say, and his widow Aline was even more anxious than he was about real or imaginary critics. For me the likely or possible disapproval of reviewers or other commentators is not a relevant consideration when making a publishing decision. The only thing that matters is whether publication is intrinsically justified. At any rate, my policy of publishing or republishing as much as possible of Berlin's most interesting work may lie behind Aline's appointment, after his death, of a series of additional trustees to the Isaiah Berlin Literary Trust, set up by Berlin in 1996 with myself, Aline and her publisher son Peter Halban as the original trustees, to own and administer his copyrights. I know that Aline, perhaps partly influenced by the scepticism of Berlin's friend Bernard Williams,[35] was initially doubtful about some of the books I published after Berlin's death, though in the light of favourable reviews she came round. So she probably felt I needed to be kept in check by more circumspect persons. After some critical reviews of the first volume of Berlin's letters (covering 18 years) in 2004, one of the other trustees, I assume at Aline's behest, instructed me to compress the remaining letters (51 years) into a single volume. Fortunately the publisher who had the series under contract refused to accept this, and Aline came round again, even allowing us to include her own letters from Berlin in the third volume, having previously withheld them from the second. I do understand her natural diffidence, but I am sure she did the right thing.

Once the last volume of Berlin's letters was published in 2015, bringing to a conclusion forty years of editorial work on Berlin, my fellow trustees decreed that no more new books by Berlin should be published, at any rate for the time being. Hubristically, I thought of the electoral rejection of Churchill after the Second World War. In 2016 the publisher of the present book offered to reprint Berlin's 1956 anthology of the writings of certain eighteenth-century philosophers, *The Age of Enlightenment*, which had gone out of print in 2003 after nearly sixty years and was the only book of his that was no longer available. At the next trustees' meeting, in July 2017, I was a lone voice in favour of acceptance, and the offer was turned down, once more for supposedly prophylactic reasons that struck me as radically misguided. Berlin's stature and the worldwide interest in his work mean, for me, that his literary trustees should, at the very least, keep any book he published himself in print if possible. He had himself agreed to a reissue of this book by OUP in 1979. Moreover, Berlin's take on the Enlightenment is at the root of his work, and this book, for all its considerable idiosyncrasies (in which I glory), is his fullest and most direct engagement with it. I mourn the loss of the chance to replace this important brick in the wall of his printed oeuvre, even though the whole text is now available online in a second edition in the IBVL, and the introduction in POI. The book is now physically published only in Chinese – Chinese! The trustees' decision reminded me of Neil Kinnock's famous description, at the 1985 Labour Party conference in Bournemouth, of the betrayal of Party values by the Militant tendency: 'the grotesque chaos of a Labour council – a Labour council! – hiring taxis to scuttle round a city handing out redundancy notices to its own workers'. Grotesque indeed.[36]

On 20 February 1979 I had occasion to return once more to the question of the importance or otherwise of Berlin's scholarly inaccuracies. Never mind what prompted my remarks (something Berlin wrote about Marx's view of Machiavelli), but here is what I wrote:

> This [accuracy in substance if not in exact wording] is a phenomenon I encounter very frequently in editing your work – that you are true to the spirit even if the letter slips. Indeed you are often truer to the spirit than the letter allows – I mean particularly your way of improving quotations so that they better express the thought that lies behind them. So I wasn't claiming that you had misrepresented Marx on Machiavelli, only that we couldn't retain that particular quotation – I've dealt with it. It is equally unimportant, for example, that you say that Machiavelli said in a letter to Francesco Guicciardini that he loved his country more than his own soul, when in fact he spoke of his native city in these terms in a letter to Francesco Vettori [AC2 68]. Nevertheless, this is the sort of thing I am dealing with in my editing.[37] One might well generalise and say that nothing I have done to your writings affects the light they shed in the smallest degree – it merely protects them to some extent from attacks by pedants who prefer to concentrate on details rather than on your central themes and theses.

My closing sentence now seems an exaggeration. Berlin did not check his sources scrupulously, and should have done. Of course it is easier to do this today by using the internet, but all the same. I should happily trade accuracy for insight, but it is better to achieve both.

While I was at OUP I also reissued both of the books of Berlin's that they already published, *Karl Marx* – in a new, fourth edition, for which he reread the text, making numerous corrections and one long addition, on alienation – and FEL. In the latter case I asked him if there were any amendments he wished to make, and received a reply whose possibly misplaced confidence in my editorial capacities touched me deeply:

> *Four Essays on Liberty*: again, this is something that I cannot bring myself to look at again. No doubt there is plenty that is wrong with it, but I do not think I can correct it now. I cannot think of any criticisms that were made of the last edition that I ought to take notice of. There was a singularly unpleasant article by one Anthony Arblaster, of the University of Sheffield, in *Political Studies*, the main method of which was to compare the original and amended texts, both in the essays and in *Karl Marx*, in order to show that I trim my sails to new winds and change my views to adapt myself to new fashions, especially politically, and am a man of no integrity or decency whatever.[38] There may be some charges of factual inaccuracy in that article, and if you would cast your eye over it – you are by now the greatest living expert on Berlinophobia in the world – and tell me if there is something to do, I shall do it. I shall rely upon you entirely and not look at the texts again. (5 March 1979)

I also published the new edition of *The Age of Enlightenment* referred to above, so that OUP had three books by Berlin on their list.

I had one more Berlinian book up my sleeve. On 2 June 1979 George Richardson, head of OUP, presented Berlin with a Festschrift, *The Idea of Freedom: Essays in Honour of Isaiah Berlin*, instigated by myself, edited by Alan Ryan and published by OUP. The event occurred at Wolfson, at a lunch in the college buttery (a menu signed by those present may be seen at A 106–7, and a photograph of the contributors is Plate 1 in this volume – the only photograph known to me of Berlin and myself together). The last word on who should be invited to contribute – it was an invidious choice – was the editor's, though at least one uninvited person blamed me for the omission. Berlin had picked up some scraps of information about the genesis of the book, and wanted to know the full story. I tried to tell this, in abbreviated form, in a letter of 19 June:

Sam Guttenplan and I had a conversation [in 1974?] during which we agreed that a Festschrift for you ought to be organised. The two of us, with Cecilia Dick, invited Stuart Hampshire to lunch, and possibly Tony Quinton as well (I fear my memory of these stages is rather hazy). In any case, we agreed that Tony should edit the book, and he accepted the commission. He then did nothing whatever for three or four years, for a reason which I can't begin to guess. Can you? Occasional proddings produced no sign of action. Eventually, in desperation, I wrote to Alan Ryan on 5 December 1977, and asked him if he would like to take over. I chose him because I knew him to be a performer, and also because he had expressed slight regret that he hadn't had the opportunity to write the introduction to AC. At this stage it seemed best to choose somebody who would actually do the job. Alan agreed to do it, if I could extricate myself from Tony.

I wrote to Tony on 16 January 1978 with this in mind, and again on 7 February when he didn't reply. I suppose eventually we must have talked on the phone (whether at my or his initiative), because on 27 February 1978 I wrote to Alan setting out plans for going ahead with him as editor. I suggested liberty or pluralism as possible subjects to organise the book around. He and I and Hugo [Brunner, by now at OUP] had lunch on 13 March to discuss the project. Before this discussion he [Ryan] and I and Pat produced lists of possible contributors. We established a shortlist [including Tony Quinton, who agreed to contribute, but failed to deliver] [...]. We decided to go for a delivery date of 1 October 1978 – i.e. a writing time of six months flat. A number of names were excluded because we didn't think they'd fit the chosen topic, liberty. Or because they were known to be non-performers, because we didn't think that you would be so keen to see them included, or for other reasons [...]. The invitations presumably went out in the second half of March 1978. Contributors were sent a list of provisional titles sometime in the summer, when most people had replied to the initial invitation. Pat agreed to do the index in November 1978.

At first we tried to arrange to have the lunch in All Souls, but this turned out to be difficult. So eventually we turned to Wolfson, who were extremely helpful in all ways. Nobody believed that we would be able to keep the secret for half an hour after we had sent out the invitations. I was sceptical myself, but we surprised everyone. We arranged everything for 9 June, only to hear shortly afterwards that a mysterious event (now revealed) [Berlin's honorary LLD at Harvard, bestowed on 7 June] made that impossible. So we changed things to 2 June, and this stuck. The contributors were (as you can imagine) deluged with a stream of circulars from me, and an occasional one from Alan. I think we all got quite excited about doing the thing so quickly, and breaking records in the process – I certainly think the book holds the record for the fastest production job by the General Division of OUP, chess books excepted. Adrian Bullock, the Production Manager, and Visual Art Productions, the typesetters, deserve much of the credit here.

There remains the Hampshire/Hart intervention. They can tell you better than I what lay behind it. At all events, I was summoned to a drink in New College with Alan Ryan and the two interveners very late in 1978 (in December, I think). This was long after everyone had been told who was contributing. I don't know why the reaction was so delayed. Herbert had been doubtful all along about whether he could contribute; he knew that if he was to contribute, his piece would have to be a lecture he was giving in Columbia. But he thought that perhaps it was improper to contribute to a Festschrift a piece that would previously have appeared in a periodical. I said that you had done the same with your essay on Namier. In the end, he asked the *Columbia Law Review* to postpone their publication of the piece until this coming August, which they kindly agreed to do. This co-operation, together with much encouragement from many sides, enabled us to persuade Herbert to contribute. But I digress. My understanding is that Herbert met Morton White in the States when he was over to give the lecture, and suddenly realised how hurt he might be not to be included. This sparked off some related reservations, and the New College meeting was called in order to persuade me and Alan that we hadn't chosen the right list, quite. There were not enough heavyweights in it. Where was Momigliano, for example? The whole case against our list rather folded at that point, because we were able to point out that Momigliano was not only in our list, but had accepted the invitation! Where was Meyer Schapiro [...]? Where, above all, was Morton White? To cut a long story short, we agreed to add Morton White to the list, and there followed a series of transatlantic telephone calls, cables etc. Morton White very graciously agreed to write a piece fast, and did so (I quote from a letter from him) 'in about two weeks'![39]

The rest is history. As I say, do ask if any omitted details intrigue you. It was all very exhilarating, and I hope that, when you have had a chance to read the volume, you will find some things in it to approve of. For what it was worth, I find Morton White's way with your views on determinism radically unconvincing.

In a letter written on the same day Berlin told me he did not want his piece on 'Einstein and Israel' included in my fourth volume: 'The piece is not important or good enough, in my view, to need bothering about.' Fortunately he later relented, for reasons that were not explained, at any rate to me.[40] Victories, though, tended to be balanced by defeats: I was not successful in my attempt to persuade Berlin to let me add his revealing 1979 Jerusalem Prize acceptance speech as an 'Autobiographical Endnote'; I was finally able to do so twenty years later in the posthumous second edition of the book (1998), using the title 'The Three Strands in My Life'.

The essay on Einstein provides an occasion to mention a striking property of most of Berlin's essays: their timelessness. This is a paradoxical property, given that his subjects are mainly historical, and his essays often written for a specific occasion. Nevertheless, his underlying interest in 'the more permanent aspects of the human world' (10) usually lifts his remarks out of their immediate context and transforms them into reflections for all seasons. When I sent him my proposed editorial adjustments to the Einstein piece I explained what I had done with reference to the permanence and universality that I perceived in his work:

I thought it best to remove the ephemeral shell, as it were, in which the remarks of enduring interest were contained (as I have done in the case of certain other pieces in the other volumes). In this way the piece will sit more comfortably in the longer-term context of your *Selected Writings*. As so often with what you write, the shell peels off comparatively easily, providing evidence once again that you use the occasions on which you are asked to speak as stimuli to formulate ideas of less occasional importance, and do not merely regard them as providing chores to be perfunctorily performed.

The characteristic touched on here is one of the main justifications of the project on which I have spent so many years. I invoked it when Berlin suggested that the blurb for PI should speak of 'commemorative pieces [...], usually in response to specific occasions or requests', since that would give the misleading impression that what he had to say was more context-specific than it actually was. All these words were retained (with one substitution), though in a different order: 'Though mostly written in response to specific occasions or requests, these commemorative pieces have a permanent value and interest.'

The publication of the second and third volumes of *Selected Writings* – CC on 7 September 1978 and AC on 7 June 1979 – left little trace on our correspondence, but Berlin did draw my attention to a 'highly favourable' review of the latter volume contributed not long before his death by Goronwy Rees (in his final column signed 'R.') to the October issue of *Encounter*. Rees's last paragraph ran: '*Against the Current* certainly represents a most remarkable intellectual achievement. There are few books published in our time which more dazzlingly illuminate some of the most crucial problems of Western culture and civilisation.' As may be imagined, this warmed the cockles of both our hearts. On 2 October Berlin warmed my own cockles further by writing: 'Herbert Hart says that you have transformed my reputation for ever, and had a more decisive effect on it and indirectly me than anyone has ever had. It may well be so. What a charge to labour under!' Indeed. In return I offered him, writing on 13 October, this from a letter I had received from my friend Willie Jones, formerly head of English at Shrewsbury School, then teaching in Japan: 'As with the other two volumes, it's marvellous work – and so encouraging: it gives such magisterial support to everything I've always held to be true. [...] I do not know the man but I love him.' On 20 October Berlin replied: 'what a splendid, warm-hearted man your friend is – I am glad to think that I shall be mentioned in Sapporo.'

At about this time I persuaded the ODQ to include a passage from Berlin's 1950 essay 'Political Ideas in the Twentieth Century' that had struck me: 'Injustice, poverty, slavery, ignorance – these may be cured by reform or revolution. But men do not live only by fighting evils. They live by positive goals, individual and collective, a vast variety of them, seldom predictable, at times incompatible.' Berlin was flattered, but thought the passage not sufficiently remarkable. Maybe he was right. I now think that some of his sentences in 'Two Concepts of Liberty' are even more resonant, as is the concluding sentence of HF.

I also persuaded the ODQ to include one of Berlin's favourite quotations, from Kant: 'Out of the crooked timber of humanity no straight thing was ever made.' This is Berlin's characteristically free and creative rendering of a more pedestrian original: 'Aus so krummem Holze, als woraus der Mensch gemacht ist, kann nichts ganz Gerades gezimmert werden.' Literally translated, this says: 'From such crooked wood as that from which man is made, nothing wholly straight can be constructed.'[41] Only because Berlin transformed this into memorable English has it become a famous quotation that fully deserves its ODQ listing. In a moment of misguided pedantry I advised the editor that Berlin's version ought to have said 'can ever be made', and this is the wording that was published. Maybe Berlin's wording can one day be restored, making this a quotation from him as well as from Kant.

The publication of PI was still a year away, waiting for the new piece on Berlin's personal encounters with Russian writers. On 2 August 1979 he had told me: 'I am agonizing about the [Russians] *now*. God knows what will emerge; & how careful, even about the dead, one has to be.' By 7 September I was able to write: 'It's good to hear the piece on Russian writers is taking shape. How has it turned out in the end?' That was a very unrealistic question: in the end he completed it in the middle of the following year, sending it to me on 16 June 1980 with a manuscript note beginning 'Here it (surprisingly) is!'

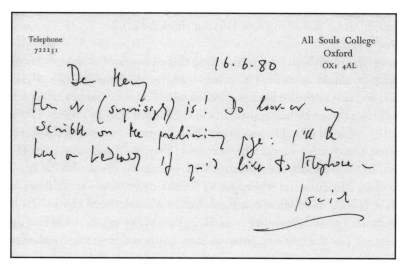

Berlin's covering note to me with the text of
'Meetings with Russian writers in 1945 and 1956'

One of the unfortunate side effects of his uncomfortable discussions with Annan was that Annan, understandably, did not feel able to add a passage about this new piece, the longest and (arguably) most important in the book. Fortunately this lack was not commented on, and was eventually supplied by Hermione Lee in her foreword to the 2014 third edition.

On 2 November Berlin wrote me a letter branded on my memory because of its second sentence: 'Let me be brief (a quality characteristic of neither of us).' A two-page letter followed, including a paragraph on the new essay, for which I had requested a more memorable title than what Berlin had offered on 20 June 1978: 'Meetings with Russian Writers in 1945: A Personal Reminiscence'. Unaware of the details of the meetings, I had on 27 October 1979 suggested 'Meetings in Moscow' as an example of the sort of thing I was after. Berlin replied on 2 November:

> 'Meetings in Moscow' is no good because the principal one was in Leningrad: 'Meetings in Moscow and Leningrad' seems absurd to me. [Why?] However, we can leave all that until you have read the piece. I gather that there is a vast myth about Akhmatova in Russia, into which I enter, and many versions of why and when I saw her, and how often, and what she said, etc.; so that whatever I write is likely to be controverted by someone. I shall have to be careful in declaring that memory may play one false but that in this case I do not think it has.

'Meetings' ends with an appendix listing the passages of Akhmatova's poems that refer or allude to Berlin's meetings with her. Uncharacteristically, Berlin took great pains with the details of this appendix, the accuracy of which was naturally important to him, especially in the face of the 'vast myth'.[42]

Berlin's awareness that the accuracy of his memory was widely disputed, and his conviction that he was recalling events as they really happened, are of some interest. In 2009 a Russian book appeared, written by researchers at the Anna Akhmatova Museum (in Akhmatova's former apartment) in St Petersburg's Fountain House, in which it is argued that, in addition to the two visits Berlin writes about (15–16 November 1945 and 5 January 1946), he made two further visits lasting, like the first one, into the early hours, on 17–18 and either 18–19 or 19–20 November, and also a daytime visit on 2 January: that is, five meetings in all, counting the interrupted first meeting as one.[43] Berlin never referred to any such additional meetings, but the circumstantial evidence cited for them is

A Cinque, Nos 415–9; I, 26 November 1945; II, 20 December 1945; 3 20 December 1945; 4, 6 January 1946; 5, 11 January 1946 (pp. 235–7; S & F. Vol I, pp. 300–302; p. 404).

B, A Sweetbriar in Blossom (Shipovnik Tsvetet) From a Burnt Notebook (Iz Sozhzhennoy Tetradi) Nos 420–33; 1, Burnt Notebook (Sozhzhennaya Tetrad') 1961; 2, In Reality (Nayavu), 13 June 1946; 3, In a Dream (Vo Snye), 15 February 1946; 4, First Song (Pervaya Pesenka), 1956; 5, Another Song (Drugaya Pesenka) 1956; 6, (Nos 420–33) & 6, A Dream (Son), 14 August 1956, near Kolomna; 7 (no title in either edition); 8, (no title in Zhirmunsky; 'A Memory (Vospominaniye) in S & F); 18 August, 1956, Starki; 9. In a Broken Mirror (V Razbitom Zerkale) 1956; 10, (no title in either edition) 1956, Komarovo; 11, (no title in Zhirmunsky; Dido Speaks (Govorit Didona) Sonet-epilogue in S & F.) 1962, Komarovo; pp. 238–243; 245, 488–9 (S & F. vol I, pp 303–8, 404–5; entire cycle dated 1946–1962).

C Midnight Verses (Polnochnyye Stikhi) Seven Poems (Sem' Stikhotvoreniy), 442–50, In Place of a Dedication (V'mesto Posvyashcheniya), Summer 1963; 1. Elegy Before the Coming of Spring (Predvesennyaya Elegiya), 10 March 1963, Komarovo; 5, The Call (Zov) 1, July 1963; 6, The Visit at Night (Nochnoye Poseshcheniye), 10–13 September 1963 Komarovo; pp. 247–50, 490; (S & F. vol I, pp 328–331, 407–8) who date Zov in 1964.

[left margin note] with an epigraph Arioso Dolente taken from Beethoven, 1 movement of the piano sonata op 110, by Beethoven.

Part of Berlin's original draft for the appendix to
'Meetings with Russian Writers in 1945 and 1956'

cumulatively not unpersuasive. Despite claims that he had visited more often, he never gave any sign of doubt on this point. We shall probably never know for sure what really happened.

However that may be, 'Meetings', the only newly written essay in *Selected Writings*, is by common consent a marvellous piece: it seems to me the coping stone of the entire enterprise. The publication of the volume containing it on 30 October 1980 completed the four-volume series, bringing this chapter of our association to an end. The book was an enormous critical success, garnering over 100 reviews, and was reprinted soon after publication.[44] Rumour had it that it was the chattering classes' favourite Christmas gift in 1980. Laurie Taylor's column in the THES on 9 January 1981 alluded to this sociological fact:

> **Got anything to swop this year?**
>
> Interested in an Isaiah Berlin?
>
> **Concepts and Categories?**
>
> No. *Personal Impressions.*
>
> **Oh dear, I doubt if you'll shift that one.**
>
> Why not? Lovely book. Just happens to be a second copy. Cost £9.50. Never been opened. I'll take five.
>
> **You'll be lucky. I tell you, in our neck of the woods, Berlins were as common this Christmas as J.R. After-shave and Soap-on-a Rope. Couldn't move for them. At one stage we had three in the same room. Two we were exporting to pretentious relatives in the Home Counties and one which had just arrived for me from the Aged P.**[45]

With good grace Berlin admitted on 19 December 1980 that he had been wrong about the likely level of interest in the project: 'The entire series of four volumes continues to astonish me. Such fame at my age!' In a letter of 7 January 1981 he added: 'I cannot understand why *Personal Impressions* should sell in such quantities.'

No doubt because of its autobiographical content, Berlin commented more on the reviews of PI than on those of the earlier volumes, writing in the same letter: 'Dan Jacobson. His speculation [on] my own Anglomania etc., whether or not I "manage my effects well", irritates me a great deal'; Jacobson had written that in 'novelistic' passages (of which he regrets that there are not more) Berlin 'manages the effects very well indeed'.[46] Berlin continues:

Tony Quinton has sent me a copy of his review[47] also, and it embarrasses me acutely, as you may very well guess. I, too, have sent him a letter, pointing out at least four major inaccuracies. All this talk about me, my outlook, my origins etc. is far too personal not to annoy me considerably. Jacobson simply thought it was an amusing theme and decided to embroider on it: Tony means well (I suppose), but cannot help appalling insensitiveness about others. He has a complete lack of moral or aesthetic antennae – worse than Annan. It must be a characteristic of Stowe School at a certain period of its development – yet it does not seem to have affected my stepson Peter. But Annan, Quinton, Robert Kee [are] all coarse-grained journalists at the very opposite end to Bloomsbury. Of the two extremes, I prefer the latter: it is further away from the apes.

The first edition of *Russian Thinkers*

5

AN UNREMARKABLE DECADE

I

Once the dust had settled after the publication of PI there followed a relatively fallow decade. I assumed that my work was done, and did not anticipate a future instalment. My contacts with Berlin became infrequent by comparison with the preceding nine years. I continued to work at OUP, first in the department which I had initially joined, and from 1985 as an academic commissioning editor for politics, sociology, and in due course social anthropology. This new position was forced upon me unwillingly after a disagreement with my managing director that does not form part of this story (though its details are not without interest),[1] except that it made me anxious to leave OUP when I could.

In 1980 the Past Masters series of short paperback introductions to important figures in the history of thought was launched by OUP on my initiative alongside the first paperback incarnation of the World's Classics series. The creation of the former series (with Keith Thomas as the external series editor) was directly inspired by my work on Berlin, and by his belief in the importance of individuals in the history of thought.[2] The first batch of (six) titles included books on Jesus and Marx by Humphrey Carpenter and Peter Singer respectively, and I remember observing to Bruce Wilcock, one of OUP's science editors, that the juxtaposition was not without its ironies. 'Yes,' he replied drily, 'a slight difference of emphasis.'

Given Berlin's interest in Giambattista Vico, the Italian thinker was naturally one of the subjects I had in mind for the series. We approached Peter Burke, who must have given us some idea of the line he would take, since on 15 December 1981 Berlin wrote:

Peter Burke: if he is right (and I mistaken) in saying that Vico was a typical seventeenth-century Neapolitan, then I should have thought that there was no case for producing a Past Master volume on him. The only interest he has for Western readers is not as a seventeenth-century Neapolitan thinker, but as a thinker *tout court*, with interesting ideas which other seventeenth-century Neapolitan thinkers certainly don't appear to have had, or else we should have heard of them. There is an enormous Italian literature tracing Vico's sources in Naples, [pre-]eminently Badaloni's book.³ It is quite interesting – some of his ideas were certainly obviously influenced by minor Neapolitan thinkers. But that is like saying that Karl Marx was a typical nineteenth-century central European intellectual – which is in a sense true, but uninteresting. If Burke wants to write a piece refuting me, that is perfectly reasonable: but he must write a proper monograph, not the kind of book you publish in this series. Moreover I do not believe that anyone can write in an illuminating fashion about Vico who does not know much about philosophy. Peter Burke is a very hard-working, meticulous historian of [the] social (and also economic) life of famous cities in the Italian Renaissance – I dare say this includes Naples. He thinks of himself as a historian of ideas, and so he is if you take ideas to be current opinions about this or that, cultural manifestations of various sorts, etc. But if Vico is of any interest at all (and surely this cannot be doubted), he is only of interest as an original source, a pioneer of ideas destined later to become influential and important. If this is wrong, then surely he deserves no place in your series? That, at any rate, is my view. I do not, of course, wish to stop Peter Burke from attacking me – on the contrary, he is not only entitled to do so but perhaps has an intellectual duty to do it, but surely not in Past Masters. Wd you include one on Muratoni, Guicciardini, Guizot, Coke, Selden, all v. important men in (& of) their day? If Vico is *that* ...

Later, when the book by Burke appeared, Berlin expanded on these views in a short article that I found among his papers, and published posthumously as 'The Reputation of Vico'.⁴ This is a particularly clear example of the way in which Berlin's methodology differed from that of the Cambridge School of intellectual historians, with their emphasis on the cultural context in which thinkers of the past wrote, and the perils of interpreting their writings in contemporary, and therefore allegedly anachronistic, terms. As Berlin wrote to Quentin Skinner on 15 March 1976,

> I cannot deny that what interests me most, both about Vico and Herder, are the ideas which still seem to me to be living, hares that are still running, issues that are of permanent concern, at least of lasting concern to other societies.

And later in the same letter: 'The thing to me about Vico and Herder is that they opened windows on to new prospects. Nothing is ever more marvellous, and men who do it are rightly excited, and indeed overwhelmed' (A 24; TCE2 491, 493).

In January 1982 Aline Berlin lent me the original manuscript of a short story Berlin had written when he was at school, aged twelve. It is a striking and astonishingly precocious document, now widely known because I published it many years later both with its original spelling and punctuation and in a version in which these are normalised.[5] Why striking, why astonishing? As I wrote to Aline at the time:

> Even if it is not in the Daisy Ashford class it has some very powerful moments. I particularly noticed a passage which clearly presages Isaiah's opposition to ruthless totalitarians. It comes in the description of the villain Uritsky [...]:

>> he possesed a clever but also cruel look and all his countenance bore an expression of a phanatic he signed death verdicts, without moving his eyebrow. his leading motto in life was "The purpose justifies the WAYS" he did not stop before anything for bringing out his plans. [FL 17; cf. L 334]

> That is splendid. And I agree with you that the story has a completely Russian feel about it despite being written in English (pretty good English if he had been learning it for such a short time!). (11 January 1982)

This is why I called the story 'The Purpose Justifies the Ways'.

In 1988 a minor commercial development occurred which lit the fuse of the next phase in the publication of Berlin's work. On 8 March I wrote to Berlin to say that OUP, which had published paperback editions of three volumes of *Selected Writings* under licence from the Hogarth Press, was being asked for a 'refresher advance' in order to extend the licence, which was about to expire. Unfortunately sales were not sufficient to justify such an advance by OUP's normal criteria, and I suggested boosting these sales by reissuing the books in new editions, 'adding in each case an essay or two written since the volumes were published'. Berlin and I met to discuss this idea, and I wrote afterwards (26 April 1988) to confirm what we had agreed, which was something quite different, namely 'that there is enough material to make a second volume of *Against the Current*'. There were two kinds of ingredient for such a volume. First, there were two essays that already existed when the initial selection was made, but which Berlin had excluded because they overlapped with his projected volume on Romanticism (26, 58). He was now prepared to waive this exclusion, perhaps realising that the likelihood of his completing this proposed work in the foreseeable future had diminished. Secondly, Berlin had written a number of new pieces in the intervening decade, and at least four of these were suitable for inclusion.

True to form, Berlin worried about overlap, and that the new volume 'may be a little thin', but otherwise accepted the plan (6 May 1988). Roger Hausheer and I (re)read the essays with these reservations in mind, and agreed that neither hesitation of Berlin's was well founded. Hausheer wrote to me that 'the essays, taken together, form a coherent and forceful statement which moves into territory not touched by *Against the Current* [...], particularly European Romanticism'; and that 'there is no greater or more serious degree of overlap among these essays than in the case of *AC*(I)'.[6] I reported our view to Berlin on 16 September, suggesting that we add 'The Bent Twig', an essay on nationalism excluded from AC because of some duplication of 'Nationalism: Past Neglect and Present Power'. I also expressed the hope that, strong as the proposed collection already was, he might strengthen it further with an unpublished work, perhaps on Joseph de Maistre. I knew he had been working on Maistre for many years, but until this point he had denied that a publishable text existed. Hausheer wondered whether there might also be a piece on the obscure eighteenth-century German pietist philosopher and forerunner of Romanticism Johann Georg Hamann, another figure we knew Berlin had worked on.

In view of subsequent developments, Berlin's comments on Hamann and Maistre in a letter of 8 October 1988 are worth reproducing:

I have never written a proper piece on Hamann, only a lecture in New York which was not recorded by anyone, so far as I know, least of all by me. De Maistre does exist – an enormous (repetitive, I need hardy say) typescript, or rather several versions, are stuck away somewhere. So much has been written on him since the 1950s when I originally wrote this [but cf. 271/13] and lectured on it,[7] and the job of condensing is so awful and the degree of originality, in my opinion, so low that I don't believe it is worth it.

However, if you want to see it, Pat may be able to dig it out after a week or so of archaeological excavation. It does exist, I cannot deny.

In fact there were two New York lectures on Hamann, the first two of the four-lecture 1965 series 'Two Enemies of the Enlightenment' already referred to (29). The bulk of the treatment of Hamann was in the second lecture, which, unlike the first (and fourth), was indeed recorded; a transcript appears in the IBVL.[8] As for a 'proper piece' on him, that belongs later in the story. There were seven successive complete drafts of his essay on Maistre, each longer than its predecessor.

In the same report to Berlin I floated the idea that the new volume should be not a second part of AC, but a free-standing new collection, and on 18 October 1988 I suggested *The Crooked Timber of Humanity* as its title. By 22 November Hausheer and I had both read the latest text of 'Joseph de Maistre and the Origins of Fascism', which had been excavated, together with several folders of notes and the six earlier drafts, presumably by Pat Utechin. It was clearly a marvellous piece, and publishable with minimal editing. However, at some 30,000 words it was not an obvious natural fit with the new volume. I pressed Berlin on Hamann, hoping to achieve a book combining the two enemies of the Enlightenment, but in a letter of 5 December he referred again to the 1965 lecture series as if it was his only venture into that terrain, and added 'I do not propose to write a separate piece on him.' Little did any of us know what would happen only five years later. As for Maistre, we eventually decided to include him in the new collection after all. The disproportionate length of the essay in fact made it the centrepiece of the volume rather than a misfit, and it has become one of Berlin's most celebrated essays. It is a little longer than HF, and could well have been – or be – published in similar stand-alone form, perhaps entitled *Violence and Terror: Joseph de Maistre and the Origins of Fascism*. One day, perhaps.

11

It was also in 1988 that I first met the historian Alan Bullock, at a party in Linacre College. I talked to him about *The Fontana Dictionary of Modern Thought*, of which he was co-editor, and complained that the entries on anthropology and sociology (by Maurice Freedman and Daniel Bell) failed to give any comparative account of how the two disciplines approached the explanation of human behaviour. I was responsible for both subjects at OUP, and wanted to understand the difference between them better. To his credit, he took my observation seriously, writing to me on 16 June:

> I looked at our new edition of the Dictionary to see if we had provided a better answer to your question the second time round. We kept Dan Bell's article on sociology, but we have a new one on anthropology written by Anna Grimshaw. I enclose a copy.
>
> It is a fascinating illustration of the blinkers in which social scientists work that there is no mention [of] or cross-reference [to] sociology in her entry. It is no less striking that a sociologist with as broad a range as Dan Bell should not have mentioned anthropology. I had a look at the *Encyclopaedia of [the] Social Sciences*, and it is exactly the same there. I shall be seeing Dan Bell in a week's time, when he comes to give a lecture here, and I shall ask him why both anthropologists and sociologists suffer from this tunnel vision. In the meantime, I accept the justice of your criticism so far as our editing is concerned.

I never heard what, if anything, Bell said, but this episode initiated a link between Bullock and myself which stood me in good stead when I needed to raise funds for the next stage of my enterprise.

Later in 1988 Berlin was revising his will, and asked me if I would be prepared to act as one of four literary executors, the others being, if I remember, his wife Aline, Michael Brock and the philosopher Patrick Gardiner. Naturally I agreed, but the request fermented in my mind, and on 22 November I wrote him a letter that would eventually lead to a radical change in my life:

> I have had an idea which may possibly be mad but I hope isn't offensive. I start from two premises which I believe to be true: (*a*) You have a

considerable volume of papers of one kind and another which, if I outlive you, it would fall to me as one of your literary executors to help sort out; (*b*) I take no great pleasure, as you know, in the task that has been assigned to me at OUP.

It would of course be in some ways far easier, as well as more fun, to work on your papers with the benefit of your advice: I am sure there will be many mysteries which you could dissolve at a stroke. You can see what I am leading up to. Supposing I could somehow arrange a salary of some sort (from an educational/charitable foundation, or a publishing firm which might finance me in return for the right to publish a volume or two of your work? or *tertium quid* [some third thing]?), how would you view the prospect of my working as your prehumous (so to speak) literary executor, perhaps part-time (if OUP would keep me on part-time), perhaps full time? Be frank: it would not greatly surprise me if this suggestion appalled you, even if I promised to restrict the enquiries arising out of my burrowings to some agreed tolerable level.

I won't say more at this stage, in case this is a non-starter. I hope, at any rate, you don't mind my boldly raising a possibility which I would not want to pursue unless you too felt positively about it.

Berlin's reply is dated 5 December:

I realise that in the vast chaos of my scattered papers there must be items which cannot be understood without some knowledge of what and whence and why, which probably only I could give in some cases – in others even I would be at a loss. It is a huge task and the idea of my past arising before me makes me feel uncomfortable. God knows what there is there – I dread to think what could float up from my fairly respectable, nevertheless confused and unremembered, past. So in a sense I fully understand that it would be a good thing if someone as sensitive as you, who knows me so well, could burden himself with this awful task. At the same time I should of course much rather that it all happened after my death, when I do not mind what is done with my remains, literary or otherwise. So I must brood on this and let you know.

On 26 January 1989 I reminded him that he was still brooding, in a letter in which I proposed 'Chapters in the History of Ideas' as a subtitle for the new volume. In his reply of 30 January Berlin accepted the subtitle, and 'The Crooked Timber of Humanity' as the main title. As for my proposal about his papers:

> I think I ought to stop brooding and let you do it if you really are so kind as to take on this hideous task. Do talk to my wife and Pat about it – I need know nothing about it while it goes on until and unless you start asking me questions about who various people are, what the dates mean, what events referred to are, which I should be only too willing to answer if faced with. I dread this dipping into my past life, but I do not think I can avoid it, and shall simulate goodwill in the matter.

With these somewhat double-edged words he opened the door to a new country where things would have to be done differently, a country full of undreamt-of riches, and a new chapter in my life.

6

THE CROOKED TIMBER OF HUMANITY

I really am grateful to you for compelling me to tell the truth, i.e. conform to my claim to remain faithful to the text[s] on which I endeavour to build the thoughts and views of various thinkers – do continue doing this! Nobody is more inaccurate than I: my quotations are caricatures, sometimes positive improvements (in my view) – but never mind, accuracy is all.

IB to HH, 13 March 1989

Before I could start in earnest on my new task, I needed to prepare CTH for the press, find funding to pay my salary, and leave OUP. The editing of CTH threw up another batch of queries about alleged quotations. In his reply Berlin spoke disarmingly of his unscholarliness, as he did in the epigraph above:

You will surely by now not be surprised by my total inaccuracy, vagueness and tremendous distortions of quotations into what I possibly regard as a better formulation. [...] Of course I do not have the reference. What do you take me for? [...] Surely you must know by now that I never annotate anything I read, never mark passages, never do anything that serious scholars do – it's a grave fault, I admit, but I am too old to mend now. [...] I don't believe you seriously expected genuine scholarly precision from me in this or any matter! How could you? (5 February 1989)

He was conscienceless about fudging quotations we could not trace. For example, the next day, about a quotation from C. I. Lewis:

I think we'll just have to say 'C. I. Lewis' and hope for the best. If anyone challenges that I shall not reply, or give some evasive answer, or [tell] some hideous lie such as that I heard him say that – at this point, I think mild cheating is perfectly in order.[1]

He was also inconsistent in this as in all matters: no doubt a virtue in a pluralist, but maddening for a pedant. When I said that I wanted to use the Kant quotation about crooked timber as an epigraph to the volume, he insisted that we printed the German original (91) – fair enough – followed by a literal translation, which he provided in this form: 'Out of the crooked timber of humanity out of which man is made, nothing completely straight can be built.' This is awful: inelegant if only because of the double occurrence of 'out of' and double translation of 'als woraus der Mensch gemacht ist' ('of humanity' and 'out of which man is made'), and inaccurate if meant to be literal. I wanted to use his own familiar version, which, after all, occurred in many places in his writings. No pleading from me could sway him, but we did tweak his 'literal' rendering, and in the first impression of the book there appeared 'Out of timber so crooked as that from which man is made nothing entirely straight can be carved.' In later impressions, after representations from Ralf Dahrendorf, a native German speaker, 'carved' became 'built'. In the second edition of the book (2013) I finally had my way, substituting Berlin's resonant 'Out of the crooked timber of humanity no straight thing was ever made' and relegating the literal version to a footnote. I am certain that this is right.

At about this time I discovered, thanks to the Collingwood scholar Jan van der Dussen, that Berlin's quotation from Kant (which did not appear in any of R. G. Collingwood's published works, as Berlin had assured me it did) came from a lecture on the philosophy of history that Collingwood gave in Oxford in Trinity Term 1929, the second term of Berlin's Greats course.[2] The manuscript reads: 'Out of the ~~crooked~~ cross-grained timber of human nature nothing quite straight can be made.'[3] Maybe he said 'crooked' when he gave the lecture. Berlin was convinced:

> Bravissimo! Marvellous Scherlockismus! I am sure that your conjecture is right, that I heard Collingwood say these words with my own ears – and as you know, they changed my life. When asked if Collingwood influenced me, which occasionally happens, I can now say 'Yes, decisively and for ever.' (3 May 1989)

It was in April 1989 that the decision was taken to include Berlin's unpublished essay on Joseph de Maistre in CTH, though he declared himself 'very dubious' about it (21 April). This text presented even more serious editorial challenges than his published work. I asked him if he would say something about its origins in an author's preface (which he had so far declined to write). In case he refused, I offered him a paragraph that might appear in my own preface:

> The essay published here for the first time, on de Maistre, has origins that require a little explanation. It is the first essay in the history of ideas that Isaiah Berlin wrote. He initially drafted it in the 1940s, and then worked on it at various times until the late 1950s, revising it very substantially more than once. Publication was discussed with a journal, but the essay was too long to appear by that means, and was then abandoned. The present text has been arrived at after a study of all the drafts (none of which provides an adequate text taken by itself), and of the voluminous notes on which they are based. Some of the quotations were referenced, and I have provided references for the others [...]. No account, however, has been taken of more recent work on de Maistre, so that the piece should be regarded as having been published in, say, 1958.[4]

Berlin demurred, writing that he saw

> no reason for saying anything about its origins [...]. At most, all that need be said is that this article mouldered in my desk for a great many years because I thought that it needed drastic revision, but old age and indolence combined to discourage me from this course. (21 April 1989)

In the end he agreed that a modified version of my paragraph could appear in the book:

> The essay published here for the first time, on Joseph de Maistre, was put aside in 1960 as needing further revision. However, it was so nearly ready for publication, and contained so much of value, that it seemed right to include it here. Although the author has added a few new passages, and redrafted others, it has not been revised in any systematic way to take full account of subsequent work on Maistre, which in any case does not affect its central theses. (CTH x; amplified at CTH2 xx)

He also insisted that he must read a new biography of Maistre, published the previous year, before the text of his essay was finalised: 'Otherwise I shall get into a tizzy.'[5]

It took me some six months to find all the passages Berlin quoted from Maistre, in some cases with help from the author of the biography he was reading. Berlin then revised the text, inserting further unreferenced quotations. One discovery is worth reporting. In his essay Berlin attributed a splendid remark to Maistre: 'Dire: les moutons sont nés carnivores, et partout ils mangent de l'herbe, serait aussi juste' ('To say that sheep are born carnivorous, and everywhere nibble grass, would be just as reasonable [as to say, with Rousseau, that man is born free, and is everywhere in chains]'). After much futile searching in Maistre's works, I discovered that this is in fact a paraphrase of Maistre by the critic Émile Faguet in an essay on him.[6] Berlin must, not unnaturally, have assumed that Faguet took it from his subject. Maistre did say a couple of things that conveyed the same thought, if less pithily: 'What does [Rousseau] mean? [...] This mad pronouncement, *Man is born free*, is the opposite of the truth.'[7] And elsewhere:

> If anybody wishes to prove that it is the nature of a viper to have wings and a tuneful song, and of a beaver to live in isolation on the summit of the highest mountains, it is up to him to prove it. Meanwhile we shall believe that what is so has to be so and has always been so.[8]

The same thought turns up in Alexander Herzen, whose analogous proposition is 'Fish were born to fly, yet everywhere they swim.'[9]

CTH was to be published by John Murray, partly because they made a better offer than Chatto/Hogarth, and partly because Hugo Brunner had been ousted at the latter house by Carmen Callil. Berlin wrote to me: 'I do hope Murray wins – I'd rather them than Chatto, I think, on no rational grounds except that although everyone else much admires her I did not find Miss Callil any more attractive than Hugo did' (12 April 1989). Roger Hausheer once more wrote an introduction, by agreement with Berlin, who in one of the more discreditable voltes-face I experienced at his hands rejected the introduction without reading it. He had forgotten that he had consented to it, but did not recant even when reminded of this. This struck, and strikes, me as an act of gratuitous cruelty, a product of the lump of ice in his heart identified by Annan, the hard diamond-like intellectual core posited by Hausheer himself. If it is not entirely out of character, it is perhaps because Berlin placed a very high value on what seemed to him the best presentation of his work. Maybe I am judging him too harshly. Here are his words:

I had completely forgotten that Roger had been asked to write something for what at the time was going to be an extra volume in the Chatto series. How embarrassing. I do not think that I can agree to an introduction by anyone simply because Roger has begun writing it and is under the impression that I had agreed. I am perfectly prepared to grovel to him, to explain that I don't want an introduction to this book because I have been over-introduced already, brilliantly by him and very well by Aileen and indeed by Bernard Williams (less so by Lord Annan). Anyway I am prepared to offer every kind of apology and in fact to reward him for the work already done.

Perhaps he could turn what he has done into some kind of review of this book, when it appears – I don't think I could persuade the TLS to print anything fairly lengthy, but I could probably do something with the NYRB, though obviously I could not promise. I realise how deeply painful this could be. I just don't feel that my wish not to have an introduction must yield to the fact that an earlier commitment had been made, as I now think unwisely. I don't think two introductions by Roger would be at all appropriate – but that is less important than the fact that I do not want any introduction by anyone.

Tell me what to do: should I write to him direct? Perhaps that would be best, and stop him in his tracks – or would you like to prepare the ground, and say that I am being unreasonable about this, that I am totally devoted to him, that he has written the best of all introductions to any-thing I have written, but that I long not to be over-introduced – that I feel very badly about this but would like him to stop – and of course am ready to reward him (and do make the suggestion about the possibility of a review somewhere – unfortunately I have no pull with any editors except Bob Silvers, but journals like *Politics* and *Political Studies* and the rest could perfectly well accommodate his essay). (19 April 1989)

I had told Berlin that Hausheer had finished the piece, polishing aside, which makes 'Roger has begun writing it' disingenuous. But what took my breath away was that Berlin declared himself, in terms, as unbound by his earlier commit-ment, which he expresses in the passive as if he could thereby distance himself from it. The fact that what was to have been a second volume of AC had been turned into a free-standing book seems far from decisive in his favour. I fought back to no avail, and advised caution in offering payment, which might seem to add insult to injury. It might be better, I suggested, if any payment came from me. Hausheer was of course mortified, feeling he had been let down by a friend. Unfortunately his text appears to have been lost: otherwise I should have added it to the second edition of the book in 2013. Maybe it will turn up one day and be included in a future impression, or posted online.

I addressed the question of funding at the same time as working on CTH. I raised the topic in a letter of 31 January 1989. Berlin could easily have afforded to pay me himself, but I did not want to ask for this, and I also sensed (rightly) that he would not want to finance my work, as this would make it too much of a vanity publishing project. If the job was worth doing, he felt, it should be possible to finance it from other sources. But I needed to be sure, and so, declaring my (genuine) sense of diffidence, wrote: 'I have not supposed, in thinking about this, that you would want to pay me yourself, but clearly I must ask you to be explicit about this before I make any serious attempt to look elsewhere.' I also enquired about the possibility of a room in his home where I could install a filing cabinet and word processor. He replied on 6 February:

> Would you talk to Aline about the ever delightful subject of money, which you must not be diffident about raising. God knows how long this hideous labour will take – obviously you will not be able to continue full-time at OUP unless you decide to take fifteen years or so over it,[10] after which I shall be safely dead, which, of course, I should greatly prefer, answering no questions and leaving you to formulate hypotheses about what the obscure references may be to. However, to be serious for a second, do ring Aline and make a date with her. I would rather she talked to you about that – she perfectly understands the issue and entirely approves. So, too, about the room. There is a room in which I propose to try and compose my last, or posthumous, work on Romanticism; I think perhaps the best plan might be for you to use my room in All Souls on days when I am not likely to use it. I use it mainly to see visitors during the weekends, when you surely would not want it – sometimes on Fridays, more rarely on Mondays, but never Tuesdays–Thursdays inclusive (and if Fridays, lateish afternoon, if Mondays, in the morning) – so we could make a contract about that: there you could have a word-processor and everything else. Would you think that was a good idea? Anyway, do let's have a talk about all this – give me a buzz and we shall make a date.

I duly had a meeting with Aline, who suggested that I might come to Headington House and look through the papers there, in order to confirm (or not) my guess that there were several years of work to be done. She was at that point thinking of this as a part-time occupation, and she also confirmed that she and Isaiah did not want to bankroll me, though they might make a contribution. We discussed possible sources of funding, including charitable foundations and publishers. After our meeting she passed me over to Isaiah, with whom I was to lunch on 3 March.

I believe, though I cannot be sure, that this was the meeting over and after lunch at All Souls of which I have an especially clear memory. Let us allocate it to this date in any case, since it certainly occurred at about this time. It may be that the lunchtime exchange I shall now describe belongs to another occasion, but never mind.

Entering the breakfast room (curved tables and backless benches), in which, suitably, lunch was served, we sat down opposite a couple who were the guests of another fellow of the college. Their host introduced them, and Berlin introduced himself and me. The husband then said, addressing Berlin: 'Yes, I know who you are: we had lunch with you in a restaurant on Tuesday.' Berlin shot back: 'Perfectly possible; perfectly possible' – and carried on regardless. I gave him marks for sangfroid but not for shame.

The weather was unseasonably warm, and when we repaired to the Smoking Room for coffee, the coal fire burning in the grate made it almost unbearably hot, even when I removed my jacket. Berlin was wearing his usual thick three-piece suit, and showed no sign of discomfort. I was not only physically hot but also apprehensive about discussing funding, which I needed to do if progress was to be made. I had a family and a mortgage, and could not afford to work for nothing. I said I had a suggestion to offer, but was diffident about doing so. Berlin brushed my hesitation aside and enjoined me to speak out. I said that the royalty earnings from any future books I might edit would go some way towards defraying the cost of my activities, and tested his understanding of how great a contribution this might make by asking him how much he thought his annual income from royalties was. He named a figure that was not just too low, but too low by several orders of magnitude. He was surprised by the true figure, but even that was not sufficient by itself, though it would make a decent start. However, he readily agreed that this income could be diverted to the project. We then discussed other sources that might be tapped to supplement it, and I undertook to explore these.

Towards the end of our conversation the subject arose of the disparity between one's chronological age and one's subjective age, and I asked him how old he felt. He said that he still felt himself to be an eighteen-year-old, dragging his eighty-year-old body behind him 'like a sack'. This inner youthfulness may be part of the explanation of his lifelong interest in philosophy. In the sense of his response to Bryan Magee's suggestion about the childishness of philosophical questions, Berlin was childish to the end.

In the wake of this meeting I made a preliminary examination of the papers at Headington House, a momentous proceeding which immediately requires a new paragraph.

In 1922 the archaeologist Howard Carter recorded in his diary that, when he first looked into Tutankhamun's tomb in Egypt's Valley of the Kings, peering with the aid of a candle through a small hole he had opened in the tomb wall,

> It was some time before one could see, the hot air escaping caused the candle to flicker, but as soon as one's eyes became accustomed to the glimmer of light the interior of the chamber gradually loomed before one, with its strange and wonderful medley of extraordinary and beautiful objects heaped upon one another.

His sponsor Lord Carnarvon was there, and asked him: 'Can you see anything?' Carter replied: 'Yes, it is wonderful.'[11] No one had set eyes on these treasures for more than three thousand years. I had my own more modest, but still intense, Howard Carter moment when I conducted my first search of Berlin's home, to see what I should have to deal with as one of his literary executors. My Tutankhamun's tomb was the capacious cellar, reached by a flight of stone steps, and filled, beyond the washing machine and dryer, with a variety of makeshift shelving, all piled high with chaotic papers, and with boxes, suitcases and trunks. The quantity of material was overwhelming, terrifying and exhilarating. I went through it the first time in a breathless, trembling, cursory fashion, but immediately found many unpublished texts that had been put aside decades ago, and which no one but Berlin had ever read. I wish I had had the presence of mind to take photographs. When I think how easily these texts might have been lost for ever, I shudder. It is thrilling to have discovered them, and hugely rewarding to see many of them now out in the world where they belong, part of Berlin's intellectual legacy to future generations.

My survey of the house was complete by 4 May, when I reported on my initial findings:

> I have now completed a swift, tantalising survey of the papers at Headington House. It would take many months, given the spare time I can currently muster, to complete even a rough inventory of the whole. But I have seen enough to reach some firm conclusions, which I will do my best to express with uncharacteristic brevity:
>
> 1. The task of sorting the papers into a usable 'archive', and cataloguing them in a rudimentary way, let alone doing any editorial work on them, would take years rather than months.
> 2. It follows, sadly, that I could not realistically undertake this task on a reasonable timescale in my spare time (which is the only option apart from finding full-time funding, given that OUP aren't willing to employ me part-time). Doubtless I shall continue to chip away at the corners, but that is all it can be as things stand.
> 3. Whether the job is done now, or posthumously by or at the behest of the literary executors, it is going to have to be a paid occupation (or undertaken by someone whose circumstances enable him to work for nothing).
> 4. There is a great deal of material that is prima facie publishable. The enclosed list, which is far from exhaustive, gives some idea of the scale of this [...].
> 5. My own enthusiasm for tackling the task, if some way of making this possible can be found, is undiminished – increased, rather – by looking more closely at the material to hand.
>
> Quite where this leaves us, I am not sure. But I promised you a report on my investigations, and this is it, in summary. Before I trouble you again with my own vague ideas of how we might make progress, I shall wait to see how you respond. I fear that the only practicable course may be to give up.

The list I enclosed ran to two pages of single-spaced A4. My somewhat deadpan letter conceals the excitement I felt at what I had discovered, though at this point the excitement was tempered by the frustration of knowing that I could not (yet) set to work. The papers were in many parts of the house, extending literally from the attic to the cellar, though the latter stood out as the principal repository. The other most fertile areas were Berlin's study (located in the dressing room that opened off the original master bedroom, which he used as his main library) and Pat Utechin's office (a small second-floor room, also originally a bedroom). Though no hoarder, Berlin was also no thrower-away, and the bulk of his papers was and is exceptional. Gathered room by room from his homes and colleges, housed at the time of transfer in some 250 boxes and several filing cabinets, they range from the dramatic 1922 short story, referred to above, to his last letter, dated less than a week before his death, to Anatoly Naiman, which refers, appropriately, to their mutual friend Anna Akhmatova, whose famous night-long meeting with Berlin in 1945 was so formative for them both. There were around 180,000 leaves, which eventually filled more than 800 archival boxes in the Bodleian Library – and the riches they yielded were beyond my most optimistic imaginings.

When Berlin's friend Patricia Gore-Booth asked him in 1986 whether his papers might eventually come to the Bodleian, Berlin replied (25 April) that he had never thought of himself as possessing any. He told her that he was leaving all decisions about the 'huge unsorted heap' to his literary trustees, but was willing to suggest Bodley to them as a fitting home. He wrote to me on the same day doing just that: 'Could you charge yourself with this when the hour strikes? I shall forget to say anything about this either to Aline or to Patrick Gardiner.' After his death we did as he wished.

Every stage of Berlin's long life is documented: his childhood in Riga and Petrograd, his time in Oxford as undergraduate, professor and founding President of Wolfson, his war work in New York and Washington, his teaching, administration, writing and broadcasting. A wealth of correspondence revealed his wide circle of friendships and contacts, from T. S. Eliot to Bertrand Russell, from Churchill to Stravinsky, from Margot Fonteyn and Lauren Bacall to Cecil Beaton and Jacqueline Kennedy.

I realised after this initial search, even more forcefully than before, that Berlin was an author in need of an editor if ever there was one. He was a reluctant publisher, and had written and said a huge amount that he had not seen into print. He had always needed intellectual impresarios to help him realise his full authorial potential, and he needed one now above all. If only I could somehow enable myself to take on the task, the most fulfilling life an editor could dream of opened before me.

I hoped, I admit, that my pessimistic assessment of my prospects might provoke Berlin into suggesting some way forward, but instead, on 8 May 1989, a month before his eightieth birthday, he accepted what I said:

> I fear that you may be right, that in your circumstances you cannot really go on in a serious fashion, and that my 'archives' had better wait for my demise; after which, if Aline is alive, she may be able to make some arrangement for some professional archivist, or perhaps do nothing at all; as you know, I am not at all enthusiastic about anything I have written, and am not depressed by the thought of letting it rest. [...] If you would like to come and look at some of these things sometime, in your spare time, and be duly paid for these labours, I should be perfectly happy to arrange that. But that is about the maximum, I fear – based on your letter – that can be contemplated, don't you think? Or have you any alternative suggestion? I hate saying all this, because I think it may cause you disappointment of some sort, although it doesn't deserve to.

The ellipsis marks an intervening commentary on my list, some of whose contents make interesting reading, especially in the light of what happened later. I give three examples.

Of 'Three Turning Points in Political Thought' (Greek individualism; Machiavelli's dualism; Romantic pluralism), his 1962 Storrs Lectures at Yale, he wrote: 'There is a certain central point about these three lectures, about the gradual development from two alternatives – politics and being unpolitical – then two alternative moralities, then the Romantic plurality', characteristically adding: 'but I don't think that alone makes it worth spending much time on'. The first of these lectures is now in *Liberty*, and the other two in the IBVL. Of 'Politics as a Descriptive Science': 'I have no idea what this is and do not think it can be by me.' It was the first chapter of *Political Ideas in the Romantic Age*, his longest continuous composition. Finally, 'My father's autobiography had better be pulped.' It has now been published in *The Book of Isaiah*. Peter Halban has suggested to me that Berlin's shade will have regretted this, but I am clear that it throws valuable light on the world from which Berlin emerged, a world not too widely known about or understood outside its own confines.

In my reply of 12 May I speculated about various possible sources of funding. I was not optimistic, but observed: 'Who knows what new doors may open in the future? If nothing else, by the time you die I shall with any luck be an elderly man in carpet slippers with limitless time at my disposal.' Berlin's reply of 15 May confirmed his earlier acceptance of my suggestion that the royalties from future books might be used as (part of) the necessary funding, and expresses doubt about another option – to seek help from a charitable foundation – while leaving that door open by suggesting the Wolfson Foundation:

> there would be no harm in trying that, providing you were careful to say that I knew nothing of it and the whole thing was a secret enterprise, needing only my permission to edit these works, which I can naturally not be requested to subsidise myself, etc.

On 6 June Berlin reached the age of eighty, and various articles about him appeared in the press, some more favourable than others, some more inaccurate than others. I myself had been asked to draft an obituary for the *Independent*, and was unsure about the summary of his work that I had attempted for this purpose. I wrote to him that I was being asked from time to time to explain his ideas (which was perfectly true), and that I should be glad to have a brief account to refer to that had his approval (also true). I sent him the relevant passage from my draft, not telling him that it was to appear in an obituary. If he smelt a rat, he gave no sign of this, but approved the passage with one minor reservation (3 July 1989).

In the same letter he raised the subject of a typescript about Hamann that had emerged from his papers. It ran to 90 triple-spaced foolscap pages plus some additional A4 sheets typed on a different machine (some 40,000 words all told), and gave the lie to his insistence that he had never written anything on this mysterious anti-rationalist figure. It is true that this text had clearly been dictated, rather than drafted by hand and then typed up, but that did not distinguish it from other material composed in this period. It is likely that it was intended as the basis for parts of his 1965 Woodbridge Lectures in New York (unless it was dictated afterwards). But neither would that count as not writing: after all, his inaugural lecture on 'Two Concepts of Liberty', one of his most important published works, had been 'written' in exactly the same fashion.

The philosopher of science Nancy Cartwright, by now married to Stuart Hampshire, was reading the text and had pronounced it 'sort of OK', as Berlin put it in his letter to me. He continued:

If it were included, as Roger insists to me it should be, in the forthcoming volume, this makes it [the volume] filled with black thinkers, disproportionately to the other stuff. Hamann obviously cannot be published separately. If he is to go in, would that take too long and drive you mad? As there is nothing in English about Hamann that is much good, I cannot deny that I am somewhat tempted. If this moves you to near-despair, would you thunder at Roger and only indirectly at me?

I replied on 7 July:

It is a question of balancing the considerable further delay which is certain to be caused by including Hamann against the benefit of having it in this volume rather than leaving it for some future as yet unplanned collection. There is no doubt, of course, that it is rescuable, and worth rescuing; I am not surprised that Lady Hampshire feels, halfway through, that it is 'sort of OK' – that's putting it at its lowest. But she will find, when she gets to the end, that the main typescript is incomplete (I may yet find the missing page(s), of course), and is followed by a series of fragments of varying lengths and states of completion to be inserted at unspecified points in the main text – which reads more or less seamlessly as it stands.

The main typescript is also in a less finished state than Maistre was, not having been worked over by you so thoroughly, as far as I can see. This surely means that, even if I manage to construct a text out of the material to hand, you are bound when you come to read it through to want to do a lot to it. I think you are contemplating rewriting even Maistre, which you originally said you would not want to look at, and which I and Roger and Professor Lebrun think could go forward as it now stands. If that is going to delay the volume by, say, six months (an optimistic estimate?), by how much the more would Hamann hold things up?

Let us be realistic. It took me six months to get Maistre straight. It will take at least as long to deal with Hamann, and after that you will presumably not have time to devote to it until the summer of 1990. (This would also be yet more time stolen from the Mellon volume, which is surely a cause for regret?) I know well that you are in absolutely no hurry on your own account, and I applaud your detachment; but do you mind at all depriving your eager readers, for an indeterminate period, of a volume which is otherwise ready to be delivered to the publisher? If not, then perhaps the argument from further delay lacks force; any frustration of my own at having to put on ice a volume I have finished editing should certainly be set aside.

Perhaps I may make a proposal: that we continue for the time being on the basis that Hamann won't go in. But in the meantime I shall beaver away at the text and see what I can do, doubtless with Roger's invaluable help. If, by the time you have finished with Maistre, I have come up with something I can show you, we can think again. Otherwise, could Hamann wait for a subsequent volume? [...]

I am going to stop apologising for the length of my letters. I might as well regret the shape of my nose.

Berlin replied in turn on 10 July 1989:

I agree with you. In the end I think you may, as always, prove right and he [Hamann] should be postponed. I have not looked at the typescript in the hands of Lady Hampshire for, I should think, about twenty years – I am sure I have not corrected it or anything like that. When she gives it back, if ever, I will take it to Italy, but I wonder [if] he will be a candidate for inclusion in this volume. Will there ever be another? [...]

As for noses, plastic surgery is always possible; but neither you nor I are likely to abbreviate our letters – nor need we, despite Pat's terrible groans. Fullness is all.

In the same letter the idea of Michael Ignatieff as his biographer was first mooted:

I think he would probably be a better biographer, if one is needed, than anyone else I know, mainly because of Russia, America, acquaintance with political controversies of the present, etc. I am prepared to send him a letter authorising him to go ahead provided there is no publication in my lifetime. Of course he will try to get you to help him as much as he can, and I hope you will not mind doing this – but that is entirely up to you. I don't really mind what happens after my death – never have – so provided nothing happens in my lifetime I don't terribly mind what is arranged now. I hope this doesn't sound too casual – but you know better than anyone else how I am.

Three days later I wrote back:

> Your dispensation re Hamann is delightfully open-ended. I shall continue
> to scratch away at the text and see what I can do. I've already arranged
> for it to be put on a word-processor, and could give you a printout from
> that to take to Italy if you wanted: it might be easier to read than the
> existing typescript, prepared as it [the original typescript] was by a lady
> who specialised in spellings such as 'diliterious'. [...]
>
> As for your enquiry about whether there will ever be another volume
> in which Hamann might appear if he is omitted from the current one:
> there is, as you know, plenty of material. Whether the potential further
> volumes, once I have prepared them, are published in your lifetime will
> be up to you. Barkis is willin'.
>
> I shall be guided by your view of Michael Ignatieff.

In October 1989 I drew up a careful statement entitled 'Isaiah Berlin's papers'
in which I explained what I had found, what I thought should be done with it,
and how I thought the necessary work might be financed. I sent it to my contacts at John Murray and the Hogarth Press. In January 1990 I sent it to Stuart
Proffitt at Collins, I think at the suggestion of Andrew Best, in preparation for
a meeting with him. Meantime I explored the possibility of subvention from
a number of charitable foundations. My path was blocked, as far as other publishers were concerned, by Berlin's reluctance to agree to the publication of any
further volumes in his lifetime: the publishers naturally wanted to see a return
on their investment in the foreseeable future. There was much toing and froing
behind the scenes, and in March 1990 Alan Bullock – whom I had presumably
contacted again because he was a trustee of the Wolfson Foundation, and thus
in a position to intercede with its chairman, Leonard Wolfson – made the
brilliant suggestion that any grant might be administered via a post at Wolfson
College, and enquiries proceeded during 1990 with this in view. But this is to
jump ahead somewhat.

On 8 November 1989 I was able to send Berlin a fair copy of the Hamann
material:

> I am at last able to send you a word-processed version of Hamann, as
> promised some time ago. I enclose it now. I am very sorry about the delay
> (even though I know it won't have caused you a moment's anxiety): I have

been badly let down by a typist. As you will see from the covering note, only first aid has been administered so far. I shall be interested to learn, in due course, whether you accept my view that it is in too unfinished a state for it to be sensible to contemplate holding up the new volume still longer in order to include it. I know that you have an enviably relaxed attitude in the matter of delivery dates, but I think that even you will acknowledge that, since it would probably take you a good year, at best, to revise the text (to say nothing of the time it would take to sort out the footnotes), it would not be reasonable to add a delay of that order. But I know well that, like Maistre, you cannot promise not to surprise me;[12] so I am prepared for (almost) anything.

Two days later Berlin replied: 'Despite Roger, I feel in my bones that you must be right. Anyhow, Maistre and Hamann would make the book too "black" and Scruton-like – I cannot say worse than that.' The reference to Roger Scruton is most immediately explained by an article Scruton had recently written for *The Times* to mark Berlin's eightieth birthday.[13] Alongside a not too grudging meed of praise it contained some nasty barbs, among which these two stand out:

Re-reading Sir Isaiah's essays, I find myself both impressed by their abundance and repelled by it. Berlin's ideas circle round the great white hope of liberation, but beneath the elegant fabric of his sentences, the self-confident rhythm of which has an almost automatic character, I sense a dearth of those experiences in which the suspicion of the liberal idea is rooted: experiences of the sacred and the erotic, of mourning and holy dread.

I feel drawn to the cause that he defends. But looking at the second-rate bigots who have advanced through the academic world during his 'reign' over it, I wonder how effective a bastion he has been against the intellectual corruption which he condemns with such cautious eloquence?

Thus was Berlin's already existing antipathy to Scruton's views reinforced.

I resisted the argument that the inclusion of both Maistre and Hamann would unbalance the book, but still believed that the delay that would be caused by including Hamann, even if the problem of the truncated text could be solved, was too great. This view prevailed. Meanwhile the Maistre essay was batted to and fro between us. Berlin changed his mind more than once about whether we should call its subject 'Maistre' or 'de Maistre', and I was glad that the age of the word processor had arrived, allowing me to implement these changes quickly by using 'Find and Replace'. He also asked me if I would remove the frequent note cues from the text (instead using lemmata, referenced by page, to cue endnotes), since in the Maistre essay they numbered 130 and therefore became increasingly obtrusive. 'Have I ruined your week, month, year, life?' (New Year's Eve 1989). I pointed out that in the book the notes would be numbered by page (not a facility available in word processing), and that they were less frequent than in parts of AC. The cues remained.

Amidst such trivia, important events were occurring. A letter from me of 9 February 1990 begins: 'The whole political order against which so many of your essays implicitly or explicitly stand seems to be evaporating! It is scarcely believable to me. I wonder if you are equally surprised.' In the margin Berlin has written *Yes*. In his reply of the next day he writes:

> Of course I was totally astonished by the course of events on the part of the political order which you rightly think I do not exactly favour; my political writings will soon seem platitudes, except, perhaps, to benighted East Europeans.

I now delivered the volume to John Murray, heading off a last-minute suggestion by Berlin that 'The Bent Twig'[14] should be dropped as too similar to 'Nationalism' in AC. I reread the essays and reported on their considerable unlikenesses. Besides, how could one resist ending a book on the crooked timber of humanity with an essay on the bent twig?

7

THE MAGUS OF THE NORTH

Next on the agenda, I think, is Hamann.

HH to IB, 23 February 1990

His meticulous regard for detail made it hard for him to satisfy himself. This went so far that he dismissed an important and scholarly book as 'worthless' on the ground that in it 'Grenoble' was printed with an accent. An editor once allowed him to review a study of his own for which no other competent critic could be found, and he increased the reputation of the journal by his severe exposure of certain minute errors which he thus took the opportunity of correcting.[1]

P. V. M. Benecke

Another hideous error: in referring to Hélène in War & Peace as relevant to (de) Maistre's Catholic converts, I call her Countess H – but I now feel sure – without daring to verify – that she is Princess. Sleepless nights![2]

IB to HH, 19 September 1990

I

My editorial experiences have sometimes been strange and exciting. Perhaps the best moment of all was the miraculous restoration of what turned out to be a long passage missing from Berlin's vivid study of Hamann. The main typescript ended mid chapter, on folio 90, with these words: 'Why are we here? What is our goal? How can we allay the'. To all appearances the missing portion was substantial, and none of the separate typed passages I had found plugged the gap. This was frustrating, since I had no confidence that Berlin would be willing, or even able, to recreate what had disappeared. Despite this major problem, of whose seriousness he was perhaps not fully aware, he wrote to me on 2 March sharply criticized for supposing that language is a natural function, that it grows like the sense of smell or taste -- for Hamann is a gift from a personal Deity. Herder, after recanting, leapt back into his naturalism towards the end of his life and attempted to give an empirical-genetic explanation of how different languages developed and what relations they had to the geographical, biological and psychological and social characteristics of their users.

Hamann thinks that there is an organic connection between all these attributes, xxxx and that history may indeed reveal them, but what is for him important is to insist that the connections created by God and by history itself is only a kind of enormous living allegory; the facts, of course, occur as they do and the events that historians uncover did indeed occur, and it is possible to re-establish them by painstaking scholarship; but the point is that we read in these patterns of fact what man is, what his purposes are, e.g. what God has created him for; and we read this in the Bible also; we read this in the economy of Nature; and that is all that for Hamann is of importance. It may be that others are interested in the facts for their own sake, to satisfy their curiosity; and invent or study sciences in order to satisfy this same xxx curiosity; or perhaps they do so the better to control material forces; all this may be so, but to him this seems trivial beside the need to answer the ultimate questions -- why are we here? what is our goal? how can we allay the

The last page of the main original typescript of *The Magus of the North*, on which I marked the transition from Dictabelt 16 to Dictabelt 15 (*sic*)

1990, 'Hamann can now go forward with my blessing', immediately qualifying this with a manuscript addition: 'But: I must read the MS – Typescript – if I find it *intolerable*, I'll tell you before action is taken!'

For his eighty-first birthday (6 June 1990), I sent Berlin a spoof list of air-raid precautions drawn up by the staff of Shrewsbury School during the Second World War. My martinet grandfather H. H. Hardy had been headmaster of Shrewsbury from 1932 to 1944, and this had led Berlin to observe justly of my character earlier in our acquaintance: 'Not for nothing is he the grandson of a famous headmaster.'³ The first item in the list of precautions reads: '1. Lock Hardy in the Chapel.' Berlin responded on 7 June: 'Time has done its work – you would not need to be locked up even in a Chapel. Still, I sigh for those days and the heroic masters of my youth.'

At about the same time Alan Bullock reported that the Wolfson Foundation would after all help financially for the initial five-year period of work that I had proposed, though only, as was their wont, to the tune of at most half of my estimated needs. Fortunately, soon afterwards the remainder of my budget was covered by an (officially) anonymous benefactor whom Bullock had enlisted. I knew from the beginning, off the record, that this was my father-in-law Geoffrey Wilkinson, Professor of Inorganic Chemistry at Imperial College, London, who had set up a charitable foundation of his own to sponsor educational projects (mainly in the sciences), funded by the income from his chemical patents and his Nobel Prize. His imaginativeness in seeing the potential of my project, which lay completely outside his comfort zone, was striking. Of course it may be said that he was simply influenced by the fact that I had married his daughter, and I am sure that this was part of the story. But I do not believe that he would have acted as he did unless he had been independently satisfied that the investment was justified. Here the role of Alan Bullock was crucial. Both Bullock and Wilkinson were Yorkshiremen, Bullock by adoption, having attended Bradford Grammar School from his early teens, when his father moved to the city, and Wilkinson by birth, as a son of the Todmorden master painter and decorator Henry Wilkinson. I cannot remember how the two were first put in touch, though I suspect that my then wife played a key role *sub rosa*, but in any event the two men clicked, and the Yorkshire mafia swung into action. For the next twenty years the Wilkinson Charitable Trust faithfully supported my work, even after my wife and I separated in 2004. Wilkinson had died in 1996, and I cannot say what view he would have taken of me had he lived longer, though the trustees of his foundation, by continuing my funding, adopted an exceedingly magnanimous interpretation of his wishes. By the time I 'retired' in 2015, only the Berlin Charitable Trust had contributed on the same scale.

On 27 September 1990 I was able to thank Berlin for an advance copy of CTH on whose front free endpaper he had inscribed: 'Henry from you know who with sentiments you must by now know. I.B'. On 11 October the book was published. On Friday 19 October, St Frideswide's Day, I left OUP. On 21 November Berlin wrote: 'I began to look at Hamann and began to correct it, and then got totally bored. [...] I'll do nothing before Christmas, I'm afraid – let us hope for better news next year.' On 18 December I told Berlin that his Mellon lectures on Romanticism were now on disk, and offered him a print-out, saying that I expected him to recoil. On 21 December he wrote: 'As you anticipated, I recoil at the moment (whether there will be another moment is not clear).' This farrago of communications gives an accurate impression of our relations at the time: relaxed, humorous, my relentless impatience thwarted by his relentless procrastination.

The Hamannian miracle occurred over a period of weeks in the early months of 1991. With considerable and uncharacteristic self-restraint I refrained from reporting it to Berlin until it had run its course and I was quite sure of my ground. On 23 April I finally wrote to explain what had happened.

11

One day, when conducting a more systematic search in Berlin's cellar, I found on a small bookcase a dusty envelope containing several 'Dictabelts' – obsolete red plastic recording devices from the 1960s, both recorded on, and played back, with a stylus on a dedicated machine made by Dictaphone. The continuous belts were supplied in brown paper sleeves, and I noticed that on one of these Berlin had written 'Haman.2' (*sic*). My heart missed a beat.[4] Could it be that these discarded pieces of plastic contained what I was looking for?

The first step towards answering this question was to find a machine to play the Dictabelts. Years later I found one hidden away in Pat Utechin's untidy office. She had forgotten that she still had it. Knowing about it earlier would have shortened the birth-pangs of the book, but also deprived the story of an intriguing episode. I contacted the National Sound Archive (NSA), then in Exhibition Road in Kensington, where, serendipitously, the Curator of Western

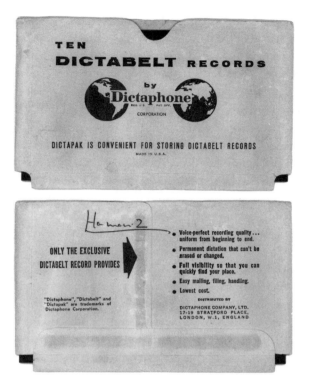

Storage envelope (front and back) for a Hamann Dictabelt

Art Music, Timothy Day, turned out to be a keen enthusiast for Berlin's work, and a great ally on this occasion and many subsequent ones. The NSA had a large collection of historical sound-reproducing devices, but not, alas, a Dictaphone machine of the relevant kind. However, the machine that Agatha Christie had used came up for auction, and hopes rose – but only briefly, as the NSA was outbid for it. Next it was discovered that there was such a machine at London's Science Museum, in the same road. This was not in working order, but the NSA borrowed it and managed to get it going.

The next problem was that the Dictabelts, of which there were seventeen for the Hamann text, had become brittle and rigid over the years, and could not be safely coaxed over the two spindles of the machine. With brilliant creativity the NSA staff put the Dictabelts in a low oven and warmed them up very slowly until they became pliable, but not so much that they melted.

They could then be loaded on to the machine, but even so they played very erratically, and had to be manually massaged through the playback process groove by groove. The stylus often jumped, causing either repetition or gaps, and picked up faint versions of the sound in neighbouring grooves. With deft fingerwork the majority of the recorded sound was painstakingly extracted from the belts and transferred to conventional cassette tapes. The delay seemed endless, and the suspense was dreadful. But in the end I received the cassettes, loaded them into my tape recorder with trembling hands, and started to listen to the extremely crackly sound recorded twenty-five years before. Finally I heard Berlin say: 'Why are we here? What is our goal? How can we allay the', and held my breath. Here it was at last: 'How can we allay the spiritual agony of those who will not rest unless they obtain true answers to these questions?' My own agony of apprehension was thus allayed, my question answered, and rest possible.

What followed was not merely the missing 1,900 words of the chapter on language (the chapter in progress at the end of the main surviving typescript), but also the first 600 words of the next chapter, which I didn't know were missing, and an appendix of 1,000 words on the similarity between Hamann's view of language and that of Wittgenstein:[5] 3,500 words in all. My excitement as I heard and transcribed all this material was intense.

Another benefit of listening to original recordings of Berlin's dictation is worth mentioning. From time to time Berlin's freelance typist, Olive Sheldon, cannot hear what Berlin says, sometimes because he uses an unusual word: so she leaves a blank for him to fill in. When Berlin checks the transcript he doesn't listen to the recording, and fills in the blanks afresh. This can lead to the loss of an interesting word or phrase, and one example sticks in my mind. In Mrs Sheldon's typescript Berlin speaks on Hamann's behalf of religious apologetics as 'an attempt to domesticate God, to place him in some tame [ ] of one's own'. Berlin writes in 'harmless formula'; but 'harmless' more or less repeats 'tame', and 'some tame, harmless formula' is not naturally preceded by 'place him in'. The recording yields 'herbarium', a much choicer term.

When I told Berlin the story about the discovery of the missing material, in an abbreviated form, he wrote (6 May 1991): 'Your story about the Dictabelts is really out of this world.' He had forgotten Olive Sheldon; he could not remember whether he had dictated the text before or after he lectured on Hamann in 1965, or whether the additional pages were dictated later, and indeed wasn't interested in these questions of intellectual archaeology and stratification: 'The

that there is an organic connection between all these attributes, and
that history may indeed reveal it, but what is important for him is to
insist that the connection created by God and history itself is only a
kind of enormous living allegory. The facts, of course, occur as they do
and the events that historians uncover did indeed occur, and it is
possible to re-establish them by painstaking scholarship; but ~~the~~ *his* point
is that we _can_ read in these patterns ~~of fact~~ *of events as facts* what man is, what his purposes
are, what God has created him for; and we _can_ read this in the Bible also;
we _can_ read this in the economy of nature; and for Hamann that is all that
is of importance.

It may be that others are interested in the facts for their own
sake, to satisfy their curiosity; and invent or study sciences in order
to satisfy this same curiosity; or perhaps they do so the better to
control material forces.[252] All this may be so, but to him this seems
trivial beside the need to answer the ultimate questions: Why are we
here? What are we at? What are our goals? How can we allay[253] the
spiritual agony of those who will not rest unless they obtain true
answers to these questions? Nature is like the Hebrew alphabet. It
contains only consonants. The vowels we must supply for ourselves,
otherwise we cannot read the words.[254] How do we supply them? By that
faith or belief of which Hume had spoken, without which we could not
live for an instant; by ~~the~~ *our* unbreakable certainty ~~that we have~~ that
there exists an external world, that there exists God, that there exist

Who is horrified? The "others" above? wↄ? can't understand the footnote: been omitted? Fine – but it's your marginale

252 {horrified when this provided an answer to real questions}
253 [at this point the original typescript breaks off, in the
middle of a sentence, at the bottom of a page; the material from here as
far as p. 115 , note 282, has been recovered from the Dictabelts]
254 B i 450.19. [repeated on p. 120]

never mind!

bravissimo !

The passage shown on p. 122, with the Dictabelt text
added, and Berlin's revisions and comments

point is the MS itself.' This he wished to read and revise over the summer at his Italian fastness in Paraggi.

Before this point I had sent the tidied typescript to James C. O'Flaherty, an expert on Hamann in the USA who had corresponded with Berlin in the past. I knew I might need ammunition from persons of this kind if I were to persuade Berlin that the text was publishable. Fortunately O'Flaherty was impressed:

> First, let me say that it was, as always, a delight to read the reflections on Hamann of this great historian of ideas. I must say that I have learned much from it, especially in regard to parallel ideas in the thought of others [...]. Many, many parts of Sir Isaiah's treatise are the best accounts of Hamann's thought I have seen [...], and of course his interpretative brilliance is everywhere evident. (26 March 1991)

I quoted this endorsement to Berlin in the letter about the Dictabelts, and also sent him a copy of the letter from which it was taken. O'Flaherty wrote to Berlin direct as well. He raised questions 'about whether Hamann was a true enemy of the Enlightenment, and whether he was an anti-Semite' – questions which Berlin regarded as 'worth reflecting about' (to HH, 6 May 1991). Berlin went on to explain to me his views on both topics, said he might modify what he had written, but in the end didn't, much. I did look up all the (very numerous) references to Jews in Hamann's writings for him, and we concocted a footnote finessing Berlin's statement in the text about Hamann's hatred of Jews (TCE2 369). But, as in the case of Maistre, Berlin didn't really reconsider his position.

It was not until the summer of 1992, in Italy, that Berlin got down to serious work on the Hamann typescript I had provided, marking up the text with corrections and dictating two cassettes of further instructions. I had supplied copies of many of the passages by Hamann that he had quoted, and of many of his other sources, so that he would have all the necessary texts to hand when answering my many questions. Even though I made this clear, for some reason he treated these copies as required reading, extracting points from them for insertion into his text, which was not at all my intention. I was embarrassed that he undertook this work, misconceived as it was. It would have been impertinent for me to suggest further reading to him, and if I had wanted to do so, I should not have selected the passages I copied for him, which were meant only to clarify my questions. But although I tried to explain the misunderstanding, he didn't seem to take the point. Not that there was anything wrong, mostly, with the resulting changes to the text.

After a great deal of reconstructive surgery, both before and after Berlin worked through the text himself, I managed to produce a publishable text. I have a clear memory of the occasion in the spring of 1993 when Berlin finally agreed to let me go ahead with this. It was at the end of a long session in his room in All Souls, which was in the south-west corner of the college, on the first floor of Staircase 5, with a bow window looking out on Oxford's High Street. We had spent some time going through my final queries on the text, and in one case Berlin had (most unusually) lost his temper, having failed to understand why a statement of his could not stand.

Mine was a small, even pedantic, point, but, it seemed to me, cut and dried. However, for some reason Berlin wouldn't accept it, finally throwing in the towel and snapping irritably: 'Put what you like.' The moment quickly passed, and harmony was restored. So much so that when, as I left the room, I asked Berlin if I might now publish his study of Hamann, he answered 'Yes.' I am sure that Alan Bullock had had a word with him, pointing out that my benefactors wanted to see something in print if they were to continue to fund my post. I told Berlin that he was, if nothing else, astonishingly unpredictable, and he merely inclined his head, with a twinkle in his eye.

Having completely forgotten that he had written any such work, Berlin was amazed by its resurrection, and pleased when John Murray finally published it in 1993 as *The Magus of the North: J. G. Hamann and the Origins of Modern Irrationalism*. It was astonishingly widely reviewed for a book on such an apparently recondite subject – though Berlin's treatment made it anything but recondite. The appreciations by Michael Rosen in the TLS and Mark Lilla in the LRB stood out.[6] Extensive extracts (again maddeningly amended by Berlin) appeared in the NYRB. There were grumblings from Germany, where in a feat of seeming perversity Hamann had come to be regarded as 'a champion of true reason and enlightenment' (TCE2 312–13) rather than as the implacable critic of the Enlightenment that Berlin had so scintillatingly brought to life.[7] I don't pretend to understand how this apparent turning of black into white is achieved, unless 'the Enlightenment' is somehow drained of its historical meaning and equated with truth. One expert on Hamann, I was told, even described the book as a scholarly scandal. But these voices were scarcely heard in the English-speaking world, and did not prevent the book appearing in a German translation.[8]

Many other Dictabelts were retrieved from the recesses of Headington House, and later played their (smaller) part in the preparation of Berlin's *Nachlass* for publication. Most notably there are recordings of early drafts of 'Two Concepts of Liberty' which amplify the surviving typescripts, and have now been made available online, and in some cases in print.[9] But the rescue of Hamann was their finest hour.

The first edition of *The Magus of the North*

8

THE SENSE OF REALITY

I

Having allowed the Hamann story to reach its conclusion without interruption, I now rewind to early 1991, since other discussions were taking place between us in parallel with my work on the magus – or 'magician', as Berlin called him in 1956 (AE 272). On 14 March I wrote Berlin a letter that I cannot now find, but Berlin's reply shows that I must have asked him what he felt about his own reputation, and when he ceased to regard himself as plain I. M. Berlin Esq. of 49 Hollycroft Avenue (his parental home in Hampstead from 1928):

> I am glad you think my view of myself is sane – I regard it as entirely realistic and I do think that I have been overestimated. I cannot really account for the honours etc. save by saying that my amiable character and anxiety to please (not a terribly good characteristic) have caused me to have few enemies; the need to give praise, honours etc. on the part of those who dispense these commodities makes me a harmless recipient of them – believe me, I am not being falsely modest, excessively self-deprecating or ironical in all this.
>
> I do think of myself as I. M. Berlin Esq. of Hollycroft Avenue. I do not think that what has happened to me is exactly mysterious, merely undeserved – lots of other people have been mistakenly praised and blamed: I can think of some. I am happy to belong to the first category: long may it last.
>
> I am afraid I have become acclimatised to the idea that I am well thought of in many quarters, and because I know that this has been much more than my due I have not, as you rightly and kindly say, 'become

rigid, like Popper, or arrogant, like Medawar, or pretentious, like [...],*
or nasty, like – no I mustn't ...' – like who? I long to know – ('like [...]'
would be the most terrible fate).

You ask, 'When did the phenomenon begin?' No idea, I am not conscious of a development, only of unexpected favours as and when they came.

I replied on 25 March:

> The source of the anxiety to please – one of the few characteristics which
> I possess in sufficient measure to be your rival – is an interesting topic
> on its own. In my view some people are just born with it, some without,
> though it can certainly be reinforced, weakened, acquired or lost too.
> In my own case I cannot be sure of the extent to which it is part of my
> genetic endowment, as compared with the extent to which it is a reaction
> to being brought up by an *Einfühlung*-less [unempathetic] stepmother
> who was impossible to please. At all events, continuous failure, despite
> one's best efforts, to be acceptable to someone at the centre of one's life
> is undoubtedly capable of strengthening an innate complaisance. What
> of your case? According to Michael I., you attribute this at least partly to
> being an outsider or exile – the expatriate Russian/Jew syndrome – but
> you seem remarkably at home to me. Perhaps this is bluff.

To this Berlin replied on 2 April:

> about anxiety to please (a relatively easy question). I still think that my
> own comes from the need, no doubt hereditary, and I daresay by now
> genetic, of outsiders exposed to peril – the Jews, for two thousand years –
> to accommodate themselves in a hostile environment, which can be done
> either by aggressive self-defence (which usually ends badly) or attempts to
> appease, which may well be undignified and pathetic but do, I suppose,
> lead to self-preservation of a minimum degree, social acceptance. It was
> so in the ancient world and the middle ages, and in the modern world
> something of that lingers. You are quite right to suppose that I am per-
> fectly comfortable in my present existence. I am not conscious of having

---

* This and the next ellipsis stands for a surname omitted out of consideration for the living.
I cannot remember whom I took to be nasty.

to make compromises or of having to appease, suck up to, potentially dangerous or powerful people or institutions; nothing of that, I admit, do I feel or practise; but my natural tendency towards trade-offs, compromise, peaceful settlement – whatever their objective justification and validity – probably does spring from unconscious efforts to fit myself into a totally new environment in 1919 [sc. 1921].[1] As it is successful, the need for it evaporates, I suppose, but its traces cannot but remain in all kinds of subconscious, unexpected and perhaps rather central ways. That's the best I can do. But I admit with some pleasure that whatever the roots of my temperament and habits, I am not conscious of them, and perhaps never was – my theory is a mere hypothesis, though I still think not implausible.

The rest of my letter of 25 March 1991 exhibits the first stirrings of a new phase in our discussion, as I begin to ask Berlin about matters of intellectual substance. My close work on his texts reopened for me questions about his thought that had long preoccupied me – even tormented me – and I began to ask these questions in my letters. I am astonished today at the patience and thoroughness with which he replied, and it seems to me that, taken together, his answers constitute an important supplement to his published work, clarifying it at certain crucial points and preventing natural misinterpretations at others.

The topic that dominated our first substantial discussion was the relationship between pluralism and religious belief. Later we discussed his conception of human nature – its contents, limits and implications. The extremely general issues we were addressing kept company with discussion of the fine detail of my work on Berlin's papers. Rather than recounting our exchanges on both sorts of topic in the order in which they occurred, making both threads more difficult to follow, I shall instead defer treatment of these demanding issues to two later chapters (10 and 11), preceding them with a chapter (9) attempting an outline of Berlin's published views on the relevant subjects, as a basis for clarifying his letters. Here I shall take the editorial story almost up to Berlin's death.

11

A letter from Berlin of 17 April 1991 ends with a somewhat uncharacteristic request from one who professed reluctance to revisit letters from long ago.

I had asked him whether he wanted regular reports on my progress, expecting the answer no. He replied:

> You ask about bulletins. I don't mind these; in fact I should be rather pleased if you let me have them from time to time – but particularly, I think, an alphabetical list of my correspondents: all those whom the Bodleian etc. have classified – it can't be all that long. I long to know, naturally, if there are any excessively personal or embarrassing letters among them, e.g. from or to a lady still alive, called never mind what, who signs her letters Tips, and similar letters of this sort. Do let me know of this. I know you collect letters *by* me: but I'd love to know the list of writers *and* recipients.

Archivists from the Bodleian had by this stage done some preliminary work on the letters Berlin had kept (or, rather, not discarded), compiling lists of his correspondents as they went, on the understanding that his papers would eventually come to the library. 'Tips' is Rachel Walker, a pupil of Berlin's at Oxford in the 1930s who fell in love with him and proposed marriage (at Paris Zoo), later becoming mentally disturbed and institutionalised (F 719–20). I did provide the lists he requested, though I have found no record, and have no memory, of any response from him to seeing them.

In a letter of 4 July I suggested, apropos a text of Berlin's, 'Four Weeks in the Soviet Union', some gaps in which he had filled, that a collection of his pieces on the USSR might appear. He was dead against this:

> About the essays on Soviet topics: no, no, no, as Mrs Thatcher said.[2] They do not amount to enough, they are occasional pieces, of which perhaps only 'The Artificial Dialectic' is worth preserving, at the moment at any rate – what happens posthumously I do not, as you know, greatly worry about. The other pieces are not disreputable, but the whole amounts to a rather lightweight affair, somewhat obsolete. [...] my great friend Hamilton Fish Armstrong, editor of *Foreign Affairs*, pressed me and pressed me to do something on a political theme, and [...] I sat down and did the piece on the artificial dialectic. And I think maybe another piece for him.[3] These deserve to survive, maybe, but not in a separate Sovietological collection, believe me!' (7 July)

I argued back, but he was unpersuadable, writing that he did not wish to dance upon the grave of the USSR.⁴ I finally had my way twenty-three years later by publishing *The Soviet Mind*. Some regard this as a substandard collection, but I disagree, as did the reviewers. It shows remarkable insight into the Soviet mentality, and is almost equally relevant to the mentality of the regime that succeeded the exhilarating collapse of Soviet Communism a few weeks after our exchange occurred.

Admitting defeat on this proposal, I began to turn my attention to other unpublished material that I had unearthed, both lecture series and individual essays or lectures, asking about their origins, of which Berlin often professed himself ignorant. I didn't expect Berlin to agree to the publication of the lecture series in his lifetime, but I did hope that a volume of the (more polished) separate essays might appear. I first reported finding three substantial essays, now published under the following titles: 'The Sense of Reality' (1953), 'Philosophy and Government Repression' (1954) and 'Woodrow Wilson on Education' (1959).⁵ I described their contents, but Berlin did not remember writing any of them: a typical exchange.

On 3 March the following year (1992) I introduced the subject of what was later published as *Political Ideas in the Romantic Age*. I had recently produced a text of this on the basis of the heavily corrected typescript I had found among his papers:

> With somewhat bated breath I enclose my provisional rendition of what is by far your longest unpublished work (about 110,000 words, or 275 printed octavo pages), the 'long version' of the Flexner Lectures [delivered at Bryn Mawr College in 1952]. Don't panic! I'm not asking you to do any work on this – not even to look at it in any detail. But since it now exists, it seemed reasonable to show it to you, if only so that you might admire its bulk. Perhaps you had no idea you had in fact written such a long book?!
>
> I have inserted after the contents page a note on the text [PIRA2 349–54] which you might find of interest. It raises one or two questions, such as: Was there ever a corresponding 'long version' of the last two lectures, or did you never have time to draft this? Why did you never publish the lectures with OUP, as you were under contract to do? Was it indeed Anna Kallin's plan that the Third Programme version should be the 1952 Reith Lectures, and if so, when and why was this notion scotched? Was there a recording of the lectures as delivered in the USA?

The first page of the original typescript of *Political Ideas in the Romantic Age*, heavily corrected by Berlin

Berlin responded on 10 March 1992:

> Flexner lectures: these were in effect that same as those delivered for the
> BBC. 275 printed pages! *Quelle horreur!* I don't know about the last two
> lectures – the BBC texts are in their own way surely complete? I have no
> recollection of a contract with OUP (remember, I shall be eighty-three in
> June). Anna Kallin did indeed wonder whether they might make Reith
> Lectures – I was only too ready. She put it up, I had a letter inviting me
> to do them, followed by a letter two days later countermanding.[6] That
> was that. I was asked to do the series seven or eight years later, and by
> that time said that I had nothing to say. That was before I thought of
> Romanticism.

On 23 April 1992 I reported on the preparation of another text on which I had
been working for a considerable time:

> My main purpose today [...] is to send you the enclosed typescript – the
> next one to go on the heap, so to speak! It constitutes my first attempt
> at your 1952 BBC lectures, 'Freedom and its Betrayal'. The text runs to
> some 60,000 words (i.e. about 10,000 words per lecture, though 'Hegel'
> is longer), as opposed to the 110,000 words of the 'long version' – the
> version you dictated in preparation for the Flexner Lectures – which was
> the last typescript I sent you. [...] (The previous one, the 'long version',
> which you cannibalised for Flexner, gave about 25,000 words to each
> topic, and lacked Saint-Simon and Maistre.)
>
> In March 1989 you wrote to me as follows about 'Freedom and its
> Betrayal':

>> These were radio talks, more or less identical with the lectures
>> delivered at Bryn Mawr in 1952. There never were any texts: it was
>> all done from notes, as usual. But I think that tidied up it might
>> produce a booklet. It was these lectures that got me the Chichele
>> Chair, so I view them with favour, though I think they are a bit
>> over-simple and in places too dogmatic and extreme. The one on
>> Hegel is really not at all good, and would need real correction. If
>> you presented me with a clean manuscript – I mean typescript –
>> of the whole thing one day, I would undertake at least to read it,
>> and scribble things on it. But not yet, oh Lord, not yet!

I hope that a delay of three years is adequately respectful of your final entreaty! I'm not quoting this letter, of course, in order to attempt to hold you to your undertaking to read the script, only to explain why I've produced it this early in my activities. Naturally, if you still felt inclined to look at it ... (aposiopesis).

I must not conceal that you also wrote: 'my natural inclination is towards the posthumous, as you may imagine'. I expect you still feel this. For what it is worth, my own view is that, whenever they were published, no bones should be made about the fact that they are closely based on a transcript of extempore lectures. That is what gives them their freshness and accessibility, and it would be wrong (even if it were possible) to try to transform them into something that you might have written long-hand. The whole style, pace, structure, atmosphere are different. That is to say, to write a new book using this material (something I know isn't in question in any case) would represent a loss. But let me say no more about this until I have your reaction.

In editing the text I 'diligently compared and revised'[7] the various transcripts that survive. The first three lectures were considerably revised at some stage, and I have usually preferred the later variants. I have listened to the recording of 'Rousseau' at the National Sound Archive, which enabled me to make some corrections. 'Fichte' is annotated by you in a way that makes it clear you planned to add some further quotations (identified by letters of the alphabet), but although I have been through all your notes, and found numerous lists of Fichte quotations, none that I have yet found seems to fit the bill. As a matter of fact I think it might be best to leave things much as they are, because if all the quotations were added, that lecture would be unbalanced in comparison to the others.[8] I don't think 'Hegel' is as weak as you say: in some ways 'Saint-Simon' was the most difficult to reconstruct, and I think it may have been less thoroughly prepared than the others.

Berlin replied on 27 April 1992:

I am sure you suspect what I am going to say. I promise to read Hamann this summer, and give you the result. This is a solemn vow and I think I shall fulfil it. But if I do that then nothing else can be done before the autumn – but even then ... I still toy with the idea of doing something about Romanticism. I realise I am too old and my mind too flickering to write the book I intended, from the Mellon Lectures, revised, re-shaped, supplied with apparatus from all the stuff I have ever read since, which is accumulated in the papers lying at the top of our house. I don't believe I shall live long enough or have strength enough to perform this, though I keep denying that to Aline, who chivvies me on the subject from time to time. What I could conceivably do is write a book about E. T. A. Hoffmann, and preface it with a huge torso drawn from the lectures and to some extent reinforced by what I should force myself to read through without taking too many notes. If I do that, I cannot possibly look at the Flexner lectures in either version, which you have so kindly, and after such unbelievable labour, supplied me with. Naturally my gratitude knows no bounds – but I don't want to hold out too much hope.

I think you are right. I think the lectures have to be corrected but not properly rewritten. If the book is ever to appear, posthumously or otherwise, it must simply be a text of the lectures as lectures, and called that; and the introduction must say that this is what it is and that like all lectures there is a certain amount of loose generalisation and possibly a certain amount of rhetoric which cannot be eliminated. Or something to assuage too much ferocity on the part of too well qualified critics. [...]

Of course if I live long enough and some rejuvenating substance can be found to stir my intermittent brain – stop me from falling asleep after even half-an-hour of not even very intensive work – that might accomplish both tasks: but not before the age of, say, ninety-four or so. Still, Ranke died about then, and he did write a rather poor world history[9] at that point – all of which he dictated. He first read Herodotus in full, then Thucydides, then I think Xenophon, and then said to his student: 'And now write!' And a not very good book was then completed. The writings of Shaw and Russell at the relevant age are not encouraging – there is no cure for old age.

Reading this, I regretted once again that my work on Berlin's papers had not occurred earlier in his life. But earlier in his life, would he have allowed me to do what I was doing now? I doubt it. I replied:

I am delighted, of course, to have your renewed promise to deal with Hamann [...]. I shall very much look forward to the upshot of that. It is also very good to know that you contemplate a book on Hoffmann. This appears to give the lie to your pessimistic remarks about your 'flickering' mind: if I believed what you say about this I should perhaps be encouraging you to devote yourself rather to the revision of things which already exist in typescript, such as those I am sending you, but I cannot deny that I am not a wholly disinterested party, and I do see that a new book might be preferred by an objective felicific calculus. Nevertheless, it would be wrong, I think, for you to feel that reading through 'Freedom and Its Betrayal', for instance, would be a major task. Though I say it myself, I have been able to produce a text that reads pretty smoothly and presents few major problems; so that, since you agree that wholesale revision/updating is unwise, it would be a question only of reading through and correcting any howlers that have eluded me. After all, if one said in a preface, as you suggest, that the published text was an only minimally doctored version of the lectures as delivered, one would free oneself from the need to attempt any more searching revisions. [...]

Finally, I should like to give you a dose of your own medicine. Who said the following of whom? 'My association with you has been in all my life the thing in which I felt more pride and moral satisfaction than anything else whatever – not to speak of the personal pleasure and the sense of justification for one's existence which it provided and provides.' I had been contemplating saying something of this kind to you apropos my new life here at Wolfson, but had been restrained by the fear that you would regard it as excessive. However, now that I find these words in a letter from you to Weizmann written in 1948, I can invoke one of my favourite principles, 'Be done by as you do', and adopt the sentiment as my own. I cannot tell you what a liberation it has been to escape OUP and enter the sunlit lands of my current activities, which I know to be of permanent value, to put it at its lowest, in a way in which commissioning works of academic 'political science' certainly wasn't. So there!

On 21 May 1992 I sent him my text of the essay eventually published as 'Philosophy and Government Repression',[10] observing:

I [...] enclose, just for you to glance at, 'The Right of the Philosopher to Self-Expression', one of the pieces I discovered recently, to which your reaction when I mentioned it to you was one of total amnesia. Does

seeing a text stir any memories? I wonder if you would still hold quite
so strongly to the view that philosophy is completely unprogressive,
like art: even in the piece itself [...] you refer to 'those great and hollow
abstractions [... and] other catchwords the exposure and destruction of
which has been one of the great glories of critical philosophy' [SR 74],
which seems to me to be one kind of progress, without doubt.

If Berlin wrote a reply, I cannot find it. A month later I sent him an edited text
of his Mellon Lectures on Romanticism, delivered in Washington in 1965. This
was the last of his unpublished book-length works that I worked on:

> When you told me that you were distantly contemplating a possible
> book on Hoffmann, incorporating the Mellon Lectures in a boiled-down
> form as a long introduction, I decided I ought to bring those lectures to
> the top of my agenda, in case it might be useful to you to have an edited
> text [...]. I have now finished going through them, and enclose the result.
> The BBC transcripts were very garbled in places, and if nothing else the
> new text is vastly more readable. Even if you can't bring yourself to look
> at it yourself, perhaps Aline would like to dip into it? I know she takes
> a special interest in these lectures.

Again no reply. In a letter of 5 July 1993, Berlin responded to the last volume of
Edmund Wilson's diaries, which I had received from its editor, Lewis Dabney,
and forwarded to him, noting the somewhat dismissive remarks about him
that it contained:

> You speak about 'a trifle sharp' – his comments on me. That I regard as a
> deliberate, courteous understatement. Of course I mind these passages
> very much indeed. I liked him, I admired him, I think he was a great
> man of sorts, certainly the best critic I have ever met – but of course
> I am indignant about e.g. being told that I behaved like royalty (my
> worst enemies I do not think have ever said that about me before, but
> who can tell?), or that I condemned Max Hayward because he was
> of humble social origin (inconceivable! there is no possibility of my
> even being misunderstood in that direction, in my opinion – so that is
> particularly wild and nasty); and a great many other passages as well. It
> springs, I think, partly from anglophobia and anti-Oxford, and regarding

me as cocooned in a horrible cosy little world, as he puts it, consisting of Maurice Bowra, Stuart Hampshire, David Cecil etc. – all of whom were as different as could be and didn't particularly like each other. All of this may have some element of truth, but is on the whole absurd; nor can I be said to be pleased at being told that I exhaust him with my interminable talk – that, I am afraid, may very well be true. I emerge as a kind of bright, quite agreeable social rattle – how can I like that? Still, he was full of prejudices, complexes, quirks, irrational lunges in all kinds of directions – so if he says these things about me, so be it; I can only hope that those who read him will make some allowance for the kind of person that he was.

Some of the essays I found Berlin tried to deny writing. On 26 July 1993 I sent him 'President Wilson on Education', commissioned for but not included in the Woodrow Wilson Foundation volume *Education in the Nation's Service: A Series of Essays on American Education Today* (New York, 1960); my guess is that his text arrived too late for inclusion. On 27 July he wrote: 'this is certainly not by me – I have no recollections of a single word of it, and I have never in my life taken the slightest interest in President Wilson on education. Very mysterious.' On 24 August I sent him his notes for the piece and a letter he had written about it to the Wilson Foundation. On 30 August he capitulated:

I could have sworn under oath in a witness box that I had never in my life written anything about President Wilson's educational views. But evidently I have. All I can deduce from the notes, which you so rightly and unkindly sent me, is that I was trying to contrast in my own mind the powerful influence which German, and to some extent French, historians in the nineteenth century sought quite deliberately to exercise on the ideology – political and social – of their nations; and, apart from Macaulay, the different situation in England, where the influence no doubt existed but was not so consciously aimed. Then I began to think about the contrast between Jowett and Mark Pattison, and their view of education – Jowett's training for the rulers of England and the Empire, Pattison's emphasis on pure scholarship, the pursuit of truth – and Jowett's victory; and the contrast between Oxford, which became worldly and politically deeply influential, and Cambridge, which remained more dedicated to pure research, particularly in the sciences. But goodness me, if there is a manuscript on Wilson and education buried ... In this case, the sleeping dog might as well be treated as a dead dog, and given quiet interment, rather than resurrecting it to embarrass me in this fashion. But there is no doubt, as always, that you were right and I was wrong – I shall never be as dogmatic in my own defence again.

After this reaction I dared not urge publication of the essay, and waited eleven years to add it to his published oeuvre.[11]

On 1 October 1993 I reported to Berlin G. A. ('Jerry') Cohen's favourable view (subject to a few criticisms) of his 1964 lecture 'Marxism and the International in the Nineteenth Century'. By 23 November I had accumulated and edited enough essays to form a solid volume, and wrote to him to propose this formally:

> With Hamann safely launched, I've been giving a good deal of thought to the question of what I should propose to you next. My guiding criteria are (*a*) to cause you as little work, and as little anxiety or displeasure, as I can; (*b*) to choose work which will do you the greatest possible credit. Fortunately these considerations reinforce one another, as I shall now explain.
>
> There are among your unpublished papers a number of polished, revised typescripts, not originating in transcripts of extempore lectures, which richly deserve publication. They require little or no attention from you before they appear in print: you don't even have to read them! With the addition of one or two published but hitherto uncollected pieces they make a very impressive volume, which I should like to call *The Sense of Reality* after the first essay, one of your very best unpublished pieces (if not the best), whose spirit presides over what follows. Here is my first shot at a contents list:

> *The Sense of Reality: Studies in Ideas and their History*

> 1. The Sense of Reality
> 2. Political Judgement
> 3. The Right of the Philosopher to Self-Expression

4. Socialism and Socialist Theories
5. The Romantic Revolution: A Crisis in the History of Modern Thought
6. Marxism and the International in the Nineteenth Century
7. Artistic Commitment: A Russian Legacy
8. Rabindranath Tagore and the Consciousness of Nationality

The subtitle reflects the fact that the first three pieces primarily give your views direct, while the others are primarily historical. Nevertheless, the volume does cohere, and I have excluded from the list a number of equally deserving items that probably ought to be reserved for other company.

I have already sent you edited texts of most of these pieces, but I think you may have re-read only no. 2 (of which more below). I have also been discussing the individual pieces, and the volume as a whole, with others, principally my old standbys Roger H[ausheer] and Patrick G[ardiner]. They both support the idea of the volume strongly, though it may yet be that I shall want to modify the contents list in one or two particulars in response to the verdicts they have promised after re-reading the set of essays as a whole. (It occurred to me that a dedication to Patrick might be appropriate: it is one in which we could both share, and it feels right to me.)[12]

Let me tell you something about each of the pieces:

1. The Sense of Reality

This is a long piece about historical realism dating, I should guess, from the mid-1950s [in fact 1953]. (To some degree 'Realism in Politics', the much shorter piece you published in the *Spectator* in 1954, is drawn from the same pool of ideas, and for that reason I haven't included it in the volume, though it might be possible to add it.) Patrick is particularly lyrical about it, and with reason. He describes it as exceptionally rich and wise; I should add that it is also very well written. Your starting point is the denial of the possibility of recreating an earlier century in our own time, but you go on from there to cover much other ground more fully than elsewhere, including the nature of historical as distinct from scientific understanding.

2. Political Judgement

This was a talk on the Third Programme in 1957, and you revised and updated it recently for a Festschrift for Arthur Schlesinger, only to withdraw it (to my regret) in favour of your piece on Edmund Wilson when you learnt that the editor(s) would accept a previously published piece. Here you apply your 'realist' insights to the realm of politics to very telling effect. It is a really excellent piece.

3. The Right of the Philosopher to Self-Expression

This is a trenchant and vigorous statement of philosophy's unique claim to escape censorship, on the grounds that it alone has the task of critically examining the presuppositions of dominant forms of thought. It has points of connection with 'Does Political Theory Still Exist?', but by no means duplicates it. I don't know its date or origins (do you?), but I should guess it too is from the 1950s [in fact 1954]. When I sent it to you some time ago you made no comment.

4. Socialism and Socialist Theories

This of course is your article from *Chambers's Encyclopaedia* (1950, revised 1966), excluded, I now suspect mistakenly, from *Against the Current* as being too encylopedia-like in tone. I have looked at it again, and can't now persuade myself that it had less claim to inclusion than 'The Counter-Enlightenment', which was after all an encyclopedia article too. In addition, as I've told you, I've discovered revisions to the 1966 version of the piece, revisions which were never published, and here is an opportunity to reprint the piece in its revised form. I have taken out all the superficial symptoms of encyclopedic origin, and it reads well.

5. The Romantic Revolution: A Crisis in the History of Modern Thought

This is the piece you are allowing Steven Lukes to publish in Italian and German[13] – so naturally I want to publish it in English! I should have included it in any case, since it gives a uniquely synoptic account of your views on Romanticism. The typescript is headed 'Lecture for Rome', but Steven says you told him the lecture was given in Venice. I wonder what the truth is? [Rome is right.] I sent you an edited typescript last year.

6. Marxism and the International in the Nineteenth Century

This is the 1964 Stanford lecture, heavily revised by you at the time, clearly with publication in mind. As you know, Jerry Cohen has read it and declared it excellent and worthy of publication. I have looked at his very few comments, and I think that some require no action, while others might deserve a brief footnote or two, whose contents I might be so bold as to suggest to you.

7. Artistic Commitment: A Russian Legacy[14]

This, in my view, is the best of the unpublished Russian pieces which you have in a folder awaiting your attention. We agreed that not all these pieces, probably, could be published together, given the degree of overlap between some of them; here, then, is an opportunity to start the process of separate publication, and why not start with the best?

8. Rabindranath Tagore and the Consciousness of Nationality

You will remember giving this carefully prepared lecture in India in 1970. It was Roger's suggestion that it be included in the volume. He feels that it presents your views on nationalism in a particularly clear and accessible way, and that the Indian dimension gives it considerable added interest. I do not dissent.

As I said earlier, I have excluded other deserving candidates.[15] I mention some of them here in case you would like me to add any of them to the list:

Synthetic A Priori Propositions (reply to Sellars)
Subjective versus Objective Ethics (ethics as sui generis)
Realism in Politics (see above under item no. 1)
The Artificial Dialectic: Generalissimo Stalin and the Art of Government (best in another context)
Jewish Slavery and Emancipation (because you steadfastly decline to have it reprinted)

1 This photo of Berlin and most of the contributors to his first Festschrift at Wolfson College, Oxford, 2 June 1979, includes some of those mentioned in this book, shown here in bold (*left to right*): **Pat Utechin, Herbert Hart**, Robby Wokler, Jerry Cohen, **Alan Ryan, HH, IB**, Chuck Taylor, **Bernard Williams**, Robin Milner-Gulland, **Richard Wollheim, Patrick Gardiner, Stuart Hampshire**, Larry Siedentop; this is the only photograph known to me of Berlin and me together

2   Headington House, Oxford, where most of Berlin's papers were stored

3   Berlin's study at Headington House

4 Berlin's heroes and villains on the door leading to his study from the library, Headington House

5 Berlin in his prime: at the BBC, London, 1964 for an episode of *Conversations for Tomorrow* with
J. B. Priestley and A. J. Ayer, available at http://berlin.wolf.ox.ac.uk/lists/nachlass/conversa.pdf

6 Berlin in the year in which I began working with him: supporting Wolfson
College during Eights Week, summer 1974, with his wife Aline

7 Berlin in his room in All Souls, 1985

8 Berlin with Imogen Cooper at the Barbican, London, 11 July 1992, after her performance of Mozart's piano concerto no. 25 with Colin Davis and the London Symphony Orchestra

9 Berlin with the Israeli novelist Amos Oz, 1994

10 Berlin during his 1995 BBC TV interview with Michael Ignatieff

A Philosophical Source of the Idea of National Freedom (an alternative to the Tagore piece?)

I am sorry, as so often, that this letter is so long. But you see why. Are you willing for me to proceed, in modified or unmodified fashion?

Berlin's reply came on 29 November:

Your approach is very kind and generous, and what can I say but that I cannot bear the thought of another book so soon, despite the unexpected success of dear old Hamann?

But if you send me the eight essays – not now! – but after we have returned from Portugal in late January – I shall, however reluctantly, take two days off and read the whole ghastly collection, and then report.

I cannot deny that you are treating me rather too well.

This exchange (and what followed) once again encapsulates our relationship in a nutshell: I propose; he demurs; later he yields; the critics approve; he is pleased; we start again no further forward. At this point I naturally agreed to wait for his return from Portugal.

At about this time I sent Berlin a transcript of 'The Lessons of History', a piece as evidently his as possible. The original text is headed 'Summary of Remarks of Sir Isaiah Berlin', which implies that it is based on notes or a recording, but although it speeds along at a faster lick than many of his lectures, it reads as if written by him. Maybe he was asked for a summary and provided one himself. Moreover, it is carefully corrected by him throughout by hand. He deferred reading it, professed no memory of it, and once again wondered if it was indeed his. I heard no more about it, and seem to have lost track of it. It covers familiar ground, on the whole, but is also vivid and trenchant, and I have published it in the IBVL and in *The Cambridge Companion to Isaiah Berlin*.

The alert reader will have noticed that our initial exchanges about a volume of unpublished essays took place three years before its appearance in 1996. This was not an unusually long delay for Berlin, but it was made longer by a decision he reported to me in a letter of 28 December 1993:

I have taken a fateful decision: I propose in January, and possibly February, to lock myself into the upstairs room and dictate, so far as I am able, whatever is suggested by reading all that mass of notes which I have accumulated on Romanticism – in case it can be incorporated into the basic BBC texts, whether by me or not remains to be seen (if you see what I mean). Consequently, I shall not deal with any of the other texts you have kindly provided until this job is done. I don't think you will disapprove of this too strongly.

There was a small bedroom containing a desk on the top floor at the back of Headington House, and here Berlin asked Pat Utechin to place the many folders of his notes on Romanticism. People had been pressing him ever since he gave his lectures on Romanticism in Washington in 1965 to write them up as a book, and he had continued to read widely since then with such a volume in mind, taking prolific notes. But his relationship to these notes was like that of George Eliot's Edward Casaubon in *Middlemarch* to his projected work on *The Key to All Mythologies*, and not a single sentence of the study of Romanticism was ever written. All he did was to dictate from his notes on to three cassette tapes, marshalling the quotations and observations he had jotted down under a series of headings for potential subsequent use. Listening to the cassettes is a poignant experience, because although Berlin hoped he was going to be able to write the book, the listener knows that nothing came of the time he spent in this way. Indeed, in my view nothing could have come of it, as he had left it too late. Here are his opening words:

Begin. Romanticism. Lots of folders or collections of papers. I have divided the themes into eight and I've given them letters –

A. Definitions of Romanticism
B. Early German Romanticism, vol. 1
C. German Romanticism, vol. 2
D. Herder etc.
E. French Romanticism
F. English Romanticism
G. General Romanticism
H. Miscellaneous

– and what I'll do is dictate fragments, odd sorts of observations which I glean from my notes, and try and give a letter to them.

Berlin's decision to get down to work on Romanticism was a blow to me, because I had no confidence that he would be able to produce anything publishable at the age of eighty-four. So his decision would only delay work on the more manageable projects which I had placed before him. However, I could not but be supportive, since I knew that this was the one book he really wanted to write before he died. So I gritted my teeth and wrote back on New Year's Day 1994:

> Thank you [...] for your letter [...] containing the exciting news that you plan to have a crack at Romanticism. I wonder what precipitated this apparently sudden development at this particular juncture? Of course I don't 'disapprove', as you put it: how could I? If your long-awaited work on Romanticism can finally appear, I shall be the first to applaud, and naturally I stand ready to give any help you are inclined to request. I don't deny that the resulting delay in your consideration of my proposed next volume is a matter for regret, but in any reasonable system of priorities Romanticism must come first. I shall keep the new volume of essays which I have prepared in cold storage for you, so that it is ready for you to look through whenever you feel able to turn to it.

In his reply of 18 January Berlin appeared to demur about his intentions:

> You speak of my "having a crack at Romanticism" – this is [only] very partially true. I never set myself the task of writing the book itself, only of dictating notes, as coherent as I can make them, based on the huge mountain of notes which I accumulated here and there, but mainly in the Library of Congress.

This puzzled me, since no purpose would be served by dictating notes unless they were to be used in the writing of the book. In a letter of 20 January I wrote:

> If what you have in mind at this stage is only 'dictating notes', do you envisage a subsequent stage when these notes will be converted into continuous prose? Perhaps I'm being too literal-minded in my understanding of what you mean by 'dictating notes'.

I find no reply to this letter, but a letter to Roger Hausheer of 8 February 1994 shows that he had in mind the possibility, hinted at in his letter of 28

December 1993 to me, that someone else might integrate his notes into the BBC transcripts.

> I am at the moment trying to read through the notes – a vast mountain of them – for the book on Romanticism; not that I shall ever write the book, I expect, but I thought if I simply dictated some of the more striking quotations and thoughts which these notes embody, that might at least form material for myself or someone else to integrate into the BBC lectures, on which my Romanticism is ultimately founded.

This plan struck, and strikes, me as entirely unrealistic; indeed, almost a form of displacement activity. Nevertheless, it seems to explain his riposte to me.

At this point another of my occasional offences was committed. I made available to OUP, as a jacket illustration for Claude Galipeau's book *Isaiah Berlin's Liberalism*, what seemed to me an affectionate caricature of Berlin drawn for me by Richard Willson in July 1989 as a substitute for a similar drawing he had done earlier that year for the eightieth birthday article in *The Times* (119). I collect drawings of Berlin, and when I enquired about this one Willson told me it had already been acquired by Charles Wilson, then editor of *The Times*.[16]

Drawings of Berlin by Richard Willson: the one on the left was in *The Times*

Most generously, he drew him again for my benefit, and Galipeau's book seemed a good opportunity to give the new drawing a public outing. Big mistake. Berlin dictated a message to Pat Utechin on 1 February 1994:

> I am not grateful to Henry for the caricature on Galipeau's book – I know that he and you like it, but I loathe it. The idea of a serious book having this awful thing on it does seem to me highly offensive. So, having given alpha plus to Henry hitherto, I am afraid I have to lower the mark to alpha. You are free to tell him this whenever you like.

I think his reaction caused greater pain to me than my error of judgement/taste did to him. But although Willson's Berlin is not my favourite, it still seems to me inoffensive. Probably unwisely, when Berlin brought the matter up again in a letter of 29 March 1994, I made an attempt to defend my conduct, but Berlin was unmoved, writing on 11 April:

> Let me inform you that Patrick Gardiner, whom I met in the High Street, told me that he was about to buy Galipeau's book, but was deterred so violently by the cover (he is, as you must know, a man of very great visual sensibility, and cares for paintings more than for anything else in the world) that he just could not touch it. And I have had unsolicited condolences from Stuart Hampshire and David Pears. No, the caricaturist may well be a worthy fellow, and a friend of yours, and an admirer of my deep wisdom, but from that it does not follow that his caricature is anything but a hideous travesty. At least I do not have to blame Galipeau. I do think the book, even though it is not by me, might have been shown me before publication.

Clearly what I had allowed OUP to do rankled with Berlin. I should have known that the drawing might wound him, and should have checked with him before allowing this use of it. My guess is that I didn't do so because I knew he would be unlikely to approve, and hoped that, presented with a fait accompli, he might come round. How wrong I was.

This and other amiable caricatures were used at my suggestion in 2013 and 2014 on the covers of the revised editions of his works published by Princeton University Press, who had asked for a fresh approach in place of the photographs that had often been used previously. Perhaps this compounds my error, but

I believed that these drawings would make the books distinctively striking, and help with sales. I also like many of them a good deal. For some reason Princeton did not use an earlier drawing by Willson (also not in his possession) which illustrated a review by Philip Toynbee of *Four Essays on Liberty* in the *Observer* in 1969.[17] It looks to me as if it is based on a 1964 photograph.

Drawing of Berlin by Richard Willson: compare Plate 8

On 27 March 1994 I wrote Berlin a letter that I cannot now find, but its contents can be to some extent deduced from his interesting reply of 11 April (the same letter from which the passage about the Willson drawing comes). The burden of my remarks must have been scepticism about his often repeated claim, already mentioned, that sincerity and authenticity were values not deployed before the eighteenth century. Of course, he knew far more about this than I did, and his reply was interesting and powerful, but not, to me, entirely convincing. As I said in my reply of 10 May, 'I still can't quite bring myself to believe that that it was impossible before 1750 to admire a person's tenacity or fidelity irrespective of its objective.' Here is what he had written:

> I cannot deny that I am liable to exaggeration, but in this case there is none. Your counter-examples to my thesis are, I fear, not very relevant.

Of course the idea of a noble enemy is quite ancient – Saladin was much admired for his courage, grandeur, magnanimity, generosity etc. by people who wrote about the Crusades. But nothing to do with sincerity. The 'pure in heart' who will see God are those who have consciences; that is, they have something in their nature which makes them more or less instinctively know the difference between good and evil, right and wrong – and follow it. *Integer vitae* simply means that a man who is such does not yield to unworthy temptations or motives, but lives by a correct principle, not just any old principle – that is certainly how it was used in the ancient world. So, too, Montaigne and [Guillaume] Postel: I have checked this, I fear, with [Michael] Screech, and he agrees with me. Of course there are many virtues in unbelievers, which Christians would do well to emulate – to be just, loving, good (Montaigne); the modesty, silence, reverence in mosques, unlike the horrid behaviour of Christians in their 'caves of robbers'. Of course Erasmus said that he was tempted to call Socrates a saint – and I daresay got into some trouble for this with the Roman Church (after his death) – but all that means is that what Socrates said appeared to Erasmus to be true, important, original, valuable, not that Socrates was sincere, said what he said from the heart and not because he was following the dictates of reason. So, too, the 'noble savage', who I suppose came into existence somewhere right at the end of the sixteenth century, and quite frequently cropped up in the seventeenth, particularly because of the number of travellers' tales from exotic countries, not America alone, which was the principal home of the noble savage. He is admired because, although not privileged to have the Christian truth revealed to him, his life and his habits are virtuous, uncorrupted by the wicked world of the observer, the traveller, very remote from the corrupt court of, say, Leo X. God has created these Indians as brave, honourable, simple, kindly, altogether near-perfect human beings, whom it would behove Christians to imitate (a proposition ferociously denied by de Maistre, as you know). But there is nothing about the quality of their beliefs, about purity of motive; pure-heartedness is not *that* at all. If you look at 'sincere' in the Oxford dictionary, you will find that the modern meaning is hardly given at all. Screech and I solemnly did that after lunch in All Souls, and he said that he thought it was a nineteenth-century concept. I am more generous and go back to the eighteenth.

I do not know the passage in Aquinas, but I assume that he means that an erring conscience binds because it is conscience but the results are extremely – all the more – unfortunate if it binds you to heresy or paganism.

It still seems to me that the value of sincerity depends on the belief that there are alternative ways of believing, behaving, being, which may not be compatible with each other, yet, even if one disapproves of them, are all ways of life which one can understand and even to some degree sympathise with, even if one is against them, because, given the circumstances of the different cultures or systems of belief or whatever, one can understand how men – perhaps no worse than oneself in attributes – given false beliefs and the like, or the pressures of a particular historical context, may come to believe, practise etc. Until then, sincerity is not so much as mentioned, so far as I know. The same really applied to the approval – our approval (the approval of liberals, I mean) – for variety in a society, in which many incompatible opinions are allowed to be held.

Toleration, which is part and parcel of this new scheme, beginning in the eighteenth century if I am right, is not a term of approval before that: it means avoiding striking down evil, putting up with what is wrong, false etc. – such as no true Christian should allow himself to do. Of course virtue, courage, wisdom are allowed to pre-Christian peoples, the Red Indians etc. – not to post-Christian Jews, because they are teachers of evil, nor by Catholics to Protestants, etc. That is why Lessing's play *Nathan the Wise* caused such shock, because in it the Jew is represented not only as wiser, but as morally better, than the Christian Patriarch in the domains of Saladin.

So I am not given pause, and I have the learned Screech with me on this. So there. I need hardly add that Aquinas, like Maimonides, finds no fault in Aristotle, nor the Christian Platonists in Plato – but nothing about Aristotle's sincerity!

[…] In case (although this may seem absurd to you) I haven't made my point absolutely clear, let me explain that in my view even those who hold false or dangerous views, especially religious ones, can possess every kind of merit, and be admirable in almost every respect, but sincerity is not among the virtues which can be attributed to them, because what makes them sinful or dangerous are, of course, their false and misleading beliefs – and sincerity is something which attaches to beliefs and their expression. This is why there is no word for this, in our sense at any rate, earlier than the nineteenth century (if you look at the Oxford dictionary you will see what I mean – there is no word for it, nor is it discussed by earlier authors). Admittedly, the wickedness and danger of heretics and unbelievers is not likely to be prominent in the thoughts of experts on, say, oriental habits like Postel, or generally sceptical and tolerant thinkers like Montaigne; but there is not a word in these authors about any possible merit in Protestants; nor will you find words of praise for, or even appreciation of, the fervour, sobriety, austerity of, say, the founder of the Jesuit Order among Protestants of the late sixteenth or seventeenth centuries, nor acknowledgment of the fervour of Philip II. No Protestant said, 'He burnt us, but one has to give it to him, he was utterly sincere' – as, no doubt, he was. No such excuse is made for anyone one is against until pretty late in the day – that is my whole point.

I am not equipped to evaluate this strong claim of Berlin's, though nothing is said about Locke's *A Letter concerning Toleration*, published in the seventeenth century; the OED, *pace* Berlin, has examples of the requisite sense of 'sincere' going back to the mid sixteenth century; and at the turn of the sixteenth century Shakespeare has Polonius say: 'This above all: to thine own self be true.'[18] But it does seem to me that Berlin explains his view better and more fully here than in his published work.

On 24 May 1994 I returned to the idea of a volume of unpublished material:

Please may I recur to the subject of what I think of as your next book? I mean the group of eight unpublished pieces I suggested to you late last year under the (to me) seductive title *The Sense of Reality*. As you'll remember, I chose these both because they are the most polished pieces I've found – right up to your best standard – and because little or no work is required on your part to make them ready for press.

These are the pieces about which Roger wrote you a very long letter [11 pages, single-spaced], endorsing them in general terms, and listing numerous small points, which I've now dealt with. The project is also warmly supported by Patrick Gardiner, who has read the typescript. In addition, since I last mentioned the book to you, truly heroic work has been done by Dr Derek Offord of Bristol University on the numerous quotations from Belinsky et al. in the essay on artistic commitment, and by Terrell Carver on those from Marx in the Stanford lecture. So things are now in pretty good shape.

You originally kindly said you'd look over the typescript on your return from Portugal, but then decided you wanted to work on Romanticism first. However, you've told me subsequently that Romanticism may now occupy a year or two, rather than the months you spoke of to start with, and so I hope it's not too impatient of me to ask whether you might be willing to take a week or two off at some stage to cast an eye over what I've prepared? My fingers are crossed.

No good. Berlin replied on 31 May 1994, arguing, characteristically, for a longer gap after *The Magus of the North* before the next volume appeared:

Too many books too frequently published diminish the attractiveness to the potential reader, of that I am sure. Hold your (and my) horses. Despite Roger and Patrick, I think we ought to wait. I am most grateful for the 'heroic work by Dr Offord', and to Carver – but it really must wait. I shall certainly not look at it now; put these things in a basket and send them to me, if you must, next year – this year is far, far too early if the appetite of potential readers is not to be weakened or destroyed. Forgive me!

I replied on 3 June 1994:

Thank you for your reply to my letter about your 'next book'. You ask me to forgive you: perhaps I too should ask for forgiveness. Believe me, I don't in the least relish asking you to do what I know you would far rather be spared. Indeed, if I knew there was no pleasure in store for you of any kind at any stage, I should desist, even though eventual publication of more of your work is of course the *raison d'être* of all my efforts. But I hope I'm right to think that once the books appear, and receive critical acclaim, as they invariably do, this is not an entirely painful experience, and may compensate, to some degree at least, for any time you have had to spend on them beforehand.

I'm not particularly trying to persuade you to change your mind, even though I disagree about the need for a longer gap: I realise that that would probably be fruitless. Instead I will come back to you next year as you suggest. I suppose you wouldn't feel differently if I suggested taking it one essay at a time? For example, Bob Silvers might publish 'The Sense of Reality' (perhaps the most brilliant piece) in the NYRB, or we might offer 'Artistic Commitment' to the *Slavonic Review* or somesuch? I hear you say 'No good' even as I write.

His reply is missing, but he stuck to his guns, as my letter of 14 June 1994 makes plain: 'I absolutely take on board your reservations about publishing another book too soon. I also know how little you enjoy reading through past work.' I then repeated the points made in the final paragraph of the previous extract, adding as another possible freestanding NYRB publication 'Political Judgement',[19] 'which would also involve you in literally no work, since you have already revised it'. I concluded: 'What do you say? Don't be cross: say no if you must. But I need to be sure that every path is blocked before I finally put my plans in cold storage.' Again I find no reply.

The following month I changed the subject and sent him a list of the shorter, more popular pieces that I had long thought deserved collection between one set of covers, and which I eventually published posthumously in 2000 as *The Power of Ideas*. This stimulated the following on a tape for Pat:

> Henry: no need to answer – I suppose I must look at it, I say in a gloomy way. You can tell him that the list of opuscula he produced embarrasses me deeply, but that sometime I'll tick the ones that I think are worth something, as opposed to those which seem to me to be worth nothing.

Pat sent this on to me on 11 July 1994 with the note: 'Doubtless this will plunge you into the depths of gloom – but I have embarked on a course of (your) character-strengthening, and therefore refuse to w'hold this kind of thing!'

Despite my agreement to wait until 1995 to ask him again about the unpublished essays, I seem to have been tipped off by Pat Utechin that he might relent and read at any rate some of the essays in Italy in the summer of 1994. I wrote on 19 August of that year:

> I gathered from Pat earlier in the summer that you had kindly agreed to steel yourself, while in Italy, to look at a couple of the pieces, at any rate, from what I propose as your next book – my collection of your best and most finished unpublished pieces, entitled, after the first and most

striking of them, *The Sense of Reality*. If you like what you find, we could either publish the pieces separately, or move on to the consideration of the remaining essays.

Here, then, is the typescript. I have flagged the two pieces I would suggest for your initial perusal – 'The Sense of Reality' itself, and 'Artistic Commitment' – but I am giving you the lot in case you prefer to look at other pieces first, or (*per impossibile* [as is impossible]) want to forge ahead and finish the job!

One point I want to emphasise: please don't think of this as a re-run of the Hamann experience, which I know was tough for you. Unlike Hamann, these pieces really are pretty well ready for the printer: if you can restrain yourself, only i's need dotting and t's crossing. No homework is needed, and no new writing. So it shouldn't be too ghastly an ordeal.

I have put at the front of the folder Roger's long letter about the essays (all his individual points have been dealt with or incorporated as footnotes) and my original letter about the volume from last year. I have also put in copies of the originals of all the Russian passages you quote in 'Artistic Commitment', just in case you want to check your translations (some of which, as noted, do perhaps need adjustment).

I leave this with you, then, afflicted, as ever, by two incompatible emotions: guilt at intruding into your other activities, and a strong desire, based on a certain conviction of its excellence, to see the work in print, and deservedly acclaimed.

He replied on 26 August 1994:

I should be terribly upset if anything further by me appeared as early as next year – 1996 at the earliest, if then. Consequently, I shall allow myself to break my promise, and not look at anything, however ready, until early next year.

As always, I am ashamed but firm. As Léon Blum said about Munich, echoed by my father, 'I feel shame and relief.'[20]

At about this time I was invited to attend a Liberty Fund conference in Oxford on James Fitzjames Stephen's *Liberty, Equality, Fraternity*, his 1873 riposte to Mill's *On Liberty*. Reading the book for the first time, I was astonished to find many passages that put forward a pluralistic theory strongly reminiscent of

Berlin's.[21] Those attending the conference were not too interested in my discovery, but I wrote to Berlin asking him whether he was aware of this anticipation of his views. I may also (the letter is missing) have taken the opportunity to ask him about some equally striking passages in Weber which I had known about for some time.[22] His reply is dated 5 October 1994:

> I am most grateful to you for exhuming J. F. Stephen's book, which Herbert Hart once wrote about as 'that gloomy book'. I know that he sharply disagreed with Mill, and indeed his brother Leslie, but although I ought to have done so I have in fact never read it. I feel sure that all you say is only too true, but believe me, I had no idea of it: as in the case of Weber, whom I did not properly read – his anticipations were new to me too, even though I refer to them here and there. I wish I could say that great minds think alike, but I cannot claim greatness even to the extent of J. F. Stephen, let alone Weber.

I returned mercilessly to the unpublished essays on the very first day of the year in which he had said that I might do so: 1995. Having wished him a happy new year, I continued:

> I immediately proceed to make the wish less likely to come true by reminding you, in my relentless way, that your most recent ruling about what I am offering as your next book was that you would look at it early in 1995. The text is in a brown folder in Pat's office ...
>
> Let me say once again that no revision is required – that's one of the reasons I chose the pieces concerned. There are a couple of specific queries in footnotes, but apart from that you have only to dip and give (or withhold) your blessing. You already know that the volume is enthusiastically supported by Roger and Patrick; much of it has now been read by Michael Ignatieff too, who adds his strong support, as he has probably told you. On the question of revision Michael goes further, indeed, and says that it would be a definite mistake to attempt to undertake to revise the essays, which are absolutely fine as they are. I agree.

If Berlin sent a reply to this nagging letter, I have not found it.

By June 1995 I was at work with Roger Hausheer on the one-volume anthology of Berlin's best essays that was published in February 1997 as *The*

Proper Study of Mankind: An Anthology of Essays. As far as I recall, the idea for this volume came from the publisher: it certainly didn't come from me, and indeed the work of preparing it brought me close to a breakdown, since it was suddenly added to everything else that I was doing, and there was pressure to complete it quickly. I turned to Hausheer to help me out, and I couldn't have managed without him. He took the lead in making the selection; drafted an overlong introduction which I edited down to the length required; and helped me to track down the sources of the many quotations in 'Herder and the Enlightenment', one of the three essays in the volume that I had not previously edited. Berlin's footnotes to the essay in *Vico and Herder* were more than usually inaccurate, and I remember many hours in the Taylorian Library in Oxford with Hausheer, examining Bernhard Suphan's monumental *Herders sämmtliche Werke*. We found most of the quotations, but by no means all, and many of the references (and the corresponding quotation marks) had to be dropped in despair. A comparison of Berlin's original footnotes with ours is as good a window as any into the kind of work needed to bring his apparatus up to scratch.

Berlin's acceptance of the suggestion that such a volume should be published contrasts starkly with his sustained reluctance to sanction *The Sense of Reality*. Gone is the argument that books should not appear too frequently. Admittedly a selection of previously published material is a different proposition from a volume of unpublished essays, but a new volume is a new volume, and I remember being frustrated by Berlin's inconsistency,[23] especially since it created so much extra work at a time when I was trying to make progress elsewhere. Moreover, an indistinguishably similar suggestion I had put to him some years earlier under the heading of a 'Berlin reader' had been vigorously rejected, I believe on the grounds that such a project would convey a status in the literary and/or academic firmament to which he did not aspire, or would be embarrassed by seeming to claim. (A subsidiary difficulty may have been that it would have involved taking extracts from essays rather than reprinting them complete, something Hausheer and I considered for PSM, only to reject it as doing violence to the integrity of his texts.) Nevertheless, I naturally welcomed the opportunity to publish a 'best of Berlin' volume as part of my campaign to make his work better known, and since he died later in its year of publication, I am glad we produced it when we did.

I proposed *The Proper Study of Mankind* as a title for the anthology in a letter of 30 June 1995, observing that 'It seems to me to capture perfectly what you are about in all your manifestations, and to do so in an unboring but also unpompous way.' Berlin replied on 3 July:

> Oh dear: you really think that *The Proper Study of Mankind* is a good title? All right, provided you quote Pope somewhere as an epigraph, and provided it is clear that the selection is not mine – I don't mean the title, but that you and Roger are entirely responsible for the contents!

I don't want to think that I foisted either the title or the selection on Berlin: both still seem to me defensible, at the very least, and he never demurred subsequently.

On 4 July 1995 I tried once again with *The Sense of Reality*, not failing to crank up the pressure:

> I'm writing in my usual relentless way to remind you that you kindly agreed to devote some of your London time this summer to looking through the unpublished essays that I want to bring out as a book. I know your heart will sink, probably into your boots, but I beg you not to postpone this ordeal this time: the essays have been ready in their brown folder in Pat's room for eighteen months, and I long to see them in print, and to share with you in the enjoyment of the acclaim they will surely attract.
>
> As I've said before, they are in good order, and little or no work is required (by contrast with Hamann). Further, you have already corrected two of the essays [...]. That leaves only six, of which you may rule out one or even two on a priori grounds: in short, the work is nearly done!
>
> My fingers are not so much crossed as in knots.

Berlin seems not to have replied directly, at any rate by letter. But he did read (most of) the essays over the summer, and a message dictated to Pat arrived after he had made a brief visit to Oxford in August:

> Henry: preliminary note from Isaiah
>
> I have looked at '[The] Sense of Reality', 'Political Judgement' and 'The Right of the Philosopher to Self-Expression'. The last two seem to me more or less OK; so does 'The Romantic Revolution' in Lukes's version (he presumably had my corrected English original – perhaps you do too).
>
> The only real difficulty is '[The] Sense of Reality'. The trouble is, I have had three or four ideas in my life, which I repeat constantly in

various forms: incompatibility of values, scientific method inapplicable to humane studies or politics, inevitability, two liberties and so on. I know that I am very repetitive, and badly need pruning, otherwise reviewers will constantly and rightly comment on this.

The trouble about '[The] Sense of Reality' is that huge chunks of the second half of it are practically identical, in idea if not in style, with my piece on 'History and Theory',[24] and some of it is echoed in 'Political Judgement'. You are kind enough to call it a 'minor masterpiece' [Berlin to Pat Utechin: Why not a major one?], but if it appears in its present form, reviewers who know my work will be bored to extinction by it (as I was when I read it).

[Some corrections to the title essay follow.]

After this I got bored and could not go on reading. It seemed to me that 'Political Judgement' also repeats all this in various ways.

Pat added:

After dictating this stuff to me, when they came down [to Oxford] and 'camped out'[25] for two days, he left a message on the answerphone for me (from London), saying:

You were quite right, Henry has left me at least six other huge pieces – I get so terribly bored looking through my own work that I can't bear to do more than one [PU: He said 'a day' – do you think he meant 'a week'?], so may not finish before going to Italy; and can't bear to take them to Italy; so he may not get the whole thing till, say, early November.[26] But he will get it. Remind him that on *no* account may anything at all be published before 1997.

My letter of 19 August 1994 also finally came back to me about a year after it was written with this MS annotation:

Wonderful! *Most* grateful. Do look at my scribbles – I've read all except Tagore – surely otiose? & Romanticism, which, you rightly surmise, I checked for Steven Lukes. We can talk about all this in the autumn I.B

On 30 October 1995 I invite him to read the essay on Tagore, which he had declared 'otiose' without, I think, looking at it. 'Roger argues strongly in its favour,' I write, 'and I should prefer, if I must disappoint him, to be able to say that your decision was made in the light of having read the text, rather than on some a priori grounds.' It was perhaps disingenuous of me to pretend that it was Hausheer and not (also) myself who would be disappointed, but I was desperate for new clothes in which to dress my importunacy. By 9 November the essay had been reprieved, but a question-mark hung over another essay in the volume, which I accordingly had to fight for. I wrote to Berlin that day:

> I am delighted that the Tagore piece has been reprieved. Thank you very much. The only major question, I think, that now hovers over the contents list of the volume of unpublished pieces is the one raised by you in your comments on your summer reading – viz. your worry about the overlap between 'The Sense of Reality' and other pieces you have published. I do not want to deny that this overlap exists, since it quite clearly does, and everyone who has read the 'new' piece is aware of it. But I do most strongly want to argue that it does not provide grounds not to publish the piece, for these main reasons:
>
> > It has been read by myself, Roger, Michael (Ignatieff) and Patrick (Gardiner), and we all agree that it is one of your very best pieces. Although you cover ground some of which you have covered elsewhere (in different words, as always), this is the most comprehensive, focused, sustained treatment of the topic you have achieved, and the peg on which it hangs (the impossibility of recreating a bygone age) is unique to this essay. I should venture to predict that, when it is published, it will swiftly become one of your most celebrated essays. The overlap is no more extensive (indeed it is less extensive) than between other essays you have already published without encountering a breath of criticism. For example, there are the three essays on Herzen in your *Selected Writings*; and there are the two essays on nationalism in *Against the Current* and *Crooked Timber* (you were most reluctant that 'The Bent Twig' should be included in the latter volume, but I was obstinate, and it has turned out to be one of the most widely valued and commented-on essays in the book).

All those who have read the essay [...] yield to no one in their anxiety not to see you publish anything that will damage your reputation. They all agree that this will not be the effect of publishing this splendid piece ('rather brilliant' was Patrick's phrase): on the contrary, it will add lustre to your name.

Finally, I attach special importance to Patrick's imprimatur ['Let it be printed'], indeed imprimandum ['It must be printed']. As you know, he is a man not given to excessive enthusiasm; he is a cautious, careful and just critic, and when he bestows praise one is particularly confident that it is well deserved.

I rest my case. I am certain that this is the *pièce de resistance* of the proposed book, and I hope you will allow me to include it.

He did. Pat annotated the letter: 'OK. Provided that somewhere there is a footnote saying that I dealt with some of these matters in "History and Theory".' On 16 November 1995 I wrote:

Thank you so much for reprieving 'The Sense of Reality'. I shall certainly mention the overlap with 'The Concept of Scientific History'; perhaps I should also mention 'The Hedgehog and the Fox', whose additional sections draw to some extent on parts of the same piece.[27]

I cannot tell you how pleased and relieved I am that the way now seems at last to be clear for me to publish this volume – the cream of your heretofore unpublished essays. If it is not a terrific success I shall eat my hat.

I also suggested an introduction by Patrick Gardiner, to which he agreed, despite his earlier protestations that he had been over-introduced; and publication in due course of one of the pieces in the NYRB, to which he also agreed.[28] On 4 December 1995 I successfully asked to add his Humayun Kabir Memorial Lecture, delivered in New Delhi in 1972, on Kant and nationalism. Its original title was 'A Philosophical Source of the Idea of National Freedom'; on 19 December I counter-proposed 'Kant and Nationalism', and Berlin scribbled on my letter that he wanted 'Kant as an Unfamiliar Source of Nationalism'. The book, the last collection of new material to appear in his lifetime, was published on 24 October 1996.

III

Through all the years I have been writing about, financial worry was never far beneath the surface. Most of the benefactions that enabled me to work full time on Berlin's writings were more or less short-term, and I had conveyed to Berlin my anxiety about the future. In December 1995 he decided that all his royalty earnings should be transferred to Wolfson to support my work. This was the first step towards the setting up of the Isaiah Berlin Literary Trust the following year. His royalty income was not enough by itself to pay my salary, but it would make a huge difference, and I was bowled over by his generosity. From that day to this his royalties have been paid into the Wolfson College fund that paid for my work until my retirement, and then for the work of my successors, Mark Pottle and (until June 2018) Nicholas Hall, on Berlin's legacy, literary and otherwise.

On 4 April 1996 Berlin wrote to me about one of a number of attempts to refute the identification of himself as Akhmatova's 'guest from the future'.[29] His letter shows how much he cared about this vexed issue:

> I enclose a copy of *Voprosy literatury* 1995, issue 6, in which V. Esipov seeks to show (pp. 57–85, 'In the Days of Vespasian ...')[30] that the dedications of Akhmatova's various poems to me, and my role as 'the guest from the future' in *Poem Without a Hero*, are mistaken; he nominates various other dedicatees as more likely on grounds of date, meaning, circumstances etc.
>
> I have no intention of replying, stating what I know to be the truth (the author makes various mistakes of fact which I do not, either, propose to correct), claiming the dedications etc. – which I know on many grounds, most of all Akhmatova's own words to me in 1964 (he says 1965),[31] to be so.
>
> But I wonder whether you, in your zeal to collect this and that about me, would want to see this, and get it roughly translated [...].
>
> Of course, if someone else wrote a thunderous refutation, e.g. if Anatoly Naiman[32] [...] would like to do it, I should not be displeased. But I don't want to suggest it to him – on the other hand, you might.
>
> There is only one other 'attack' on my identity in Akhmatova, by a man called Kralin,[33] who has written a good deal about this, but who is

regarded by most reputable Russian critics as somewhat crazy and not to be taken notice of – except that he is by the author of this article. [...] Goodness! How Brodsky wd have expostulated in not v. parliamentary language.

On 5 September 1996 I sent Berlin an advance copy of *The Sense of Reality*, observing:

> I haven't forgotten that you hated going through the essays when they were in typescript: but I hope very much that the reception of the resulting book turns out to compensate for this agony to some degree. I hardly need to say, perhaps, that it gives me enormous satisfaction to see it finished at last, after all the vicissitudes of its genesis.

He replied on 23 September 1996: 'The book looks splendid – unreadable according to me, but I expect kind persons may find otherwise. Very heavy stuff, I consider.' I disagreed two days later:

> Of course I think you are far too hard on the contents of the new book, but this is only true to form! I wait for reviewers and others to back me up, as I'm sure they will. Indeed, some recipients of early copies have already written enthusiastically.

On 6 January 1997 I was able to add:

> I am happy to report that *The Sense of Reality* has sold so well that it has already been reprinted once, and may well be reprinted again at any moment. You will assert as usual that this only shows a deplorable lack of taste and judgement on the part of your readers, and I shall as characteristically repudiate your modesty.

When I reflect that most of its contents are the product of my archaeological dig through the piles of discarded papers in his Oxford home, its existence seems a minor miracle, and it occupies a special place in my affections.

PROBING IDEAS

You ask, as is your wont, important – central and difficult – questions, to which I do not know of any firm answer.

IB to HH, 2 April 1991 (189)

9

NOT ANGELS OR LUNATICS:
BERLIN ON HUMAN NATURE

I am no good [...] at [...] isolating the permanent characteristics of mankind.

IB to E. V. ('Peter') Gatacre, 20 October 1969

What, then, do I mean by saying that men do have a common nature? Well, I think that common ground between human beings must exist if there is to be any meaning in the concept of human being at all. I think that it is true to say that there are certain basic needs – for example, for food, shelter, security and, if we accept Herder, for belonging to a group of one's own – which anyone qualifying for the description of human being must be held to possess.

IB to Beata Polanowska-Sygulska, 24 February 1986
(UD 40/A 280)

Before we plunge too deeply into the sometimes mildly turbid waters of the exchanges between Berlin and myself about basic human issues, it may be helpful to set up a framework for discussion, in the form of a summary of his view of the human predicament, if I may put it in such portentous terms.

I

Social and political terms are necessarily vague. The attempt to make the vocabulary of politics too precise may render it useless. But it is no service to the truth to loosen usage beyond necessity. (L 204)

An immediate problem arises at the outset. What Berlin has to say is sometimes imprecise or equivocal, and different statements of his view can be inconsistent with one another, or even internally. What he says, what he means, and what he ought to say in the service of his overall outlook are not always the same. So we need to undertake some sympathetic reconstruction, favouring those of his statements which seem truer to life, or a closer fit with better or fuller statements made at other times. Such reconstruction (his own policy when writing about others) is more fruitful than fault-finding, though there are ingredients in his thought which, even when he is given the benefit of the doubt, remain problematic. We also have to fill in some gaps. Both the reconstruction and the gap-filling should be done as far as possible in a way that is sensitive to his general approach, but there are times when we cannot be sure what he would have said, and times when we do know what he said, or would have said, but believe him to be mistaken.

Interpretation and supplement should not be confused, but I believe that there is a coherent vision of human nature and human life underlying all that he said, and that we can tease this out without departing from the spirit of his own words. However, because he does not always use terms consistently, or define them clearly enough, we need to refine his conceptual toolkit if we are not to be distracted into semantic disputes – what he called 'words about words' as opposed to 'words about things' (B 147; L 95; TCE2 398–9), one of the most important distinctions, he believed, that philosophers should make. So in this and following chapters I shall make use of a few new terms (not multiplied beyond necessity) to mark some neglected distinctions.

Why did Berlin not provide a more careful, complete, unambiguous account of his vision of human life? Part of the answer derives from the nature of the subject matter, which, as Berlin stressed, does not lend itself to cut-and-dried, $2 + 2 = 4$ description. The timber of humanity is crooked, as Solomon knew before Kant: 'Consider the work of God: for who can make that straight, which he hath made crooked?' (Ecclesiastes 7:13). Berlin wrote of 'the fleeting, broken, infinitely various wisps and fragments that make up life at any level' – 'a vast amalgam of constantly changing, multicoloured, evanescent, perpetually overlapping data, too many, too swift, too intermingled to be caught and pinned down and labelled like so many individual butterflies' (SR 47, 46; cf. SR 24). Despite this unpromising, apparently ungraspable, raw material, he could sometimes have been a good deal clearer than he was, especially given his claim that Frank Hardie, his tutor in ancient philosophy at Oxford, had pressed him so relentlessly to eschew vagueness and obscurity that lucidity became one of his leading values.[1] Berlin's early philosophical papers are beautifully clear and precise: why then did he become murkier later?

I have one tentative hypothesis to offer. When Berlin turned from pure philosophy to the history of ideas, and increasingly took on the role of a public moralist, he moved into territory that was sparsely populated in his immediate intellectual environment, and populated, if at all, by persons not specially inclined or able to subject his observations to the exact and exacting challenge of a Frank Hardie. In short, he became intellectually imprecise because no one stood up to him. Later, people began to do so, but by then he had lost his edge, and had gained a celebrity status that protected him from the need fully to engage his critics on their own terms. This is perhaps an uncharitable suggestion, but I believe it to be just, and a partial explanation of the difficulties we encounter in his mature work. Again and again I have had occasion to regret that Berlin was not challenged earlier and more rigorously. If he had been, we might today be less puzzled about some features of his outlook.

It should be added, in fairness, that the construction of a systematic account of the human terrain was not a project for him. For the most part his focus is on specific thinkers, or specific aspects of the history of ideas, and his underlying vision of life emerges incidentally and in passing remarks rather than being laid out fully and explicitly, head-on. The same or similar insights pepper his work, always in slightly different words, usually suggestive, approximate and impressionistic rather than careful, unambiguous and precise. There are some valuable exceptions to this generalisation, especially in L and SR, but he gives us no single, canonical account of his fundamental beliefs to which we can appeal when in doubt. Indeed, it would have been foreign to his temperament to attempt this, as well as inconsistent with his fluid view of his subject matter. He both liked untidiness, and believed that it is an ineliminable feature of reality.

Having got that off my chest, I shall try to reconstruct the broad outlines of the conception of humanity that informed Berlin's writings.

II

The ideas of every philosopher concerned with human affairs in the end rest on his conception of what man is and can be. To understand such thinkers, it is more important to grasp this central notion or image (which may be implicit, but determines their picture of the world) than even the most forceful arguments with which they defend their views and refute actual and possible objections. (AC2 376)

One of Berlin's basic guiding lights was his empiricist mindset. He was a doubting Thomas of philosophy who put his trust in the deliverances of his senses (including his own rich stream of consciousness, which may be regarded as an internal sense) rather than in the fabrications of metaphysicians. I suspect that this was to some extent a genetic trait, but also one strengthened by his formative encounter with the no-nonsense English temperament, and with the dry light of Oxford philosophy. He was suspicious of all metaphysical constructions, from rampant fantasies such as Hegel's Absolute Spirit to the unsubstantiated inventions of theologians and other religious personnel. This made him a natural ally of the Enlightenment, and of its resistance to superstition, prejudice, 'appeals to mystery and darkness and authority to justify arbitrary behaviour' (AE 29/POI2 62; cf. L 277). His mind was commonsensical, realistic, down to earth. He told Beata Polanowska-Sygulska:

> For me, in the end, everything is empirical.[2] Experience is all we have. Where else can you turn, if you are not a Christian, if you don't believe in God's word, if you don't have an intuition of certain things as absolute (which I don't)? That's what it means to be an empiricist. That's why people attack me, people who really believe in an a priori conception of certain things. (UD 222-3)

And he told Ramin Jahanbegloo:

> I think that all there is in the world is persons and things and ideas in people's heads – goals, emotions, hopes, fears, choices, imaginative visions[3] and all other forms of human experience. That is all I am acquainted with. But I cannot claim omniscience. Perhaps there is a world of eternal truths, values, which the magic eye of the true thinker can perceive – surely this can only belong to an elite to which I fear I have never been admitted. (CIB 32)

Of course he didn't really believe in such an elite or such a metaphysical world, and this unbelief attracts me greatly. His empiricism, together with his cultural pluralism, liberated me personally from a suffocating religious upbringing. That may be an uninteresting autobiographical fact by itself, but it points to a wider Berlinian message. His clear-eyed sense of reality, reinforced by his recognition of and devotion to the irreducible plurality of human goals and cultures, made him a settled opponent of any claim to have found *the* single, certain, final answer to all the deepest human questions – what to be and do, what to strive for, what values to accept or adopt, how to live. This made him an equally firm opponent of any attempt by those who believed they had found such an answer to impose it on others, above all by force. If we accept his rejection of inflexible, one-size-fits-all panaceas, as I do with the greatest conviction, and if we add to this that it is part of the essence of the leading world religions and of totalitarian political ideologies to offer us just such panaceas, then we have the tools we need to stand against the panacea-peddlers. I return to this topic in greater detail in the next chapter.

Berlin's vision of human nature – of 'the more permanent aspects of the human world' (10) – was rooted in the conviction that the most important and distinctive human characteristic is freedom of the will, because it enables us to make the necessary deliberate, conscious choices between our conflicting ends, and so forge our own identities. (He sometimes called this 'basic freedom', as opposed to the specifically political concepts of negative and positive liberty.) There are two main aspects of this conviction that should immediately be noted. First, he did not claim to be able to prove that free will existed. Rather he argued, principally in 'Historical Inevitability', that our whole conceptual repertoire is inextricably committed to its existence, so that it is not an option from within this repertoire to discard our belief in free will. It may be an illusion, but if so it is a necessary illusion, unless we are to abandon human linguistic communication as it now is, and the view of the world that it embodies. But to do this is not an option for us, given the way we are made. We cannot help thinking as we do. If we deny free will, large parts of our conceptual scheme collapse. Berlin drew particular attention to the notions of praise, blame, responsibility and desert, which presuppose freedom of choice, but it goes further than that: the very notion of rational assent depends on acceptance of freedom of the will; without free will we could not argue and reason at all except in the attenuated sense in which an automaton can.[4] This would mean, among other things, that we could not assess the arguments in favour of or against the existence of free will, could not rationally decide which arguments are stronger. If there were no free will, a statement that it exists or does not exist would be empty noise, or at best true by accident: determinism is not meaningfully statable if true.

Second, Berlin did not offer any proof of his belief that free will is the most fundamental aspect of human nature. Nor, I suspect, is such a proof possible. A number of other candidates have been put forward as the distinguishing criterion of humanity: for example, rationality, the use of language, or even the absence of body hair. There seems to be a certain arbitrariness about such claims. Why, indeed, should there be only one basic criterion of humanity? If there should, then perhaps it may be the increased cerebral evolution of our species, which makes many of our other distinctive characteristics possible. Again, there are rival theories as to why this evolution occurred (and occurred only once), and again none of these may be provable. It is perhaps safer to construe Berlin's emphasis on freedom of the will as an expression of what he personally finds most essential in human beings. But even if it is unsusceptible to proof, his claim seems attractive, as plausible as any of its rivals, and consistent with the sense of reality that he champions. It certainly explains much of the more detailed account of humanity that he builds upon it.

Berlin's liberalism flows from his belief in the centrality of free will. He held that people are most fully able to be and become themselves when they are not hemmed in by restrictions on their freedom of action and opinion. This is the source of his emphasis on 'negative' liberty, the freedom from interference by others, though he also accepted the value of the 'positive' liberty of being one's own master, freedom *to* as opposed to freedom *from*, the freedom to construct one's life and identity in accordance with one's own wishes and vision of life, without external direction or pressure.

Berlin's liberalism is also linked to and strengthened by his moral individualism, his belief in the moral sense of individuals as the only source of value:

> all that is ultimately valuable are the particular purposes of particular persons; and to trample on these is always a crime because there is, and can be, no principle or value higher than the ends of the individual, and therefore no principle in the name of which one could be permitted to do violence to or degrade or destroy individuals – the sole authors of all principles and all values. Unless a minimum area is guaranteed to all men within which they can act as they wish, the only principles and values left will be those guaranteed by theological or metaphysical or scientific systems claiming to know the final truth about man's place in the universe, and his functions and goals therein. (RT2 128)

In case this seems too starkly uncommunitarian, it should be added that Berlin also stressed cultural belonging, which strongly influences individual moral values, as a basic human need. But the values of the group are a construction out of individual values, not vice versa, and do not replace or trump those of the person.

Berlin's morally individualistic liberalism led him to endorse Kant's insistence that other people should always be treated with respect, as ends in themselves, and not as a means to one's own ends, or to collective ends, especially those prescribed by authority. The freedom and dignity of the individual were for him among the highest of all values, essential to any decent society.

Equally important to him, and intimately connected to freedom, was variety, plurality, especially in human life. He was entirely free of the wish to organise and regiment people, to suppress their natural exuberance and idiosyncrasy. On the contrary, he gloried in personal variousness. Any attempt to impose a rigid schema on human beings, suppressing their differences, was anathema to him. So greatly, indeed, did he value unrestricted differences between people that he believed it more important for us to be able to go to the bad, if that is the result of our free choice, than to conform to some external (or, for that matter, internal) notion of what all people should be and do. Some might find this preference for freedom over prudence and discipline a step too far, but it was a preference that Berlin regularly asserted.

Berlin's sense of, and responsiveness to, human plurality was underwritten by his belief in the plurality of value. He held that ultimate human values – values we pursue for their own sakes rather than as a means to some higher end[5] – are plural. This thesis is what is now generally known as *value pluralism* (not Berlin's term: he called it simply *pluralism*). It means not just that there are many values, but that they are irreducibly distinct – that is, they cannot be interpreted as versions of a smaller set of values, still less translated into the terms of a single master value such as utility or happiness. Each end or value makes its own distinctive demands on us (absolute demands, he sometimes says, but why?), and when values come into conflict, as they often do, we cannot always arbitrate between them according to some generally defensible abstract formula for adjudicating such conflicts. Sometimes we cannot measure one value against another on a common scale (*incommensurability*) in order to resolve our dilemma. Do we prefer freedom or equality? Happiness or knowledge? Spontaneity or organisation? Justice or mercy? There can also be conflict *within* values, pitting, for example, freedom of speech against freedom from abuse. We have to do our best in the specific situation in which we find ourselves: 'The concrete situation is almost everything' (CTH2 19; cf. CC2 126). However we decide, we may suffer a loss in terms of a value allocated a lower priority in the particular case, and this loss may be tragic.[6] On the other hand, this predicament is part of the same fabric of reality that gives rise to the broad panoply of personal difference, and this is part of the glory of human life.

What, we may ask, does Berlin mean by 'values', and is it these that we should regard as the primary locus of pluralist conflict? He speaks at different times of ends, goals, goods, values, ideals, principles, demands, and offers very little by way of definition. In particular he sometimes seems to equate values and ends, which are surely not self-evidently identical; the same might be said of the other members of this list (except perhaps ends and goals). A more systematic and explicit account of ultimate human values is devoutly to be wished, in Berlin's philosophy as well as in the public arena. The OED definition, 'worth based on esteem', is unhelpfully circular.

There is much pious talk of values on the lips of politicians, but what it is to be a value is scarcely ever examined in the media. 'Our values' is a term with a pejorative underbelly, used to promote the interests of a nation, presumably on the basis that values are a nobler yardstick than mere self-interest. The unspoken assumption seems to be that 'our' values differ, to their credit, from those of whoever is cast in the role of enemies of our culture, today typically terrorists.

Much has been written by philosophers about the nature and origin of values, and it is a rash fool who rushes into this angel-resistant territory. But some preliminary platitudes are suggested by what Berlin has to say about another vexed (and not unrelated) issue, that of human rights. He does not discuss human rights formally in his published work, but his views emerge from interviews and letters, and they are astringent and disarmingly straightforward. Here is what he said to Beata Polanowska-Sygulska in 1986:

> Rights, for me, are simply things which, according to some code, it is right to do, and which happen to be something which I want done, which are in my interest. [...] A right always means something which I want; so rights are simply those things which people owe me because the law says so, or the ruler says so, or the Ten Commandments say so, or God says so, or the prince says so, or I say so – it doesn't matter – and which happen to be the sort of things I need or want, or that are in my interest. What rights are in an absolute sense I've never understood. Rights can only be explained in terms of rules, and the rules simply say: this is right, this is wrong. (UD 158; cf. UD 174, L4 445–6, L 210–11)

In other words, rights are simply interests – 'what makes life tolerable for normal individuals' (L4 453), 'the permanent interests of man' (L 210) – codified by rules, typically legal rules.

Something closely analogous to this, I suggest, can be said about values. Indeed Berlin more or less says it himself when explaining the views of others, and as so often we may suspect that he to some extent shares the views he is expounding. So, for example, when discussing Hume he writes:

> Values are what men seek: they seek satisfaction of their needs. The science of empirical psychology will tell you what men want, what they approve and disapprove, and sociology or social anthropology will tell you about the differences and similarities between the needs and the moral and political values of (and within) different nations, groups, classes, civilisations. (SR 172)

And in an analysis of Kant he writes:

> a goal or a value is something that a man sets himself to aim at, it is not an independent entity that can be stumbled upon. Values are not natural growths that a science, say psychology or sociology, can study, but are made by men, are forms of free action or creation. (SR 178)

Just as rights are interests codified in law, so values are interests, purposes, ends codified in morality – that is, they are sanctioned by a moral code which recognises the interests in question as beneficial for normal human beings, and therefore as proper objects of moral approval and promotion. Disagreements about values will then represent disagreements about our common human nature, or different cultural priorities (and it will be important to tell the two sources of difference apart). There is much more, of course, to be said about values, especially their phenomenology and the appetitive psychophysiological mechanisms by which they operate in our lives, but this basic picture of the logic of value seems to give us a start. We have a number of natural needs, and naturally pursue a range of ends, and values are supervenient on these needs and ends. It is natural for us to value the things we need or desire, and valued ends become imbued with an instinctive emotional sense of approval or assent which strengthens our attachment to and pursuit of what is valued. This goes beyond the instinctive drives that we share with other animals, perhaps because it is tied to the use of language. Values, we might say, are self-conscious instincts. Morality is constructed from our values, and basic moral principles reflect our shared needs. These principles are invested with great psychological power, and the flouting of them can cause great revulsion.

If I am right, the primary source of value pluralism is not the plural values themselves, but the plural ends they sponsor. The plurality of value is parasitic on the plurality of ends. Indeed, although I have not made a systematic count, it is my impression that Berlin writes more often of clashes between ends or goods than of conflict between values. 'Some among the Great Goods cannot live together' (CTH2 14); 'not all good things are compatible' (L 213). Not everything that we want can be had at the same time, at least not completely, and the values that endorse our most cherished ends can be expected to reflect this. Ends and values clash because ends are irreducibly plural.

This plurality leads in turn to the plurality of lives and cultures constructed out of this plural raw material (*cultural pluralism*). Different ends or values can be given different priorities, can be elements in different combinations, with different weightings and different principles of interaction, can be excluded from or included within different personal or cultural amalgams, 'constellations of values' (CC2 280). In this way enormous individual and cultural variation arises – but not unlimited variation. Human nature sets certain limits that arise from the basic shared needs and desires of the human condition.[7] We all need (and want) at least food, drink, shelter, companionship, membership of a social unit to which we feel we belong, and no doubt indefinitely many other things too. The idea that human beings are blank slates, limitlessly malleable vessels whose innate structure imposes no restrictions on what they can do or be, is self-evidently absurd, even if some philosophers have tried to assert as much; but then the history of philosophy is littered with the denial by allegedly intelligent persons of basic truths known to everyone, even to philosophers in their non-philosophical moments.

Berlin calls humanity's shared principles 'an empirical version of "natural law" [...], namely, that minimum of moral values accepted by all men without which human societies would disintegrate, and from which, for quasi-biological causes, men cannot depart without perishing' (L4 206).[8] He never attempts to provide a complete list of basic human needs, though he often gives examples: food, clothing, shelter, security, belonging, unity, culture, education, self-knowledge, responsibility, harmony, order, peace, happiness, performance of duty, wisdom, justice, honour, dignity, power, action, mercy, knowledge, freedom, equality, efficiency, independence, reason, self-development, (rational) self-government, truth, virtue, self-sacrifice, moral perfection, *humanitas*, self-expression, creation, love, worship, communication, self-description, beauty, goodness, spontaneity, originality, genius, mental energy, (moral) courage, cooperation in the pursuit of common purposes. If we wish to pursue the question of what should be on the list, we might turn to Abraham Maslow's hierarchy of needs,[9] often depicted as a pyramid with physiological needs at its base and 'self-actualisation' at its apex. If we prefer to think in terms of human potentialities rather than needs, we can turn to Martha Nussbaum's work.[10] One might ask which approach is better, and why. But I shall not pursue these lines of enquiry here, since Berlin's underlying view does not require full listings of values in order to be understood or evaluated.

The different constellations of value exhibited by different cultures inherit the incommensurability of their constituent values: *value incommensurability* generates *cultural incommensurability*. Houses built in different architectural styles cannot be ranked in an objective order of approximation to some one ideal structure, since there is no such single ideal. A given house may have identifiable defects which make it in that respect inferior to another; but such defects can be rectified, and the house cannot be judged to be *as a whole* superior to all others. Similarly, most cultures cannot be ranked objectively as wholes, even if they score higher in terms of a given value.

The nature of the connection, if any, between plurality and freedom is widely and deeply contested, and there is now an unmanageably large secondary literature on the topic. Some see a logical entailment of liberalism by pluralism, some only a psychological connection – a link between the sensibilities that are drawn to liberalism and pluralism – and there are intermediate positions of various kinds. Suffice it for present purposes to say that Berlin, though his specific remarks on the topic in different places are inconsistent, sees the two positions as natural if not inevitable bedfellows. The link is strongest at the level of 'basic freedom', or free will. If the possession and exercise of this faculty is a defining property of human beings, some minimum degree of 'negative' freedom is required in any human life worthy of the name. As Berlin writes, 'liberty in one sense is basic, the one value which is presupposed by all others in human life – without that no choice, no action, [no] subject or object of moral thought; in my sense, no humanity' (A 345). This is enough of an answer to extreme forms of illiberalism, especially totalitarian repression and thought-control. And it gets us safely into the ground floor of liberalism.

How much further than this we can go in arguing positively from pluralism to liberalism is what is so hotly debated. Why can a pluralist not reasonably opt for an illiberal option? Berlin does not argue that liberty always trumps other values: there are circumstances in which it must be sacrificed to a more urgent end. But someone who recognises or, even more, celebrates the plurality of value is likely also, in general, to endorse the freedom to choose that enables us to navigate this plurality by our own lights, rather than in deference to outside guidance or compulsion. And someone who values freedom of choice as an instrument of self-government or self-creation is likely to be receptive to the view that many doors are open before us, some of which close if we walk through others, and none of which beckons us ineluctably in by offering a knock-down argument in its sole favour. But there are exceptions to both these generalisations, and in any case they are not sufficient to justify full-blown liberalism on pluralist grounds. Other priorities too can be reasonable.

Berlin calls the limit set by human nature to what we can value the *human horizon*, a fence which encloses both our basic shared values and a wide variety of other possible values that are recognisably human but not universally subscribed to. It circumscribes too, for Berlin, the limits of empathy, because we can empathise with any unpathological human aspiration, with any end 'of more or less sane human beings and not angels or lunatics' (L4 208), even if it is not one that we pursue ourselves. Our shared humanity enables us to place ourselves imaginatively in the position not only of our relatives and friends, our neighbours, contemporaries and fellow citizens (who can differ from us quite enough), but of humans from other times, places and cultures, and to see that we ourselves might share their values if we were placed as they were or are. This kind of empathy is crucial for Berlin, because it distinguishes his pluralism of values from relativism or subjectivism, the view that values have no standing outside the society which, or even the individual who, espouses them. For him values are 'objective' in the sense that they are either shared by, or comprehensible to, the whole of humanity: 'The minimum values needed for intercommunication are [...] an objective, not a subjective, need: part of the objective world which we inhabit together, which we literally cannot do without' (L4 207). They arise out of human nature and are not just matters of individual taste[11] like a preference for coffee over champagne (CTH2 11), or kindness over concentration camps (POI2 14). We do not live in hermetically sealed bubbles, pursuing values that make no sense to others and disagreeing radically about what the basic principles of decent human behaviour are, or indeed whether such principles exist at all. If we did, social life, still more international cooperation or an understanding of history, would be impossible, because we could not communicate about or in terms of values that make sense to everyone simply in virtue of membership of the human species. It is evident that this is not our predicament: communication and some agreement about values do occur. We share 'common assumptions, sufficient for some communication [...], for some degree of understanding and being understood' (L 152).

If this picture is right, then all acceptable systems of value, individual or collective, will share certain basic features derived from human nature, but will also display variation within the peripheral areas left open by the shared principles. For Berlin, 'There is a finite variety of values and attitudes, some of which one society, some another, have made their own' (CTH2 82). It is not clear why the available values are finite in number, especially given Berlin's belief that new values (such as sincerity, authenticity and variety) arise historically. We cannot predict how many more new values may arise in the future. Nor are values biologically definable natural kinds like botanical species, which means that the fineness of our subdivision of the territory of value is logically arbitrary, so that values can be sliced indefinitely smaller by different possible conceptual systems, rather as the Eskimo subdivide the concept of snow. Alternatively they can be amalgamated under more capacious labels, ultimately all being examples of 'good'. It seems best to regard Berlin's statement as a vivid way of saying that human nature sets limits to the kinds of value we are likely to pursue. For present purposes this is good enough. All we need for an exposition of Berlin is a variety of value-flora growing in the shared soil of human nature.

But there is one ingredient so far missing, and it is one which Berlin does not speak of as much as we might wish. I mean the inbuilt tendency towards malignity that is at least as much part of human nature as any tendency towards the benign. This is what theologians call original sin, which, like the poor, is always with us. When Berlin talks of conduct that defies normal human values, his examples tend to be of behaviour that is psychotic rather than malign. In chapter 11 I cite one of his favourite cases, that of the man who sticks pins into others because it gives him pleasure to insert sharp objects into resilient surfaces, with no regard to the pain he causes (230–1). He also speaks of someone who collects green objects simply because they are green (L4 204; cf. L4 207 on collecting matchboxes), though this is less clearly outside the human horizon, given the perfectly familiar phenomenon of favourite colours. A third example concerns someone who worships wooden objects simply because they are wooden, without being able to rationalise this activity in more intelligible terms (CTH2 12).

Malign acts do not belong in this company, but we know that malignity (sometimes called *evil*) exists. Perhaps because he is specially interested in the power of ideas, in particular the power of ideas to mislead us into wrong behaviour, Berlin tends to emphasise cases where we have been misled rather than cases where we deliberately do what we know to be wrong, or at any rate generally regarded as wrong. This distorts his map of the territory of human action, and produces some counter-intuitive results. For instance, he explains the behaviour of the Nazis as based on an empirical mistake about the nature of Jews and other human groups marked down for obliteration. This may be part of the truth, but most people feel there is also a strong element of malignity or evil at work here. It is not that Berlin systematically fails to recognise evil: on the contrary, he sees it clearly for what it is. But his laudable insistence that we should understand before we condemn can lead him to be more indulgent towards the perpetrators of nefarious actions than some of them deserve, and to under-represent the role of malignity in his discussions of human motivation. At any rate, as we shall see, he admitted when pressed that he did accept the category of the malign, and believed in (a secular version of) original sin. So it is safe to add this category to our toolbox for interpreting what he says. Indeed, I should argue that without it we cannot make sense either of human behaviour or of Berlin's ideas about humanity.

Much more could be said about Berlin on human nature; indeed everything he wrote could be said to fall under this heading. But we have now set out the bare bones of his account, which are a sufficient backdrop for the discussion of the specific points at issue in our 1990s correspondence, to which I now turn.

10

PLURALISM AND RELIGION

Croyez ceux qui cherchent la vérité, doutez de ceux qui la trouvent.
(Believe those who seek the truth, doubt those who find it.)

André Gide [1]

Tantum religio potuit suadere malorum.
(So great is the evil that religion could induce.)

Lucretius [2]

I now turn to continuous accounts, in the next two chapters, of my exchanges with Berlin on pluralism and religion, and on the 'moral core' and the 'human horizon'. This division into two chapters is not completely tidy, since our discussions of the two themes overlapped both chronologically and substantively. But the main treatment of each topic does occur in the suitably named chapter.

I

The questions I put to Berlin about the relationship between cultural pluralism and religious belief seemed to me then, and seem to me now, central for anyone who wishes to think intelligently about the human predicament. Cultural pluralism's recognition and celebration of different visions of life, many of them valid in their own way, is for me in fatal tension with the insistence of at any rate the major world religions on a single true path for all mankind, which puts pluralism and religion at odds. Berlin seemed never quite to accept this, and, despite our extended discussion, his reasons are still not entirely clear to me. I hope that our exchanges will enable readers to understand his view better than I have so far managed to do.

Whether we are concerned with Christianity or Islam, or Communism, to name only three examples, there exists a permanent potential, built into the very nature of such enterprises, for over-enthusiastic adherents to get carried away by the conviction that they know the truth, that they have the final solution to all human ills, and that this justifies doing almost anything that will persuade, or compel, non-believers to fall in with them. In the past this was one rationale for the Crusades and the Inquisition. In our own time we see this tendency in its most extreme form in the terrorism of extremist jihadist fanatics, as well as in totalitarian political systems like those of North Korea or Vietnam;[3] and Berlin's ideas provide important intellectual ammunition to use against the beliefs that lead in these directions.

Berlin himself was reluctant to draw the general conclusion about religious belief that I have suggested. His experiences in life made him more immediately concerned with political than with religious totalitarianism, though the two are closely related. And he had not suffered at the hands of excessive, importunate religious certainty, so that there is a biographical reason why he didn't directly address it. But one can reasonably deduce from scattered remarks, some of which I have quoted or shall quote, that he would have agreed with me about this. Indeed, he once effectively told me he did when I published something about it myself, as will emerge.

Berlin himself was a non-believer, in a special sense that he explained in words that I quote below. He was also an anti-believer. He wrote to his friend Irving Singer in 1984:

> As for the meaning of life, I do not believe that it has any: I do not at all ask what it is, for I suspect it has none, and this is a source of great comfort to me – we make of it what we can, and that is all there is about it. Those who seek for some deep, cosmic, all-embracing, teleologically arguable libretto or god are, believe me, pathetically mistaken. (L4 246)

But at the same time he recognised that religious belief is in some way hard-wired into human nature. Though he declared himself personally 'tone-deaf' to God, he could write to me:

> I find that those who, like Freddie Ayer or [Hugh] Trevor-Roper, are bone-dry atheists and simply deny and denounce the whole thing [...]

do not begin to understand what men live by, which I claim to be able to do, because of this understanding, which I believe I possess, of religious emotion and the effect and influence which it has upon people's characters and lives. (10 February 1992)

Of course, religious emotion is not the same as religious belief, but the former typically springs from, or leads to, the latter, and there is a paradox in Berlin's thinking here that I am not sure how to resolve. What he says appears to imply that human beings are bound to live by an illusion. Perhaps they are, and perhaps this is only one of many illusions that we are reluctant or unable to shed. Others might be that we have free will (see previous chapter) or that we are not going to die. In the case of belief in god, maybe the natural human desire to understand and explain misfires when it is extended beyond specific phenomena and applied to reality as a whole; as if we were to ask, not where a particular piece of the jigsaw puzzle fits in, but where the puzzle as a whole fits in. There is no necessity to believe that the mental equipment that has evolved in us will not contain imperfections, especially when applied outside the context which drove its evolution. We may find that our instincts create expectations that our reason tells us to discount. (A more extreme thesis is that beliefs created by evolutionary pressures cannot lay any claim to truth.)

How does an acceptance of cultural pluralism bear on our attitude to religious believers who hold that one universal creed is true for all mankind, for all time? Of course cultural pluralists should not seek to censor religious believers unless they turn aggressive, but should they argue that they are mistaken? Cultural pluralism asserts that no single overall account of what human beings should be and do can claim to be uniquely true. It seems to me to follow from this – indeed to be almost a restatement of it – that a cultural pluralist is bound to reject all universalist creeds and ideologies, because they make a claim of just this kind.

Berlin strongly argued just such a case against political universalism, and the intolerance that can flow from it, and the same arguments apply in the religious arena. Part of the reason for his unwillingness to accept this may be a failure to keep the question of toleration distinct from that of rational assent, but I suspect that there was a deeper source of reluctance that I should find it hard to identify, though it may have had something to do with his strong sense of rootedness in the Jewish tradition, which would scarcely survive without its religious roots. Not that this is a justification for preserving the religion, as I argued in a 2008 interview:

> [Berlin's] attitude to religious practice seems to have been that this is a valuable vehicle of cultural identity. For him the ceremonies and practices of Judaism kept the collective identity of the Jews alive. And he was perfectly happy, indeed anxious, to join in with them on this basis without subscribing to any of the doctrinal, metaphysical claims that they entailed. This seems to me an intellectually and morally unacceptable conjunction of views. [...] it means, in effect, wishing for the preservation of a religious tradition based on beliefs you do not share, beliefs that have a life-forming effect on many people, just so that one of its side-effects that you value can continue in play. I remember Mary Warnock saying once on the radio something to the effect that she believed none of the theological propositions in the Prayer Book, but wanted the Church of England to continue in being so that the beauty of Evensong could be preserved. More seriously, if you believe, as I do, that religious belief at least has the potential to become oppressive and destructive, then anything which encourages religion to exist and to thrive seems to me regrettable.
>
> Berlin once wrote that a new dimension of horror was opened up when the Nazis loaded people 'into trains bound for gas chambers, telling them that they were going to emigrate to some happier place' (L 339). Well, the logic of that situation seems to me comparable to that of Berlin's attitude to religion. It's too close for comfort to Marx's characterisation of religion as the opium of the people. And opium is an enslaver, not a liberator. (BI 142)

At times Berlin did virtually concede my point, agreeing, for example, that the religious imperative was universalising, and that it is reasonable for pluralists to challenge universalists. 'Of course one has the right to be an "evangelist" for the abandonment of universalist beliefs: it is certainly legitimate, and in my opinion desirable.'⁴ But at other times he resisted my argument. I suspect his view was both more complicated and less thought through than I wanted it to be.

I now turn to our correspondence on this topic, allowing issues to arise in the order in which we addressed them.

11

My first salvo came in my letter of 25 March 1991:

> I'd like to change the subject and ask you a couple of questions about
> your views. These [...] have been lurking at the back of my mind, but
> were crystallised when Michael [Ignatieff] asked me to comment on a
> very interesting piece he's written for *New Republic* on *Crooked Timber*.
> The first point concerns the scope of your view of the common human
> moral core[5] (if I may so describe it) – the bulwark against relativism.
> I have always assumed that, though your examples have naturally most
> often been Western ones, your canvas is (at least potentially) the whole
> of humanity. Indeed, I would be greatly disappointed if you were to say
> that your observations had no application, or none that you knew of,
> beyond Western limitations. One of the attractive features of what you
> have to say is that it offers some guidance as to how one should think
> about the behaviour and intellectual claims of, for instance, Islam, or
> Chinese Communism, or the current behaviour of those in power in
> Sudan – not to mention more exotic cultural manifestations of the kind
> studied by social anthropologists. Perry Anderson[6] (if I remember rightly)
> and perhaps Michael have been misled (I hope) by remarks in *Crooked
> Timber* into wondering whether you might wish to restrict yourself to
> the Western tradition. But in that case do not the discussions of the
> nature and extent of the common human core, and of the associated
> limits of tolerance and acceptable variety, become far less interesting,
> to put it at its lowest?
>
> The second point is connected. I have often wondered how far the
> tolerant attitude to different priorities which is one of the consequences
> of your pluralism should be extended to creeds of a universalist kind –
> pan-Islam, old-style Communism, many varieties of religion (including
> Christianity?), etc. Is it a case of 'I will tolerate anything but intolerance'?
> Certainly your repeated rejection of totalitarianism might lead one to
> suppose so. If pluralism is true, then no form of monism will do?
>
> On the other hand, do you not accept religious belief in others,
> without restricting this acceptance to faiths that themselves espouse
> or accept pluralism? Many faiths, one suspects, would be denatured

if their universalist aspirations were pruned away. So much the worse
for the faiths; but is it really consistent for a pluralist to hold that they
are acceptable manifestations of human variety? To 'stand for [one's
convictions] unflinchingly' may be civilised, but only, surely, if one also
realises their 'relative validity'[7]? (I'm worried by that 'relative', incidentally, especially when people start accusing pluralism of collapsing into
relativism: shouldn't it be 'optional validity' or somesuch?)

Universalism isn't totalitarianism, though it's often one of its largest
foundation-stones. It is, however, inconsistent with pluralism, is it not?
So if, for example, it is an essential ingredient in Christianity that its
teachings are true for all men, at all times, does it not self-destruct?
One can I suppose continue to tolerate it so long as it does no harm, but
should one accept it as one of the legitimate options open to those who
wish their beliefs to be in accord with reality?

My 'second point' does not distinguish the following questions as clearly as it
should (as I soon realised):

1. Should cultural pluralists tolerate universalist creeds (a political question)?
2. Should cultural pluralists include universalist creeds among the plural
   approaches to life they regard as valid (a logical question)?
3. Can a universalist creed be compatible with the truth of cultural pluralism (a different way of asking question 2)?

I should say that the answer to question 1 is yes, to questions 2 and 3, no. I return
to these distinctions and questions below.

Berlin's long reply of 2 April 1991, as I told him on 11 April, was 'wonderful –
a richly informative response to my questions', though its treatment of what has
for me long been a central paradox in his thought – that we can simultaneously
understand and yet condemn the views and behaviour of others – was not completely satisfying. To this conundrum too I shall return. I reproduce most of
this important letter below, interjecting comments where they seem required,
as a running commentary on what strike me as difficulties in Berlin's account.
Anthony Quinton used to describe Berlin's expositions as like a rickety train
with luggage insecurely lashed to the roofs of its carriages, speeding along an
uneven track, shedding suitcases as it goes.[8] I shall try to catch the suitcases as
they fall. It would be possible instead to drive along in the wake of the train,

loading the discarded luggage into a trailer for later wholesale attention. But this would involve repeating the problematic passages in the course of the retrospective report, and it seems best to proceed on a piecemeal basis.

> You ask, as is your wont, important – central and difficult – questions, to which I do not know of any firm answer. I'll do my best to reply to you, but it is all, as you will see, painfully tentative. [...]
>
> My God, what do I answer about 'the common human moral core'? All general propositions of the kind I utter about that kind of thing are in a sense amateur observations, general reflections not founded on accurate knowledge of history, sociology, psychology etc., which in theory would be needed to give them any kind of objective or scientific respectability. One just says 'Most human beings, at most times, in most places, surely ...' etc. What is this founded on? A general sense of what human beings are like – which may well not merely have gaps but be seriously mistaken in places – but that cannot be helped: all vast generalisations of this kind are neither avoidable nor demonstrable.

It is of some importance what is omitted after 'surely'. Berlin often uses the 'Most people' formula, and elsewhere it is clear that he is speaking of widespread *acceptance* of moral principles based on shared beliefs. For example: 'I think there are certain common principles which human beings, in a great many places and a great many ages, have almost universally accepted' (199). The difficulty with this account of the core is that it is too conservative. There are some principles that have been widely accepted but later discarded, such as the principle that women should be subservient to men. In order to allow for moral progress, it seems better to speak of the core as composed of *needs* or *interests*, which we may come to understand better, revising our principles accordingly. It is entirely plausible to suppose that human beings of all times, places and cultures have certain needs and interests in common, simply in virtue of their species membership. These shared needs and interests, we may suppose, generate a minimum of shared values and principles, which apply everywhere in the world, as Berlin now confirms:

> You ask if they apply to the non-Western world – in my opinion, they do. Japanese culture, for example, which seems to me remoter than any other I have ever encountered, and its values, which differ sharply from

our own, nevertheless is a culture of human beings – that is, *nos sembla-bles* [people like us]. I mean something very simple: that unless there are common values, however different in detail, twisted this way or that by circumstances, genes or whatever – unless there are these, communication becomes impossible; but it is not impossible. Missionaries correctly assumed that they could try to convert Trobriand Islanders or, for all I know, African pygmies, in spite of the vast chasm which lay between their forms of life. They could only do this by appealing to something which in the end the others understood – in some cases allowed themselves to be persuaded by, in other cases not, but [which was] in both cases in some degree intelligible.

Here Berlin asserts that communication can occur between human beings anywhere in the world. Elsewhere he makes a similar claim about the possibility of understanding human beings of different times, even though a great effort may be required to step into the shoes of people in the remote past. He may be right, but a question is begged. It is not absurd to suppose that there may be limits to such communication and understanding. Shared biological species membership does not automatically entail the possibility of mutual understanding, and cultures, as he says, can 'differ sharply' from one another. One must also, of course, allow for historical development: the needs and interests of cavemen will hardly be identical with our own. But let us speak ahistorically for the purposes of this discussion, for simplicity's sake. Let us assume that no historical or cultural limits to communication and understanding exist, but note that this assumption merits further examination.

The next question concerns the *range* of the common core: how many principles does it contain?

> The question is, how widely does this go? Herbert Hart, as you probably know, once tried to work out an empirical theory of natural law,[9] by saying that there were certain principles which all men accepted because otherwise society would collapse, and there was an almost biological need to continue living together: e.g. no murder, otherwise society couldn't go on; no lying, otherwise nobody could believe anyone else (again, no communication); presumably food, drink, shelter etc. etc., without which men would perish. But in the end, although these things are true, they form too thin a basis for what we like to think of as human

rights, which are presumably founded on some kind of general moral acceptance.

Here Berlin seems to mean that even the whole minimum content of natural law (what we are calling the core) is not sufficient to generate a complete list of the human rights we now wish to assert. Without examples it is difficult to assess this claim. As I said in the last chapter, for Berlin human rights are simply human interests codified in law (see also A 445–6, UD 43, 91), which makes them sound closely related to the core. A more plausible claim, which Berlin would certainly accept ('too thin a basis'), is that by itself the core does not a culture make. Fully fledged cultures include principles and values that go beyond the shared minimum human needs, and different cultures display different additional elements. But Berlin believes that they have enough in common to underwrite cross-cultural understanding, as he next confirms:

So what can I say? Only that in my opinion – but only in my opinion – differences between nations, cultures, different ages of human life have been exaggerated. We do not, surely, entirely misunderstand Plato, though we don't know what Athens looked like (was it like Beirut, or like an African kraal?), even though [Quentin] Skinner would have us believe that, unless we do know such things, we don't really understand what thinkers mean.[10] If this is so, then there is a pretty wide common ground between human beings as such, upon which one can build. It must be possible to preach to Muslim bigots, or Communist fanatics, in terms of values which they have in common with the preacher – they may reject, they may argue, they may murder and torture, but they have to construct special hypotheses in order to account for the fact that the preacher is mistaken, and explain the cause or root of the mistake, which entails some degree of common understanding. At some times, of course, the preacher is successful, at least in weakening, if not refuting, violently held views. This I firmly believe, and this applies to the whole of mankind. If Michael Ignatieff thinks differently, do correct him.

Now, about pluralism and toleration. My God, another terrible question. Your formula is the well-known – and in my opinion correct – one, that democracies should tolerate all doctrines save those which threaten to subvert democracy; liberalism should tolerate everything except what will put an end to liberal thought and action; etc. All that is true, and

I do accept that. But it does not go far enough. I do not wish to say that I tolerate, and do not wish to suppress, the opinions of those who think it all right to torture children to amuse themselves, or preach or practise other enormities – even racial or national hatreds – even if my presumably tolerant society is not actually endangered by it in a serious degree. You ask me, do I want to imprison David Irving or the National Front? Not imprison, perhaps, because that is not needed: I would not in the least mind a degree of censorship which would not permit certain things to be published, much as the race relations legislation does. And yet society is not in serious danger: it is not the kind of intolerance which might subvert the foundations of our liberal society.

On the other hand, I can't say that I wish to suppress all intolerance, as such. All believers in universal values are presumably at some point intolerant of what they regard as falsehood or perversion – but far be it from me to say that a check ought to be put on the preaching or practice of Islam, Christianity, Buddhism or whatever. I believe Judaism also believes in universal truths, which those who depart from them do at their own peril and should if possible be stopped from doing. But some Jews maintain that Judaism is only for the Jews, and they take no interest in anybody else – about that there is some controversy. I cannot say that I wish to tolerate everything except intolerance: only either (*a*) your case – intolerance which endangers pluralism, tolerance etc. – or (*b*) what I regard as evil (which others may not so regard) because I do have the sort of beliefs that I have, I do believe that there is a certain interwoven set of values – a horizon of them which underlies a form of life – without which, in my opinion, my life (and that of people who think like me, i.e. the society communication and life in which is part of my own life and thought and feeling) would be impossible.

The phrase 'universal values' in the second sentence of the last paragraph is slippery. It could apply to the universal values of the core, but here Berlin is using it of religious believers who hold that their particular doctrines are true for everybody, everywhere, at all times, and that those who reject these doctrines are guilty of 'falsehood or perversion'. Let us call such persons *religious universalists* to distinguish them from those who merely accept the principles of the core.

The more important issue arising from this paragraph concerns what Berlin says in (*b*), where he seems to confuse the core with what is culturally specific. This is important not only in itself, but also because the same confusion occurs repeatedly in what he writes. Here he speaks of 'what I regard as evil' as culturally specific, as if members of other cultures might take a different view of what counts as evil. This seems wrong to me. If I take the strong view that something is *evil*, it seems more natural to take this as the view that it offends against the principles of the core, not just against principles peculiar to my own society. Indeed, this is part of what 'evil' means, for me. It is a strong, universalist label, because there are universal human considerations which make certain behaviour deeply reprehensible in any society. But Berlin's account in this letter places evil outside the core, in the area of cultural variation, making it an offence against 'a certain interwoven set of values' rather than against *any* normal set of values – against humanity as such.

Berlin may have been confusing an offence against humanity with a different case: one where we are indeed defending a culturally specific standard against a rival standard from another culture. In this case it may be that neither standard flouts the core, so that we cannot appeal to the core as a basis for defending our own way against its competitor. Here the basis of our defence will be that it is our right to defend our own ways, the ways of our own culture, when they conflict with the ways of, say, outsiders or immigrants. This is the position typically adopted by the dominant culture in a given nation or territory, and it is a position that Berlin too defends, as we shall see. From a pluralist viewpoint, both cultures have a valid take on the situation, since both invoke principles that are consistent with the core; but their approaches are inconsistent with one another, and a choice must be made between them. This is done by reference to the prevailing majority culture, and evil does not enter into the matter.

Berlin now turns to my key question of how one can combine understanding with rejection:

> You will ask, but what about pluralism, what about life in societies which hack off limbs for theft or send people to torture and death? I maintain the somewhat uncomfortable, but to me nevertheless fairly clear, notion that, while pluralism entails that I can understand other cultures (because they are human and because with a sufficient degree of imaginative empathy I can enter into them at times – at least, I think

I can, though this may be an illusion), I remain wedded to my own, and am prepared to fight, or exterminate if extreme cases arise, forms of life which I understand but abhor. Pluralism is the remedy against relativism, not against intolerance of what I regard as evil.

Again, this seems too cautious. I should drop 'what I regard as' before 'evil'. Otherwise 'societies which hack off limbs for theft or send people to torture and death' are evil only in relation to my own culture, not in relation to humanity. There may of course be cases where I reject certain values for myself, or for my culture, without claiming that this rejection is or should be universal; but the case Berlin describes is not one of them. Evil is evil, without qualification.

Another repeated difficulty arises here. Berlin writes that 'pluralism entails that I can understand other cultures'. What does this mean? Berlin's picture is of a multiplicity of values subscribed to in different combinations within a 'human horizon' that delimits the values comprehensible to a normal human. So it is part of the definition of pluralism that the plural values are cross-culturally comprehensible. This means that the entailment that Berlin speaks of here is trivially analytic, not a further claim somehow deduced from pluralism. It would be clearer to say that 'pluralism claims that I can understand the values of other cultures'. This claim I dub *pluralist empathy*, to distinguish it from *value pluralism*, the claim that ultimate human values are irreducibly plural etc. Berlin oscillates between the two, sometimes even appearing to treat pluralist empathy as primary, so that 'pluralism' then *means* the empathetic understanding of unshared values rather than the plurality of value. The two claims should not be confused, even if they are related. However this may be, what has pluralism to offer here? If Berlin understands evil forms of life, surely this is not because they are part of the pluralistically acceptable smorgasbord of cultural options, but because he knows that human beings can be, and often are, vindictively evil. Pluralism has nothing to do with the case.

Similar difficulties afflict Berlin's account of Nazism:

In other words, I do not believe, as, for example, Hampshire does, in the existence of 'absolute evil', in an objective way. I don't know what this would mean: objectivity of values is an old conundrum, and I don't quite understand what people believe who believe that; I only know that they believe it – perhaps my empathy doesn't go far enough for this.[11] But I claim (*a*) that I understand why the Nazis believed what they believed (at least, the genuine ones among them) – namely that Jews, or gypsies, were subhuman, and termites, who undermined the only societies worth preserving – their own – and therefore had to be exterminated. This in the end is an empirical error (though it sounds tame to call it that): there are no subhumans; there are no gammas; Jews etc. don't undermine, nor does anyone else, etc. But if you really believe that they do, then of course you do what the Nazis did, and it is not insane (people too easily said they were mad, i.e. unintelligible): it is sane but founded on a colossal delusion, which had to be exterminated, very likely by force – as, indeed, it more or less was. 'Understanding', however, does not preclude a violent 'battle against'. I defend my – our – form of life against the enemy. The fact that I understand the enemy does not make me more tolerant towards him – but the fact that I do understand him precludes relativism.

This seems to repeat the previous confusion. I can understand 'the enemy' in one or both of two ways: (1) he is empirically mistaken in the way Berlin describes; and/or (2) he is evil. These two forms of understanding are quite different. So their relation to pluralism/relativism cannot be treated as a single issue. Pluralism again seems irrelevant in either case. Empirical error is empirical error, not adherence to values that differ from mine; evil is evil, and its rejection is not to do with pluralism, but with the universal values of the core. In neither case is the understanding involved a pluralist understanding.

Berlin now turns to universalist religious doctrines:

> You ask about universalist doctrines, e.g. Christianity. Of course I am not prepared to exterminate it, or even argue against it, particularly vehemently. Pluralism does not entail intolerance of non-pluralism, only, as you yourself say, the kind which does too much harm – harm towards what I regard as the minimum set of values which makes life worth living for me and mine – i.e. the culture in which I live, the nation, society etc. of which I see myself as a member.

Once more, I should replace 'worth living for me and mine' with 'worth living for any recognisably human being', and argue that a doctrine that does 'too much harm' is to be opposed because it offends against the core, not because it is inimical to a particular local culture.

My next question was about Berlin's celebrated quotation from Schumpeter:

> Now, about 'relative'. I suppose that was a quotation from Schumpeter –
> which I could not alter. But I agree, it is not what I would say. Nor would
> I say 'optional validity'. I think what I would have to say is something
> like 'even though it is not eternal or universal'. I think that's all that
> Schumpeter meant – not that it is relative to me, but that it may pass,
> that in two hundred years' time it may not seem worth dying for, as we
> do not think that some forms of martyrdom were worth undergoing even
> if we respect them and yet perhaps reject them – like the Old Believers
> in Russia, who burnt themselves; or terrorism in our time everywhere –
> how much do I respect Palestinian, Irish, Basque terrorists? I hate them
> all; but I cannot deny that if they risk their lives one owes them a certain
> degree of extremely reluctant respect because one puts a value on integrity,
> however misconceived.

Again, Berlin seems too sceptical here about the durability of his principles.
The convictions for which we are willing to die are not those we think may be
abandoned in the future, or may not be subscribed to universally even now.
They are convictions we believe to be underwritten by human nature, which is
universal (though contingent). Being an empirical phenomenon, human nature
cannot be guaranteed against change; but if it were to change fundamentally
things would fall apart, and we should be concerned not with an adjustment in
our list of basic convictions, but with a whole new conceptual and moral world.

Shortly before he quotes Schumpeter, Berlin writes: 'Principles are not less
sacred because their duration cannot be guaranteed.' I discuss this perplexing
statement at some length at FIB2 264–7, suggesting that the absence of a guarantee that principles will endure is really a way of saying that even our most
basic values are part of the empirical world, not of some ideal Platonic realm:

> The world might have been different [CC2 157], and might not have
> contained human beings as we know them, but it is in fact what it is, and
> has always been so, and human beings have always possessed the same
> underlying nature since they emerged.[12] [...] our values are empirical,
> not a priori – not metaphysically guaranteed against change, for all that
> many of them may in fact apply through human history. This still leaves
> us able to stand unflinchingly for our commitments, or at least those

among them that we regard as basic requirements of humane conduct: we do not, [Berlin] believes, need the values we stand for to be part of the fabric of eternity;[13] nor are they. (FIB2 264–5)

Berlin ends his letter: 'Have I answered your questions? I expect not, but it's the best I can do – if Michael Ignatieff has got me wrong, do put him right.'

His closing enquiry was rash. My reply of 11 April 1991 attempts to clarify some of the questions which still troubled me. I had plainly not got the measure at the time of the questions about core values that I discuss above (maybe I have still not got the measure of them), even though I was indefinably uneasy about some of the things Berlin said about them. I fastened instead on the questions about religious universalism, which were of particular personal importance to me:

I failed to distinguish clearly enough the following four separate questions:
1. To what extent could Christianity and other universalist religions be said to retain their integrity if they dropped their universalism? (Cf. those Jews who maintain, as you tell me, that Judaism is only for the Jews.)
I think the answer has to be that they would be hopelessly compromised: i.e. a non-universalist Christianity (e.g.) is a contradiction in terms, whatever certain modern Christian apologists may urge to the contrary. This in turn would mean that a pluralist doesn't have the option of subscribing to them (see question 2). Jonathan Sacks in his recent Reith Lectures said something to the effect that the major problem faced today by the world religions was that they have not come to terms with being part of a pluralist world.[14] If I am right, that is tantamount to saying that they have not come to terms with the fact that they have become untenable – which is hardly surprising.
2. Is it consistent at the same time to be a pluralist and to belong to a universalist religion? Here my answer (and presumably yours) has to be negative.
3. Is it possible for a pluralist to recognise, as one of the many different options/priorities/cultures/value-systems open to those who wish not to fly in the face of the truth about human nature, membership of a universalist religion?
Here again it seems the answer must be no. You say, rightly, 'pluralism does not entail intolerance of non-pluralism'; but it does presumably entail its intellectual rejection.

4. Whatever pluralism may say, people do subscribe to universalist religions. Should this be tolerated (this side of its causing suffering to others)?

This is the question I put most explicitly, and you have given a full and enlarging answer. If there is a loose end in my mind, it concerns the degree to which it is legitimate or desirable to be an evangelist for the abandonment of universalist beliefs, given their ever-present potential for causing intolerance and pain.

Berlin's reply is dated 17 April 1991. Here is his answer to my first question:

Can Christianity and other universalist religions retain their integrity if they drop their universalism? Certainly not. You are perfectly right. A non-universalist Christianity and a non-universalist Judaism are equally absurd. What I think people like Sacks and such mean (apart from a certain degree of political tact, to which they are committed) is that all religions are basically universal in their appeal, and not ethnic* – they express truths and an outlook which are valid for all men, everywhere, at all times. But some religious denominations believe that all men seek the truth (which is one and not many), each by his own route, and that it is wrong to force people, against their conviction, to seek the truth by a favoured route; that every effort must be made to understand and explain to oneself and to the others what it is that the goals which they pursue have in common, [that they] are, indeed, paths to the same goal, etc. That, I think, is what is at the back of religious toleration on the part of true believers.

My difficulty here is that some religions appear to claim that only *their* route to the one truth is valid: 'I am the way, the truth, and the life: no man cometh unto the Father, but by me' (John 14:6). As an earlier commentator has put it, 'Religious ethics has often tended to brand as immoral and prompted of the devil all codes different from one absolute code regarded as given for all time.'[15] Such attitudes have certainly been typical of religious authorities throughout history – think, again, of the Crusades and the Inquisition – and are familiar in our own time, especially on the part of Islamic extremists, echoing past

* Is not Judaism ethnic, at any rate by origin?

Christian extremism. Whether insistence on one unique true path ought be regarded as essential to all contemporary mainstream universalist religions is less clear, but the monistic temperament that fosters universalist religious belief creates the permanent risk of absolutism, and the conflict and violence that can follow from it.

Berlin continues, in answer to question 2:

> Can a pluralist belong to a universalist religion? Yes (unlike your answer), he can. That only means that he professes the universalist religion of his own [*sc.* his own universalist religion?], but allows other religions or views or whatever to be expressed, unless they offend against what must be called the large minimum accepted as a common moral code, in at any rate the Western world, but maybe beyond – but I don't know much about the East or Africa.[16] However, I think that, pluralist or not, one is entitled to suppress (to use the harshest term I can think of), or in some cases, where it is possible, to dissuade, people from committing crimes, acts subversive of, or too disturbing to, a given society, whatever the agent's religious beliefs. The British were right to suppress suttee in India, and other forms of physical interference. They were also right to suppress the thuggees [*sc.* Thugs]. I am quite happy to say that, no matter how pluralist a society is, it is entitled to resist, make illegal, any form of terrorism – IRA, Shamir or whatever. In other words, I think there are certain common principles which human beings, in a great many places and a great many ages, have almost universally accepted. That must act as a barrier to excess of pluralist freedom. However, I believe there is such a thing as a dominant culture in every society, and that that society has a right to preserve that dominant culture and prevent it from being too far eroded by religious or ethnic persuasions which are not compatible with it. This is a typical clash of incompatible values, but I can only say what I myself believe: namely, that a degree of solidarity and peace is something that every society is fully entitled to; morally, politically and socially entitled to; and therefore, as I have had to reply to another correspondent of mine, religious practices which go against accepted morality (encourage murder, or various forms of oppression of certain human beings – infidels, women, blacks, whites) can be legitimately resisted in a pluralist liberal society. Indeed, a liberal (pluralist) society is one in which such practices ought to be excluded. But, of course, a

wide variety of practices which do not threaten the moral foundations of the dominant culture should be freely permitted, even if not positively encouraged.

This I cannot entirely follow. It seems to confuse *political tolerance*, if that is the right term, with *religious pluralism* (I had the latter in mind): toleration with intellectual assent. Of course someone who believes in toleration will not seek to suppress rivals to his own religious beliefs, even if the latter are held to be the only true beliefs for all of humankind. But if he is a religious pluralist, that is, accepts that no one creed has the monopoly of truth, then to espouse a universalist creed involves a contradiction in terms (on this the beginnings of Berlin's first two replies above are inconsistent).

The way in which Berlin elaborates his reply seems to show that we are somewhat at cross purposes here. Berlin is talking about the core, the shared moral consensus that is accepted by, and applies to, the whole of humanity, and the limits that this consensus places upon reasonable toleration. I, on the other hand, am talking about what logical limits an acceptance of cultural plural-ism places upon the kind of religious beliefs that can be consistently held by the cultural pluralist. I am asking whether it is rational for a cultural pluralist to be a universalist, a position that seems, at the very least, close to a formal contradiction. Of course, we need to be clear what kind of universalism we are considering: a cultural pluralist may well, indeed ought to, be universalist about a single principle or *universal value* such as the proscription of gratuitous cruelty. But when it comes to the whole value system inherent in a culture or a religion, universalism and cultural pluralism are opposed.

In any event, Berlin answers a different question, namely whether a cultural pluralist should be tolerant of universalist beliefs (which will of course conflict with his own). He answers in the affirmative, and we may therefore be tempted to see at work yet another sense of 'pluralism'. But there is nothing distinctively pluralist about such toleration: toleration is open to all, whatever their own view of the nature of values may be. Of course, if toleration is strengthened by the belief that the rival views may be as true as one's own, then pluralism has a role, and the label *pluralist tolerance* might be appropriate – toleration, that is, that does not view the tolerated views as erroneous. But this form of tolerance cannot be extended by the pluralist to universalist beliefs.

Berlin here also introduces the idea of a dominant culture, and what this implies, but that is a separate issue. Indeed, he almost immediately slides back to the previous issue, listing practices which are excluded not merely by the dominant culture, but by humanity's shared moral consensus. Of course, he was dictating his remarks extempore, and it is unfair to expect them to be logically watertight; all the same, I believe that even a sympathetic reading does reveal a confusion here.

Berlin now moves on to question 3, which is very close to the previous one:

> Yes, it is possible, given the conditions I have stated, among which there are bound to be, for example in educational practice, the need for a curriculum which overlaps between various religions, ethnic etc. groups sufficiently not to distort – or what the dominant culture would think to be likely to distort – the education of children; so ethnic or religious schools must not be permitted to forbid the dominant language, or the teaching of what might be called general history as certified by impartial judges taken from the dominant community, or mathematics – whatever we take to be the general need of human beings for being adequately educated. Pluralism certainly does not demand freedom in this respect, or other respects of a similar kind, if you see what I mean.
>
> You speak of 'flying in the face of the truth about human nature', but it is narrower than that – flying in the face of a minimum of commonly accepted moral and political ideas. So the answer to your question 3 is the following: 'A pluralist society has the right to oppose views which are those of a given individual or group, but not [to oppose] the right to follow them, unless they offend against the conditions given above.'

The same confusion seems to be operating here as in the previous case. I was asking about the logical consequences of a belief in the truth of value pluralism (part of 'the truth about human nature'), one of which, surely, has to be that a universalist religion, because it rejects the plurality of humanly possible value systems (a plurality which is nevertheless limited by the general requirements of our shared humanity), cannot consistently be entertained by anyone who recognises such a truth. Berlin, once again, is discussing the limits that our common humanity places upon the practices we tolerate or permit. These are two entirely different questions.

A further possible confusion ought to be cleared up here. I see no reason in principle why a religious universalist should not be a value pluralist, in the sense of believing that the values he recognises are irreducibly plural and sometimes incommensurable when they conflict (*internal pluralism*). Can all the virtues listed in the Sermon on the Mount be maximally developed simultaneously? This kind of difficulty is not something that religions often emphasise, so far as I am aware, perhaps because they prefer to sponsor the notion that each moral problem has a unique solution. (Is this the view of the Koran and/or the Torah?) But the idea of praying for guidance when faced with a moral quandary is a natural fit with value pluralism, except that the decision between competing values is in this case allegedly made by the divinity who answers the prayer, not by the suppliant. I return to this issue below when I ask whether Jesus could have been a pluralist. The universalist cannot, on the other hand, have a pluralistic attitude to rival universalisms (*external pluralism*).

We come to Berlin's answer to my last question (4):

> Of course they should be tolerated – as you say, this side of causing suffering to others. If too much suffering is caused – perhaps a very small amount of irritation doesn't matter – then not. Of course one has the right to be 'an evangelist' for the abandonment of universalist beliefs: it is certainly legitimate, and in my opinion desirable, but that is only *my* opinion – I recognise the need to tolerate those who reject this as desirable, provided ... etc.
>
> Is this satisfactory? I do hope so. If not, do go on pressing me, I don't mind a bit, it is only Pat upon whose shoulders the dreadful burden of my answers lies.

This seems more straightforward, and I accept it (with some misgivings, admittedly), even though it doesn't clear up the confusion I identify in Berlin's replies to my questions 2 and 3. I think it also shows that Berlin was instinctively more tolerant than I am, and that is to his credit.

I replied to Berlin on 25 April 1991. Addressing myself specifically to his answer to my second question ('Is it consistent at the same time to be a pluralist and to belong to a universalist religion?'), I wrote:

> I asked you to confirm that a pluralist cannot in your view consistently belong to a universalist religion, and you brought me up short by saying that he can. But how? A pluralist maintains that there is no single,

objective, demonstrable etc. answer to ultimate questions, e.g. 'How should we live?' But a universalist religion lays down just such answers, true for everyone, everywhere, always, *mutatis mutandis*. Therefore a pluralist who claims to belong to such a religion is guilty of self-contradiction. What have I missed?

Perhaps we don't disagree at all, but are using 'pluralism' in different senses? You explain your response thus: 'That only means that he professes the [*sc.* a?]* universalist religion of his own, but allows other religions [...] to be expressed.' This makes me think that you are talking of pluralism in the sense of an attitude to *how one should behave towards* those with different moral viewpoints; but I meant it in the sense (which I took to be your usual one) of *how one should assess the validity* of those other viewpoints. In the latter sense your pluralism is very capacious and tolerant, subject to the limits you state – but it does not, centrally, endorse any form of monism, a category to which all universalist religions belong. If I'm wrong about this, I'm further off beam than I thought.

That is to say, again, that I was asking about the logical consequences of a belief in religious pluralism, whereas Berlin was speaking about the limits of pluralist tolerance – tolerance on the part of a religious pluralist towards value systems that differ from the one to which he subscribes himself. Note also that when I say universalist religions are monist I don't mean monist in the sense that utilitarians are monist – that is *value monism*, to which, as far as I can see, such religions do not (have to) subscribe. I mean *religious monism*, the view that there is only one true religion, which is therefore universal.

Berlin's reply is dated 6 May 1991:

> Pluralism and universalism: let me explain. A pluralist does not need to maintain that there are no single, objective answers to ultimate questions.

This statement is astonishing, given that one of the most constant burdens of Berlin's song is precisely its denial. I suppose he may be thinking of answers to questions about single issues rather than about wider forms of life. So, for example, the belief that cruelty is wrong might be regarded as an answer of the kind here referred to, whereas Marxism wouldn't. Berlin continues:

---

* Added at the time in my letter.

All he has to say is that he holds certain beliefs which for him are, if not absolute, held as part of his general *Weltanschauung*, which he believes to be correct. When I say 'believes to be', that means that unless it is refuted he will hold on to it through thick and thin, and even perhaps give up his life for its central values or principles. At the same time, he has to say that this may one day have to be modified, changed – that there is no guarantee of anything absolute in the empirical world. Nevertheless, so far as he is concerned, that is what he finally believes and there's an end on't. At the same time, he is aware that other people have similarly strong convictions of a different kind. He believes them to be mistaken; but what makes him a pluralist is that he is able to understand, by some kind of imaginative empathy, how it is that people living under the circumstances of these others, or brought up as they have been, or having the character or the mind that they have, should believe in these other things; they are certainly mistaken, in his view, but it is not an unworthy thing to believe these things – one must tolerate them, unless they threaten the very bases of the existence of himself and his culture, etc. Certainly a universalist cannot be a pluralist;[17] but one can be a pluralist and believe in the universal validity of one's own views, and in the error of other views – but not in the impermissibility of holding them. And also one must be able to sympathise with the kind of people who hold those kinds of views, and see what kind of worlds these people live in, what kind of outlook they have – and perhaps find something of value in it. What one must not do is to assert one's view to be absolute for all time and every universe in an a priori, utterly incorrigible fashion – in that sense of course a pluralist can't be a universalist. It is not simply a question of toleration, it goes further – it denies the validity of views different from one's own, while at the same time understanding how one might live [by] and believe what these mistaken persons believe. Is that all right?

This struck me as somewhat confused (though of course the confusion may be my own), and to conflate various distinct points:

1. Nothing in the empirical world can be guaranteed not to change. I take it that this applies to scientific theories (and 'facts'?) as well as to moral beliefs – indeed one reason for a change in moral beliefs would be a change in scientific beliefs – but since we are here concerned only with morality, let us call this *moral empiricism* as opposed to *moral absolutism*.

2. People may be moral empiricists and yet be prepared to fight to the death for their deepest (moral, ethical, religious) beliefs. This is the attitude to one's fundamental convictions which Schumpeter regarded as civilised, and which we have already examined. Schumpeter's dictum isn't, I assume, the same as saying that one's attitude to one's deepest convictions has to be *ironic*, as some philosophers prefer, though perhaps a touch of irony is no bad thing if one is to be immunised against the moral absolutism of the barbarian, for whom there is an absolute guarantee (whether scriptural or traditional) that his beliefs are true universally and for ever. Let us call this *civilised conviction* as opposed to *barbaric conviction*. However, as before, Berlin surely here presents adherence to core values as if it were adherence to culturally particular values. The values we are willing to defend to the death are the ones we believe apply to the whole of mankind. A pluralist may vigorously defend culturally particular values (and the right to hold them), but not in a way that is captured by saying 'that is what he finally believes and there's an end on't', or 'one can be a pluralist and believe in the universal validity of one's own views'.

3. A pluralist is (defined as?) one who can empathise with those whose beliefs and values differ from his own: 'what makes him a pluralist is that he is able to understand [...]'. We have called this *pluralist empathy*. We can understand values we do not share, values that fall within Berlin's 'human horizon' but are not part of our own constellation of values. Pluralist empathy is related to value pluralism, because if values were not plural, the question of value empathy would not arise: instead our values would all boil down to the same thing (*monism*), in which case we should disagree only about means, not about ends; or we should live in private universes of value, incomprehensible to outsiders (*relativism*).

As I have suggested, it is confusing to call pluralist empathy simply 'pluralism', as Berlin does here and elsewhere, since the latter term is primarily used of the thesis that values are plural, and for clarity's sake it should be reserved for that use. It is unclear, too, whether pluralist empathy is supposed to apply to values, or cultures, or both. But since values are typically situated in cultural wholes rather than existing in isolation, maybe this distinction doesn't matter too much.

4. A pluralist is one who believes that there can be more than one acceptable moral or cultural outlook. Let us call this *participatory cultural pluralism*, or just *cultural pluralism* for short. (We cannot sensibly call it 'multiculturalism', which is either a descriptive term, pointing to the reality of cultural variety, whether within one political jurisdiction or in separate geographical locations – what we might dub *descriptive cultural pluralism* – or a normative term, applauding

this variety.) Cultural pluralism is not the view that *all* cultures are valid, perhaps equally so. If this were the case, we should never be able to criticise other cultures, but this is something we must be free to do, and able to do with good reason. We might call an uncritical stance towards other cultures *cultural relativism*: 'Liberalism for the liberals, cannibalism for the cannibals.'[18] This stance is incompatible with the existence of a moral core, which provides the leverage we need to form judgements of those who flout it in one way or another.

The last two points are importantly distinct, cultural pluralism being about what a pluralist *believes*, and pluralist empathy about the kind of *understanding* that pluralism accounts for (whether or not those who understand are conscious pluralists). In addition, Berlin appears to elide (*a*) empathy with views that are different from mine but valid (pluralist empathy) and (*b*) empathy with views that are mistaken, presumably because they flout the core. One does not need to be a cultural pluralist to understand the holding of beliefs that one feels sure are mistaken ('He believes them to be mistaken'): the world is full of this familiar contingency, which even a monist can understand. So it is problematic that Berlin here talks of the beliefs we empathise with as *mistaken*. We know that people make mistakes all the time, within and outside our own culture, and we often understand why they do so, whether or not we are pluralists. The special kind of empathetic understanding of alien values that Berlin derives from our shared human nature applies, rather, to values that are *different*.

Such understanding is for him obviously a central feature or consequence of a pluralist outlook, even if it is not part of its definition. Perhaps it *is* part of its definition, for him: I should have asked him. At any rate, this pluralist understanding is contrasted with and ruled out by relativism, for which the unshared beliefs of others are opaque.

I replied on 9 May 1991:

> Your remarks did indeed clarify matters, but they also disappoint my excessively tidy mind, which wants pluralism to exclude universalism, even of the empathetic kind you describe, straightforwardly. I don't know if I can explain what my dissatisfaction consists in. If you were suddenly to announce that you had become a committed Christian, for instance, I should be surprised and shocked; but according to your account I should be wrong to say that you had betrayed your pluralist beliefs. I should rather not be wrong about this. You say: 'Certainly a universalist cannot be a pluralist; but one can be a pluralist and believe

in the universal validity of one's own views.' *That's* what I can't quite take in: in fact it seems tantamount to a self-contradiction. It also seems to weaken the sense of 'pluralist' too much, so that it means only the ability to empathise with viewpoints one rejects; but I don't want to lose its stronger sense (which you espouse on other occasions?), in which it means the claim that ultimate values necessarily conflict; from which it follows (or does it?) that no universalist creed, however hedged about with empathy for other views, can be even coherent, let alone true. Or am I confusing universalism with monism? Monism is ruled out by pluralism, I take it, as a matter of definition. But perhaps non-monist universalism is conceivable.[19] What I want, in short, is that all universalist creeds should be ruled out a priori. (This does not mean ruling out individual universal *principles* – especially second-order ones of the kind I've just enunciated: I am talking rather of systems of belief which claim to lay down what is right for everyone everywhere always.) But it sounds from what you say as if I may have taken an illegitimate step, and be squeezing out of your pluralism more than it was intended to deliver. Alas.

I suspect that greater clarity here would require an explicit agreed definition of crucial terms – pluralism, universalism, monism, ultimate values, etc. – a project I defer ... [...]

PS I confess that my remarks about pluralism etc. above fall short of expressing what I want to say. Your writings repeatedly reject totalitarianism and authoritarianism of all kinds on the grounds that they are incompatible with the recognition of the truth of pluralism, and the consequent need for negative liberty. That's why I'm surprised to find you now saying that universalist religious systems aren't ruled out too,[20] since they seem to me to have a necessary streak of totalitarianism in them.

I am bound to confess that, twenty-seven years later, I still struggle with this issue, and am still unclear whether the confusion is my own or Berlin's, or perhaps both. I am reminded of a sentence that Berlin quotes from Hamann: 'On this marrowbone I gnaw, and shall gnaw myself to death on it.'[21] Even with the aid of clearer definitions and more consistent use of terms, I am not sure that clear understanding emerges. But that is no reason not to make the attempt.

Let me make a start by suggesting that value pluralism and cultural pluralism are more analogous than is sometimes allowed. Value pluralism is a thesis about the relationship between individual values, cultural pluralism about that between the constellations of value that constitute cultures. If cultures are simply additive constructs composed of individual values, nothing distinctive is achieved by talking in terms of cultures rather than values. But if cultures have a gestalt quality, whereby the wholes are greater than, and to that extent different from, the sum of their parts, then what is true at the cultural level may mimic what is true at the level of individual values, though without being reducible to statements at the latter level. This issue is addressed, for example, in Berlin's essay 'The Sense of Reality':

> [T]here is a Greek or German way of talking, eating, concluding treaties, engaging in commerce, dancing, gesturing, tying shoelaces, building ships, explaining the past, worshipping God, permeated by some common quality which cannot be analysed in terms of instances of general laws or effects of discoverable causes, recurrent uniformities, repetitions which allow common elements to be abstracted and sometimes experimented upon. (SR 19)

Elsewhere he suggests the somewhat bizarre hypothesis that the various components of a culture are more closely related to one another than they are to the equivalent components of other cultures, because they stem from an overall cultural essence, or centre of gravity (Herder's *Schwerpunkt*),[22] that infuses all its ingredients with the flavour, so to speak, of the culture in which they participate, so that 'it is no use judging these things from the point of view of some other century or some other culture' (RR2 73):

> There is a way in which Germans eat, drink, pass legislation, sit down, get up, do their hair, write poetry, dance – all these various activities, although they resemble the activities of other people who also do these things, have something in common which is impalpable, unanalysable, and German in character. The way in which the Portuguese eat and drink and dance, the way in which they produce their laws, study their history, the way they look, the way they get up and sit down, the kind of moral and political beliefs which they hold – these things have more in common with each other than they have with the corresponding behaviour on the part of the Germans. That is to say, the way in which the Portuguese do their hair is more like the way in which the Portuguese speak or move

or think or feel than it is like the way the Germans do *their* hair. There is something in common, no doubt, to the ways in which the Portuguese and the Germans eat, or the ways in which they walk, but there is something which is also not common.²³

Taken literally, the suggestion that (for instance) a German's walk is more like his way of drinking than it is like the walk of a Portuguese strikes me as comically exaggerated. But then, as Berlin observed, 'few new truths have ever won their way against the resistance of established ideas save by being overstated' (TCE2 149). We don't need to follow Berlin all the way here to recognise that a culture forms a coherent whole that differs from a mere list of its ingredients. In which case we can also acknowledge that cultures can be incommensurable, just like individual values. This doesn't mean that we cannot identify some features of a culture as better or worse than their equivalents (if any) in other cultures. It may even be that a culture (e.g. Nazism, if that may be called a culture) includes at its heart so many inhuman practices and false beliefs that we are unable to endorse it as a whole even after reform: it is rotten to the core and beyond rescue. But apart from such extreme cases, and leaving aside specific points of legitimate comparison and preference, we cannot rank cultures in the abstract: it is not better overall to be German than to be Portuguese, or vice versa.

Religious belief is sometimes supposed to be like culture in this regard, and this is one basis for religious toleration. Just as a German is not superior to a Portuguese just in virtue of being a German, so a Christian is not automatically superior to a Buddhist. The trouble with this analogy is that religions typically have at their heart, in a way that cultures don't, or needn't, quite specific factual or quasi-factual claims or beliefs that are incompatible with the claims or beliefs of other religions, and in this way are more like scientific theories than like cultures. Of course, one can treat all religious beliefs as myths, 'the poetry of the tribe',²⁴ but this is not the understanding of religious belief in the mind of crusaders and jihadists; nor would it work for them as a justification of their military campaigns if it were. Throughout history the great world religions have espoused fiercely held beliefs that are of their very essence incompatible with the beliefs of their rivals.

For this reason rival religious beliefs seem to me to operate, at any rate in part, more like rival scientific theories than like differing cultures. Of course, according to the Popperian demarcation of science, they cannot actually *be* scientific, because they are not open to empirical testing in the required manner.

But they ape scientific theories by claiming to rule out their competitors, which cultures don't, at any rate when not infected by aggressive nationalism. It is this understanding of religion that lies behind my doubts about Berlin's too tolerant (as I see it) attitude to universalist religious belief. This may become clearer when I quote from later exchanges between us, in which we continued to talk past each other, it seemed to me; and I blame myself for not being better able to clarify, at the time, what separated us.

I say 'at any rate in part' at the beginning of the previous paragraph because there is another aspect of religions in terms of which they are more like cultures, and so more susceptible to being held pluralistically. That is, religions combine assertions of alleged fact – 'There is no god but Allah', and 'Muhammad is the messenger of Allah' (Koran 3. 62, 37. 35, 38. 65, 47. 19; 48. 29); 'Jesus is the son of God' (Acts 9:20, 1 John 4:15, 1 John 5:5) – with moral teachings (alms-giving; 'as ye would that men should do to you, do ye also to them likewise', Luke 6:31). Some of the moral teachings of religion have a universal character, so that they are found in some form in almost any mainstream religious code (perhaps the 'golden rule' cited above is one of these); others are peculiar to specific religions (wearing the hijab). Different cultures emphasise different aspects of humanity (meekness, shame, service; power, military glory, self-assertion), and this goes for their religious traditions too. The extremist fanatic may regard every aspect of his religion as non-negotiable, but there is also an area within the tent of religion where it is possible to regard different moral paths as incommensurably valid, at least as far as we can tell: complete certainty in such matters is not available to us, or not available at all, whatever 'true believers' may claim.

This double nature of religion – this mix of quasi-factual assertion and moral precept (the boundary between the two is not always clear) – is one of the factors that complicates discussion of the relationship between pluralism and religion. To the extent that a religion makes factual claims that conflict with the scientific consensus (creationism), it does not make sense to view it pluralistically. Saying that the Earth is flat is not just another take on things that cannot be compared with rival views. But to the extent that religion is a source of moral guidance, very different approaches to life may be hard or impossible to rank. For this reason we should be on our guard against confusions that stem from an elision of religion's two aspects. Let us call them *religious articles* (of faith) and *religious precepts*.

I now return to my discussion with Berlin, bearing this distinction in mind in the hope that it may add a measure of clarity.

On 3 June 1991 Berlin reiterated his position in terms that didn't seem to advance matters greatly:

> I believe that if one is a pluralist, one can believe that one's position (normally deeply connected with one's *Kulturkreis*, as Schlick calls it) is that one can pursue a constellation of values in which one completely believes, but does not regard as objective, a priori etc.; and that, based on this, one can approve, condemn, doubt, question other people's constellations. What makes one a pluralist is that one can, by empathetic imagination, sometimes grasp what other people, in other circumstances, have come to pursue, and not simply rule it out as objectively valueless, only, at most, as disgusting, repellent, dangerous to all that one believes and is willing to live or die for, and therefore sometimes to be fought, perhaps to the point of killing.
>
> I do not regard the Nazis, e.g., as mad. The idea of sub-men is intelligible but grotesquely false. But if you accept it, then the horrors about the Jews may follow. You may have to kill people one regards as totally evil and dangerous from the point of view of one's own beliefs, and justify this by basing one's action on what a great many people, in a great many places and times, [have] accepted without question. But even that does not make this eternal, a priori, etc. Of course pluralism and monism are totally incompatible.
>
> Is this OK?

Here there seems once again to be a confusion between rejecting the values of others because they offend against our shared humanity, and rejecting them only because they are not the values of our own culture. Whether the values to which we appeal in either case are empirical or a priori seems at most a marginal issue. If what other people do seems 'disgusting, repellent, dangerous to all that one believes and is willing to live or die for, and therefore [...] to be fought, perhaps to the point of killing', surely one is deploying values that we derive from our common human needs and desires, not just values that belong to our own culture but not to that of the people whose conduct we abhor? Again, it is logically possible to be willing to die for culturally specific values, but I find it virtually impossible to imagine a case of this unless the holder of the values is mistaken about their status. Indeed, the willingness to die for a value seems to me a very good criterion of a belief that the value is central to the human condition.

However this may be, I tried again on 11 June 1991:

> I had a strongly Christian upbringing, and on that account, like so many others, experienced considerable anguish in the slow process of relinquishing (at Corpus) the beliefs I had been taught. I did this initially for pragmatic as much as for intellectual reasons: the evangelicals active in Oxford at the time maintained, plausibly I thought, that Christianity, if true, required one's total and uncompromising allegiance; I knew I was unequal to this challenge, like the rich man who was asked to give away all that he had.
>
> This was the main reason why I found your writings so exciting when I first encountered them. Your pluralism seemed to me (and still seems) to provide the intellectual endorsement I sought for my abandonment of the full-blooded religious beliefs offered me by parents and school (Lancing). If pluralism means that ultimate ends necessarily conflict, no moral system which provides otherwise can be espoused by a pluralist (though its espousal by others may certainly, *ceteris paribus*, be tolerated – this is a different matter).
>
> You repeatedly argue against all forms of monism, and the totalitarianisms based on them, on these grounds. Universalist religions seem to be clear cases of monism; and we know, of course, that they often turn totalitarian. What still puzzles me, therefore, is that you are not willing to agree without reservation to the proposition that a pluralist cannot in logical consistency subscribe to such a religion.
>
> You speak of our most central values as being in some sense not objective – a sort of halfway house between objectivity and relativity, though closer to objectivity. But the truth of pluralism, at least, is surely fully objective, as a logical truth? (It is a second-order truth, certainly, which perhaps counters the paradox that, though ruling out universalism, it is itself universally true.) If so, then whatever is inconsistent with it must be objectively false.

I am not sure what I had in mind in the last paragraph. Berlin described his own view as 'objective pluralism' (280/9). He did sometimes refer to Vico, Herder and others as relativists, but when it was pointed out that this got him into difficulties, he withdrew the label.

Leaving that aside, at this point we need to deploy a distinction introduced above, one that I hadn't formulated clearly to myself at this point, as the second paragraph of this extract shows. A religion (or a culture) is *internally pluralistic* if it allows that its rules, ideals, values can conflict with one another in incommensurable ways. It is *externally pluralistic* if it allows that rival religions (or cultures) have a claim to be no less valid. I remember once asking Bernard Williams if Jesus would have accepted pluralism. I ought to have distinguished between these two kinds of pluralism when I posed this question, because I suspect that Jesus would have been more likely to subscribe to one than to the other. Of course, mine was a ludicrously anachronistic enquiry, which Williams signalled by telling me that Jesus would not have accepted (or understood?) the terms in which it was made. Rather he would have said something like 'A man had three handfuls of sand ...'. Fair enough, but I should like to suggest that there is no reason why Jesus could not have been an internal pluralist, particularly given the way he distanced himself from the rule-bound morality of the Old Testament – 'Ye have heard that it hath been said, Thou shalt love thy neighbour, and hate thine enemy. But I say unto you, Love your enemies, bless them that curse you, do good to them that hate you, and pray for them which despitefully use you, and persecute you' (Matthew 5:43–4) – but that he could not have been an external pluralist, since he believed in only one way to salvation – again, 'I am the way, the truth, and the life: no man cometh unto the Father, but by me' (198).

Berlin's reply is dated 18 June 1991:

> I believe that one can be totally dedicated to a particular set of opinions, beliefs, loyalties, outlook and, at the same time, recognise the possibility of other such, which one rejects but believes to be equally semi-objective (as you more or less put it) – only not objective because, save for real fixities, things we cannot escape from, categories, time, space, material objects, incompatibility of values, truth, goodness etc. – save for these, nothing is. So I agree with you: if you wish to be a total Christian, you must reject everything else as falsehood; but you can be one if you allow the possibility of other faiths, provided that you reject them for yourself but do not regard others, who hold them, as inhuman or even inferior, but simply as different and to some degree incapable of full communication with yourself.

This does add something, by clarifying what the 'fixities' are by comparison with which everything else is unguaranteeable, and (importantly) including the incompatibility of values among them. But the last clause seems unsatisfactory because, for the Christian, adherents of other faiths must surely be not just different and impenetrable, but mistaken, even if venially so – either because of the lack of opportunity to know the truth, or because of the inability to recognise it. My reply (21 June 1991) addresses Berlin's last sentence:

> What you say after the semi-colon almost seems to take back what you say before it. Although the Christian can understand how others may come to hold other faiths, he cannot allow that their beliefs might be true. Non-Christians to him are indeed not inhuman or inferior, but they are nevertheless mistaken; not 'simply different', but wrong too. In short, a Christian, as a universalist, cannot be a pluralist, least of all in regard to other universalist faiths, which are necessarily incompatible with his own.
>
> But what really interests me is the obverse of this, which I might perhaps dub the limit of pluralist assent. [...] I wonder, in a word, whether your capacious natural inclination to applaud the maximum of cultural variety doesn't exceed the support available to it from your pluralism. Let me try to put this more clearly.
>
> If ultimate values collide, this is true universally. Therefore any constellation of values which necessarily involves the denial of this universal truth is in error. Just as the Fascists held an empirically false view about sub-men, so Islam, say, is mistaken because its proselytism rests on a false monist assumption, that one way is right for all mankind. As you point out, empathy, a key asset for a pluralist, allows us to understand from within how Fascists and Muslims reached their views; but where these views entail a falsehood, we cannot allow that they are logically legitimate. To understand is not to assent.
>
> Although, then, one of course wants to allow the maximum of cultural variety, one must not give intellectual assent to necessarily monist political or religious creeds. Toleration is another matter; but toleration, on the part of one who endorses cultural variety, easily looks like approval. It's a nice distinction, but important, it seems to me. I press it because sometimes what you write gives the impression that there are no credal (as opposed to behavioural) limits to cultural variety. I think you don't want to deny the validity of any outlook unless you have to, and this is surely to put the burden of proof in the right place; but I hope you won't deny that sometimes the answer *is* no.

My penultimate paragraph here confuses a denial of value pluralism ('ultimate values [do not] collide') with religious universalism ('one way is right for all mankind'), which are arguably logically independent, despite the prima facie oddity of saying that the one right way includes value-pluralist clashes. Nevertheless, one of the most regular targets of Berlin's criticism (too weak a word here: 'anathemas' is better) was indeed the belief in one right way. Because of this I find his more cautious approach in these exchanges with me puzzling. The major world religions surely have in common the conviction that there is indeed one right way; therefore one would expect Berlin to reject them (intellectually) without reservation. But he doesn't. Why not?

Berlin's final reply is dated 1 July 1991:

> I agree that, if you are a Christian and a universalist, then you think that persons who hold other faiths are mistaken and wrong. But it is possible to be sympathetic to false or implausible beliefs. If I were a Christian missionary, say in the eighteenth century, and found a sympathetic Red Indian, of course I would believe that what he believed was rubbish, but, quite apart from the probability of conversion, I could believe that his general spiritual attitude, set of values (supposing he was not keen on murder, scalping etc.) was sympathetic, moving, interesting and revealed certain things about reality which my faith perhaps did not. That is perfectly compatible with thinking that what he believed fundamentally was totally false. That is what I mean by imaginative insight, etc.
>
> Now for your obverse. Certainly to understand is not to assent; and even if I understand how Fascists or Muslims reached their views, I am not sure that I know what you mean by 'logically legitimate' – do you mean that it is logically possible both to believe what one does believe and also regard their views as legitimate? If so, I agree. But illegitimate views may also reveal and appeal. So I don't begin to assent to monist views – as you say, toleration is another matter. But toleration does not entail approval. The Catholic who decided to tolerate Protestantism cannot be accused of approving it. And I agree that there probably are credal limits to cultural variety – there are beliefs and attitudes which one rules out absolutely – understands but totally condemns, and would wish to eliminate, ideally. Is that OK? I hope so: if it isn't, I can do no more.

I signed off on 4 July 1991:

I will now spare you, both because of your implicit cry for mercy, and because we have probably got about as far as we can. Your latest remarks once again added a great deal, and reminded me that you are by nature more tolerant of what you see as intellectual misguidedness than I am.

III

Nevertheless, I continued to ask Berlin questions about large issues, and he continued to provide patient answers. One that struck me at the time was a response to my asking whether he was an atheist or an agnostic:

> I am neither an agnostic nor an atheist. My difficulty is that for me God is either an old man with a beard, in which I do not believe, or else something I do not understand – a spiritual presence, the timeless creator of the world (if impersonal), a transcendent being – I simply do not know what is meant. I am like a tone-deaf person who realises that other people can be moved by music; I respect this phenomenon but I have no idea what it is they experience. I am like a child faced with trigonometry. Since I don't know what 'God' means, I cannot be described as either denying or doubting him. (15 November 1991)

I replied on 19 November:

> Your description of your position on God is most welcome, if only because it almost exactly coincides with my own. I have long believed that we need an extra word: 'agnostic' means one who doesn't know; 'atheist' means one who doesn't believe; but there is no word for one who doesn't understand.

I also continued to pick away at my understanding of Berlin's pluralism and of his complementary belief in some form of common human morality. He had not written a systematic account of this topic, central though it was to his thought, and his scattered remarks were tantalisingly incomplete and, at times, frustratingly unclear or even (it seemed) contradictory. On 19 November 1991 I wrote:

In a letter to Beata Polanowska-Sygulska [A 281] you explain your view of the differing moralities of different people and groups by invoking Wittgenstein's metaphor of family resemblance. This brought me up short, because if face A resembles face B ... and face Y resembles face Z, it is possible for there to be no resemblance between face A and face Z. But surely it is essential to your view of the common core of human morality that some minimal content is common to all human moral outlooks properly so called? In that case isn't family resemblance too loose an image?

To this he replied on 22 November 1991:

> I think I do believe in some minimal identical content to all human moral outlooks. But even if this weren't so, and A was like B and B was like C and A was not in the least like P, let alone R and S, there would still be enough common element[s?] to any given series of cultures for there to be something intercommunicative. But it is true that if A and B had nothing in common, communication would break down and they could not be regarded as part of the same human race. I am not sure what follows – that you might work out.

This does not satisfy me. A family resemblance of this non-transitive kind is not enough to underpin the universal human ability to understand and communicate with all other human beings – an ability which Berlin repeatedly insists on. His second sentence, it seems to me, cannot be accepted.

On 28 January 1992 I ask: 'Do you regard religious belief as a private matter?' and 'Do you believe in evil?' The first question arose because Martin Gardner, in his review of CTH, asked various questions, one of which was about Berlin's religious beliefs, which he was puzzled not to find specified in a context where (in his view) they would have been entirely relevant.[25] He invited readers to provide answers, and I wrote telling him what I knew. He asked, surprisingly, to publish my letter (which I thought insufficiently interesting), and Berlin made no objection, except to a short sentence about his not being a believer. The sentence seemed harmless to me, and I expressed to Berlin the view that 'it is legitimate to ask writers who tackle large human issues what their religious views are, and why, and whether they think them of importance to their professional activities', adding 'but perhaps you would dissent?' Berlin annotated:

'Like J. S. Mill after a similar question, I dissent.' As for evil, here is what I wrote, with Berlin's annotations in square brackets:

> Do you believe in evil? I don't mean as an objective entity of any kind, but as an explanation for certain unacceptable actions, individual [yes] or collective. Your view that the Holocaust was to some extent based on an empirical error about the nature of Jews makes me wonder whether evil isn't so to speak a hypothesis of last resort for you [not quite]. Am I wrong [yes] to detect in your writings a preference for believing that men are mistaken rather than that they are bad? When confronted with someone like Saddam Hussein – or indeed any one of a mass of 'ordinary' criminals, murderers etc. – it seems more natural simply to say that we are concerned with a nasty piece of work. Do you regard such an explanation as a cop-out? [No. Saddam Hussein *is* evil.]

I was not satisfied with his Millian refusal of an answer on religious belief, and, on 7 February 1992, pressed the point:

> I'm intrigued that you join Mill in thinking that a man's religious views are private, and should like to know why. This is not, of course, because I want to dissuade you, but because I want to understand why you take this view. I can see that it is an arguable position for an ordinary private citizen (though even in that case questions of bearing witness might arise), but it seems far less easy to defend in the case of someone (like yourself) professionally concerned with the history and explanation of social and political affairs. Throughout history, after all, the deity has been supposed to be a crucial consideration in these spheres – even atheists argue that he is significant by his absence – so that it seems entirely natural to want to know what a social/political thinker's religious beliefs are, and why, and what their importance is in his theoretical views, and, if they seem to him to be irrelevant, why this is so. Or do you think that this sort of enquiry is guilty of a sort of taxi-driver naivety? If so, I take it most of the great philosophers of the past would disagree.

In the same letter I introduced a new topic:

Do you believe that it should be a democratic right to elect an anti-democratic government? I have in mind the case of Algeria, of course.[26] This problem is a paradox I can't get my mind round: it has the character of those self-referential logical paradoxes with which we are both familiar.

Berlin replied at length on 10 February 1992, expanding splendidly on the account of his religious beliefs that I have already quoted:

The privacy of religious views. My inspirer is John Stuart Mill, who, when he stood for Parliament, said he was ready to answer all questions except those about his religious views, which he said were no business of the public.[27] Rightly or wrongly, I admire that very much. There are certain things which people are not prepared to talk about, and why on earth should people who may be thinkers confess these things, even if they have had an influence on their views? After all, one may have all kinds of complicated views about one's parents – hatreds, resentments, sexual complications, God knows what, according to modern psychopathology. Yet even now I think probing enquiries about whether [John] Major could be said to have an Oedipus complex would not be regarded as altogether proper, at least by me and people who think like me.

However, I am perfectly prepared to tell you about myself and my religion. It is really quite simple. I was brought up in a Jewish family which was not strictly Orthodox – rather relaxed, like the kind of Church of England families who go to church once in a while but certainly not every Sunday, and have a vague belief about what Anglican Christianity teaches but don't allow it to disturb their daily thoughts. I remember that Lord Melbourne once said something like 'What are things coming to if religion is allowed to interfere with one's private life? That will never do.'[28] Anyway, I used to be taken to synagogue in Russia and in London, found it frightfully boring but not disagreeable, and rather enjoyed the hymns.

My difficulty was that when I began thinking about these things I could attach no meaning to the concept of 'God'. To me, he is either an old man with a beard, as Michelangelo paints him, and in that I cannot believe any more than a very, very great many other people of even a mildly sophisticated kind; or I don't know what is meant. The idea of a transcendent spiritual person, or a divine force which rules the world, or someone who created all things and directs the course of them, etc., means absolutely nothing to me. With my rigid, I fear, empiricism, I can attach no meaning to it.

So it's no good saying I'm an atheist – they know what the word 'God' means and just deny his existence. Nor an agnostic, who is not sure whether he exists or not. I am well beyond these things: I simply don't know what is meant. I am like a tone-deaf person who realises that other people listen to music with pleasure or even total absorption – I have no idea what the experience is.

On the other hand, I understand what are called religious feelings, up to a point, as expressed, let us say, in the cantatas or oratorios of Bach, or the masses of Mozart or Beethoven or Bruckner, and I have a certain empathy with that – the feelings, but not their object. Moreover, I go to synagogue, say four times a year at most, partly for sentimental reasons, to say a prayer for my parents when their anniversary falls, as they would have liked me to; partly because I like the hymns; also I like to identify myself with the Jewish community – I like to feel a member of a community which has existed continuously for three thousand years. But I perfectly understand the feelings of those of my Jewish friends who don't want to feel any of this, and never go.

How am I to explain all this, particularly in relation to my social, political, philosophical views? I don't see that it has much relevance.

The only occasions, I think, on which I am filled with religious feelings are not at church or mosque or synagogue services (all of which I enjoy up to a point), but when listening to certain types of music – say the Beethoven posthumous quartets.

On the other hand, I find that those who, like Freddie Ayer or Trevor-Roper, are bone-dry atheists and simply deny and denounce the whole thing (as Freddie used to, and Trevor-Roper, more cautiously, still does) – they do not begin to understand what men live by, which I claim to be able to do, because of this understanding, which I believe I possess, of religious emotion and the effect and influence which it has upon people's characters and lives. What more can I say to you?

You speak of great philosophers. Some would have agreed with me – Spinoza certainly, though God knows what he meant by 'God'. I don't know what *deus sive natura*[29] meant to him or to anyone. Matthew Arnold's description of him as a God-intoxicated man[30] seems to me absurd. I doubt whether Kant, who theoretically believed in God, or Hegel, who claimed to be Lutheran, could have made plain what they actually believed in. My master in this, as always, is David Hume, who would have agreed with me. I ought to add that religious poetry, say parts of the Bible, or the poetry of people like Herbert and Crashaw and Vaughan, certainly moves me; but what this has to do with my philosophical or political views, only God (if he exists – whatever that may mean) knows. [...]

Do democrats have a right to elect an anti-democratic government? In a democracy, where people have a right to vote for anyone they please, they certainly do. They'd be bloody fools if they did, and every legal step should be taken to dissuade them from doing so; but if they want to commit suicide I cannot see how this can be prevented, except by depriving democratic voters of the right to vote for anti-democratic governments – and that seems to me to go too far. This is hard on the democratic minority which is overcome by a huge, let us say pro-Fascist, majority – quite apart from Algeria – which is nearly what happened in Germany. But nobody can deny that the appointment of Hitler as Chancellor was legitimate in terms of the democratic laws of the Weimar Republic. It's rather like the question of censorship: should there be censorship of anti-social films, writings etc.? Why should pornography be censored, or racist attacks?

I have to modify the above statement. If there is a party, say the National Front, which begins to threaten to take over British institutions, then I think there is a case for trying to prevent it from doing so, by legislation of a non-democratic kind. But when this point is reached it is very difficult to say, and democrats might well disagree with me about this. Let me cite an old story to you. German conservatives in the Weimar Republic with authoritarian inclinations said to liberals, 'Under the liberal system, we are allowed to say whatever we like and vote whichever way we want to vote; that is your principle. Under us, you will be forbidden to express your views or vote in the wrong direction, because that's our principle. Anything wrong with that?' So we go back to the old business of having to ban, in free countries, any forces which seriously threaten freedom. Make of that what you will.

I replied on St Valentine's Day:

> Your account of your religious views is extremely interesting, and I am
> very glad and grateful to have it: the exact correspondence between your
> own rejection of the labels 'atheist' and 'agnostic' and my own gives me
> great satisfaction. Nevertheless, there remains a partial disagreement
> between us as to the privacy of religious views, and I fear I may be to
> blame for this, if, as I suspect, I did not make sufficiently clear exactly
> what I meant by saying that a political philosopher is surely bound to
> give an account of his religious opinions. [...]
>
> First of all, I was not urging that autobiographical details of one's
> religious background, experiences, feelings etc. should be made public:
> that, I readily concede, is a private area (though I have no inclination to
> insist on the point in my own case). What I meant was that one's meta-
> physical position on the deity (if I may so put it) – whether this position
> is positive, negative, open-minded or whatever – cannot help being a part
> of one's theoretical views if one is a political thinker, especially one who
> is interested in the history of his subject. Part of one's task, after all, is
> to describe and evaluate the political views of the great thinkers of the
> past, for many of whom God played a central role, without which their
> intellectual constructions would have collapsed. How can one avoid,
> then, delivering some sort of verdict on the theological content, so to
> speak, of the political ideas of the past?
>
> You do of course do this, by implication, a great deal. But I don't
> think you ever directly criticise religious beliefs, in the way that you do
> criticise, say, Communism and Fascism. And yet, is not religious belief,
> at any rate in its widespread universalist guises, as potent a source of
> intolerance, authoritarianism, totalitarianism, repression of negative
> liberty as any of the more specifically political creeds against which
> you rightly inveigh? If so, it deserves to be tarred with the same brush,
> possibly even more vigorously.
>
> I do not, of course, wish to claim (still less invite you to agree) that
> religion is all bad: that would be ludicrous. Like you, I do not want
> to deny the spiritual dimension, or holiness, or any of the panoply
> of goods whose origin is in some sense religious. Even though, also
> like you, I am somewhat tone-deaf on this wavelength, I agree in not
> wishing to be a Freddie Ayer on the subject. Equally, I don't suppose

you would wish to deny that many of the instincts that lie behind Communism are good ones. But it still seems clear to me that, once religious stirrings become co-ordinated into a body of universalist dogma, then we necessarily have the seeds of repression of freedom, and do not even have to wait for the dogmas to be distorted or perverted before they bear their repressive fruit. I have a strong suspicion that you will wish to dissent, but I don't understand why. For the same reason I don't understand why religion doesn't play a more leading role in your demonology of illiberalisms.

In the same letter I asked the first question in what eventually became a long series of attempts on my part, never entirely successful, to clarify Berlin's pluralism: 'Why is it not a consequence of pluralism that there can be no rational ordering of values? On what grounds can we say that a dedication to trainspotting is less noble than a dedication to the relief of suffering?'

Berlin replied on 18 February 1992:

I am the last person to deny that fearful crimes have been committed by religious intolerance. Everyone knows that: Jews, the Inquisition, Muslims, Catholics in seventeenth-century Paris, etc. etc. I think only Buddhists are comparatively innocent. But I don't think it is religion that is at fault, but clericalism – religion in authority, institutional religion. I am not engaged in writing the history of political doctrines, or giving marks to political thinkers, or analysing their views altogether. My writings, I should have thought, if anyone was interested in them, are enough to convey that I take an interest in the perversion of words such as 'liberty', that I am opposed to despotism, particularly of those who believe in the perfect solution (e.g. theologians), and therefore need not be explicit about all this. Of course if I had to write about Locke I'd have to bring in his views of the Church and Christianity, ditto Hobbes; but if I write about Kant, of course he did have religious views of sorts, but they are very extrinsic to what is most important, or considered to be most influential, most important, in his writings. Hegel said he was a Lutheran, but it is not very important that he said this, it doesn't appear to make much difference to what otherwise he says.

Of course philosophers' views of God make a difference to their views; but I don't see why I need go into that; I am not writing biographies of philosophers, and I don't attack Fascism as such, except indirectly; Communism, yes, because that depends on misuse of certain liberal concepts. In general my position with regard to persecution is clear enough, I think. What is not so clear is what room should be made by people like me for religious sects: is it all right for Muslims to insulate themselves and take very little part in general English culture? What do I feel about Sikhs and their battles against (Muslim) Pakistan and (Hindu) India? Or about the union of a certain section of the Russian Church with nationalism and neo-Fascism, as well as the Communist *nomenklatura*? I don't think I need go into that: it is quite clear, if one is a liberal, what one's views must be about all that, and there I rest it. The part played by religion in the thought of political philosophers is a subject for philosophical biography or motivation of their political views, not of great interest to me.

There is no need for a pluralist not to prefer one ultimate value to another, if they come into conflict; nor to condemn somebody else's values if they are opposed to, or even intolerant of, his own – they remain objective nevertheless. The fact that there is no overarching principle does not entail that individuals, groups, parties, Churches etc. can't create one for themselves. I am prepared to say that, as Vico said, Homeric values are not ours, but they are ultimate values; and you can give reasons for saying that, ultimate as they may be, they clash with one's own, and therefore must take second, third, fourth place. I see no contradiction there. In the end one sometimes has to plump – one just believes what one believes, acts as one acts. If you are asked for the reason, you cannot always give it – but that again does not entail non-rating.

The last paragraph reiterates some of the problematic views that I have already discussed, without answering my specific question directly. Evidently I could not face repeating my difficulties at the time; nor can I face doing so now. I replied on 3 March 1992:

Thank you very much for your letter of 18 February, in which you explain (most helpfully) why you do not inveigh against religion more specifically or at greater length than you do. Though I understand what you say, there remains a difference between us on this, whose explanation may perhaps be partly autobiographical rather than intellectual. Briefly, religion seems to me to have illiberalism far more deeply in its bones, so to speak, than you allow. It seems to me not to need clericalism etc. to make it go bad. Its very espousal of revelation as against empiricism, and still more its ineradicably monist and perfectibilian tendencies, mean for me that I cannot regard it as a neutral ingredient of life with no inbuilt bias towards the good or the bad. As in all cases where I cling to a view which you do not endorse, I expect that I shall in the end see that (and why) you are right; but there's no good pretending one believes something before one actually does.

To an extent one might say that the political message of your writings has now become orthodox – see Fukuyama on the end of history? – but that its implications for religion have still to come to fruition, certainly as regards Islam and other fundamentalist movements. That's another reason why I am tempted to place greater emphasis on this aspect of what you have written.

Goodness knows what I meant about Fukuyama: I cannot now make sense of this, unless I was simply referring (I hope ironically) to the alleged final worldwide triumph of liberal democracy as viewed by Fukuyama. In his reply of 10 March 1992 Berlin wrote: 'Fukuyama is talking nonsense: his prophecies cannot be fulfilled in either the short or long term. I have not [read], and shall not read, his book.'

It was at this point that my attempt fully and clearly to understand Berlin's view of the relationship between pluralism and religious belief was effectively abandoned. It seems to me now that I ought to have tried harder to set out my reasons for being dissatisfied with his explanations; and that, had I succeeded in this, we might have come nearer to an understanding. That we didn't remains one of the greatest regrets I have about our correspondence.

However, one last exchange took place which made me feel that the gap between us might not be so wide as I felt. At some point in the early 1990s, I wrote a piece about pluralism and religion entitled 'Taking Pluralism Seriously', to try to settle my accounts with the frustrating discussions reported in this chapter. I could not relinquish the belief that Berlin's pluralist ideas had clear implications for religious belief, even though he had not made these explicit in his published writings, and appeared to resist them when I made my case to him. This was the one Berlinian topic on which I felt I had something to say, possibly even something new; I had chewed it over in my mind endlessly, and pressed Berlin on it relentlessly. It was time to go public and expose my argument to criticism.

I tried and failed to publish the piece in a philosophical journal (it was rejected, ostensibly, on what seem to me the comical grounds that it did not adequately discuss the secondary literature: so much for the works of Aristotle, Plato and Wittgenstein, among others), but it did appear in 1995 in a Dutch translation in the cultural periodical *Nexus*.[31] My thesis was the same as the one I had put to Berlin: that, if one took his pluralism seriously, then most mainstream varieties of religious belief had to be rejected, since they were inherently monistic. This is a very politically incorrect thing to say, but that is of course irrelevant to the question of whether it is true. As should by now be clear, I was not advocating (nor do I support) intolerance of religious belief and practice: my challenge was intellectual, logical. I did not at this stage make the distinction between internal and external pluralism that I introduced above. I should now say that it is cultural pluralism rather than value pluralism that is inconsistent with religion, since a religion may perhaps be internally pluralistic. But I believe that this clarification can be grafted on to the argument without invalidating it.

In 1996 I showed the piece to a philosopher who had asked me if I had written anything in this area, and received a somewhat negative response. This came to Berlin's notice in the form of a letter telling him, on the basis of my piece, that I was no philosopher, and he asked to see what I had written. I sent him the piece, and he wrote me a letter about it dated 21 January 1997. It would be entirely characteristic of him if this letter is more generous than just, but I do not believe that he would have written as he did if he had seriously disagreed with me. Naturally I was pleased that he didn't, and felt that at last, perhaps, I had managed to make clear to him my argument about this topic, and to secure his assent to it.

> I have read your piece on 'Taking Pluralism Seriously' with great interest, and indeed admiration. I think it is a splendid piece, you need not be too modest about it – I am glad it was published, even if only in Dutch – and I think I agree with almost every word you say. There are points where I might deviate from you, or think you hadn't got it quite right, but they are so minor that I am not going to list them; if you really want me to do that, I'll read it again and then we can go through them when we next meet – but honestly, they are so small that it's not worth doing.

The only point that struck me at all was that you give the impression (without positively saying so – you deny it to begin with, but then give the opposite impression) that all ultimate values collide. As you know, they do not: there is nothing wrong with happiness and liberty, knowledge and equality, etc. That is the only place where I think you slightly mislead the reader about your own view. Anyway, I congratulate you on it, I think it is a fine piece, I really do.

In my reply of 30 January 1997 I said that I should be interested to know where he thought there were mistakes, but in the event we did not discuss the piece further.

11

THE MORAL CORE AND THE HUMAN HORIZON

In early 1992 Berlin was asked to write a philosophical self-portrait for Thomas Mautner's *A Dictionary of Philosophy*,[1] which was to contain several such entries by living philosophers. He dictated a piece that was far too long, and asked Roger Hausheer and me to reduce it to the requisite 750 words. We prepared separate versions, and mine was used, probably only because it observed the word limit. The article contains a discussion of pluralism and relativism that led me to pose a question to Berlin on Friday 13 March 1992:

> I don't even know if the question makes sense, but let me put it to you. Briefly, it is this: What is it, for you, that plays the principal (exclusive?) role in rebutting relativism? Is it the 'moral core', the fact that all known value systems share a minimal conception of the demands of common humanity? Or is it the capacity for empathy with values we don't share? Is it perhaps sometimes one, sometimes the other, depending on which values are claimed to be relative? I could expand the question, but won't at this stage, in case your answer takes the wind out of my sails.
>
> You may say that my two candidates are different aspects of the same phenomenon, so that it is artificial to prise them apart. Perhaps you believe that our common humanity both gives rise to a shared core of basic values, and enables us to empathise with the unshared values at the periphery of this core. Relativism, then, is false as it is ordinarily understood because it is true in a wider sense – i.e. because our values are relative to our humanity – rather than because our values are prescribed by some suprahuman edict.
>
> I attach a diagrammatic representation of your view, drawn up in an attempt to clarify my own thoughts, and I should be interested to know how wide of the mark this is. On it you will find [...] some other questions that occur to me, e.g. in connection with your notions of objective value and ultimate value. If I am talking complete drivel, you must say so! [...]

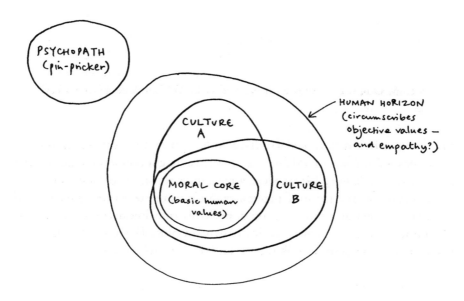

Rules:

Nothing within the human horizon conflicts with the moral core.

To be an objective value, a value must be part of a
constellation of values which includes the moral core.

Queries:

If this view is true, are there such things as subjective
values, or only pseudo-values? If the latter, all true values
are objective, and the epithet 'objective', used of values,
is redundant?

Are the limits of empathy indeed the same as the human
horizon, or can we empathise with the psychopath?

Are all true values ultimate, or are there non-ultimate
values (such as?)?

My 1992 Euler diagram, allegedly depicting some
aspects of Berlin's view of cultural pluralism

In [*Conversations with Isaiah Berlin*] you say (p. 114) that your belief in general moral truths doesn't assume something unalterable, that you cannot guarantee anything against change. It seems to me that the change that would be needed to upset these truths would be so vast that, if it took place, we should not be dealing with a world that was recognisably continuous with the one we know; but, leaving that aside, would it not be true to say that, although you don't assume something unalterable, you do assume something essential to human beings as we know them? That is, if the faculty of intuition into the truths of reason (the faculty you say you lack) is seen not as giving access to some sort of a priori truth independent of experience, but only to truths that hold, as a matter of experience, of all humans that have yet lived (with possible qualifications to cover primitive or pre-civilised cultures), then it is no longer something mysterious. Truths of reason would by that account be just true generalisations about human nature, in other words. You may reply that that is exactly what truths of reason are supposed not to be.

A little explanation may help to make sense of the diagram. When discussing what I call the 'moral core', Berlin standardly used the formulation (of Catholic orthodoxy, ironically) due to St Vincent of Lérins, 'what has been believed everywhere, always, by everyone'.[2] I note in passing that the criterion for moral universality implied here is agreement, not contribution to the common human good. The two criteria do not necessarily produce the same results, and attention to the second in preference to the first is one of the sources of moral progress. Berlin often fails to keep them separate.

The psychopathic 'pin-pricker' is the figure Berlin often used to illustrate what he meant by attitudes and/or behaviour that would fall outside the 'human horizon'. Here is one version of this recurrent example:

> Supposing a man comes along and he pushes pins into people, and I say to him: 'Why do you do this?' The man says: 'Because I enjoy it.' I say: 'Are you enjoying giving pain to people?' 'No, not particularly.' That would be an intelligible aim. Sadism I understand. Then I ask him: 'But why do you do it?' And he says: 'Because I rather like it.' 'But you realise that it causes them great pain?' And he says: 'Yes, I do.' 'But then, they might do it to you.' 'No, they wouldn't, because I am stronger than they are, and I would stop them.' So far so good. But then I say: 'But why

do you do it?' And he answers: 'But I like doing it. I like pushing pins into resilient surfaces.' 'If I give you a tennis ball, would that be just as good?' 'Of course, just as good', he replies, 'as human skin.' At this point I stop understanding him. To talk to a man for whom inflicting pain is something of no importance, doesn't make any difference, is totally puzzling. I repeat: 'You are inflicting pain'; and he says: 'So what? Why do you mention it?' This 'So what?' means that we do not live in the same world. I call him mad. People in his kind of mental condition are locked up in asylums, not prisons.[3]

The human horizon, then, is the outer limit of what counts as human or sane, the limit beyond which empathy cannot penetrate. The values that fall within it are called 'objective' by Berlin because they are not arbitrary, varying from person to person (as some relativists hold), unintelligible to others, but stable features of the world based in human nature, open to public empirical view like the world's other contents. Because we are human, we can understand what other humans are up to even if they are pursuing values different from our own: we can imagine ourselves in their shoes, and see the world from where they are standing. Berlin also regards these values as 'ultimate', non-instrumental: 'There is a world of objective values. By this I mean those ends that men pursue for their own sakes, to which other things are means' (CTH2 11, PSM 9).

It has to be said that Berlin's use of the metaphors of core and horizon was sometimes muddled and inconsistent, as are some of the letters he wrote to me on this topic. Sometimes Berlin presents the two metaphors as different accounts of the same phenomenon: the 'corizon', as one might call it. But this is a problematic view, if only because the metaphors don't work well together, each representing only part of the situation in need of characterisation. To posit a core of shared values is to imply a periphery of unshared values, values which on Berlin's account we can nevertheless understand. But to posit a horizon within which all comprehensible values fall leaves open the question of whether the values within it can be divided into those we all share and those we don't. In order not to get bogged down in tedious semantic discussions, one simply has to make a decision, for the purposes of exposition, about how one will describe the landscape of human values. My diagram is an attempt to do just that.

To leave the diagram, the core and the horizon aside for a moment, let me attempt to (re)state Berlin's view head-on. There is such a thing as human nature, and this sets limits to what is recognisably human; our shared nature enables us to understand, to empathise with, other human beings, however remote they may be from us in time or space or conviction. People do understand one another, even across great divides, and this is a rebuttal of relativism, which holds that there is no common ground between us that enables us to communicate with, understand and identify with others. The common ground that does exist need not lead to agreement, but it does prevent blank incomprehension of the inner life and motivations of others, the incomprehension that we can experience with regard to other species, or an alleged divinity, or aliens, or the material world. One may doubt just how wide this mutual comprehension between ourselves and others really is, particularly when the others are at an extreme historical or anthropological distance from us: Berlin often mentions Vico's belief that 'appalling effort'[4] (TCE2 147; cf. POI2 72) is required to enter the minds of such people, but he takes it as read, without argument, that it can be done. For the purposes of this discussion I assume that he is right.

I should make clear at this point that my account of Berlin's view, though accepted by Berlin himself when I put it to him, is not universally accepted by his critics.[5] In particular, George Crowder, author of one of the best books about Berlin's ideas, *Isaiah Berlin: Liberty and Pluralism* (2004), doubts whether it represents either Berlin's view, or the true state of affairs, as perspicuously as it might. He suggests that it does not fit a plausible alternative understanding of moral universals, according to which what really differentiates one culture from another is not that it endorses a different subset of possible human values, but that it interprets the same, universal, 'thin' values in different 'thick' ways. 'Thin' and 'thick', roughly speaking, refer to the degree of abstractness or specificity of a value: so a thin value would be consideration of others, and a thick interpretation of that value would be giving up one's seat on a bus for someone whose need to sit down was greater than one's own.

How can we decide between these two interpretations? It depends on our criteria for individuating values. And since values are not natural kinds, as I have already noted, the choice of criteria is bound to be somewhat arbitrary. We can say that culture A pursues thick value X and culture B thick value Y, or that cultures A and B both pursue thin value P, though in the different thick forms P_x and P_y. If X and Y are intuitively related, the latter locution may be more natural; if not, the former. In borderline cases it may be hard to choose. Let us leave both options open for the moment, and return to this issue shortly.

On Crowder's understanding, the 'moral core' in the diagram would be much wider, perhaps coextensive with the human horizon (in which case the notion of a 'core' becomes inappropriate), but at any rate containing, rather than contained by, the different cultures. For Crowder, such a view has the advantage of emphasising, as the diagram does not, that the shared values of the 'moral core' must be very thin, or highly generic, compared with the thicker, more specific, values of particular cultures. But must they? How thin is 'Thou shalt not kill' (Exodus 20:13)?

Crowder also sees in this alternative view advantages for interpreting Berlin's position. In particular, he argues, it helps to answer two questions. First, how can we empathise with the values of other cultures without sharing those values? Crowder interprets Berlin's 'human horizon' as meaning that we are identified as human by the fact that there are certain generic ends that are pursued by all human beings. It is because we have 'values in common with these distant figures' that we can understand them (CTH 11). On this reading, the shared moral core is coextensive with the human horizon, and the metaphor of the core might simply be dropped.

I disagree with Crowder's characterisation of the human horizon *as an account of Berlin's view*, whatever its independent plausibility may be. In Berlin's usage the horizon circumscribes not the values we all pursue, but the values that make sense to us all because of our humanity. As Berlin says, we don't all actually pursue all the values that are comprehensible to us: 'There is a finite variety of values and attitudes, some of which one society, some another, have made their own' (CTH 79). And again: 'all human beings must have some common values or they cease to be human, and also some different values else they cease to differ, as in fact they do' (POI 12). If this is right, the proposed equivalence between core and horizon fails. Crowder's response is that values we understand but don't pursue are in fact just different thick versions of thin values we pursue in other forms: which returns us to the question of whether there is in fact a substantive difference between our two views. I think there is. To use one of Berlin's examples, the Homeric values of martial valour, honour and glory are often contrasted with negative contemporary attitudes to militarism. It strikes me as artificial to say that pacifism and militarism are present in all personal value systems in some more or less disguised form; but if I am a pacifist I can still *understand* a warmonger, even if there is not a warlike bone in my body.

A second question, conversely, is this: How is our capacity to empathise with other cultures whose particular values we do not share evidence (as Berlin thinks it is) of universal values that we share or ought to share? Crowder's answer is that we are able to empathise with the values of other cultures because they are differing specific interpretations of more generic values that we do share – that is, even in the most alien practices we can recognise, if only dimly, our own most fundamental purposes.[6] For example, the Aztec practice of human sacrifice can be understood as a particular expression, however wrong-headed, of a universal concern with fertility and regeneration. Edward Westermarck takes this view when he describes human sacrifice as 'a method of life-insurance – absurd, no doubt, according to our ideas, but not an act of wanton cruelty'.[7]

Crowder allows that not all values may be explicable in this way – as either thin human values or particular expressions of these – but suggests this as a possible hypothesis for future investigation. He believes that Berlin might have been attracted to it, despite his approval of my diagram. Such thoughts remain speculative because Berlin's actual comments in this area are so scattered, unsystematic and lacking in concrete examples. However, there is one Berlinian case to which the Crowder model seems clearly not to apply, and that is the case of new values that emerge historically, such as sincerity, authenticity and variety, which are not found, according to Berlin, until the eighteenth century. If Berlin is right, what are the thin values of which these are thick versions? On my own account such new values (of which there may be more still to come) are potentially recognisable by human beings, given human nature, but are not discovered or invented until the cultural or technological conditions are right for them to emerge. Human nature contains within it unactualised potentialities which, when realised, are recognisable as authentically human, just as revolutionary developments in music and art cannot be anticipated, but may eventually win recognition when they occur. The land reclaimed from the sea in the Netherlands can be used for agriculture, but not until the dykes are built and the sea excluded.

I now return to my 1992 exchange with Berlin, who replied on 13 April:

> The basic reason for rejecting relativism is the 'moral core', but the reason for pluralism, which is also incompatible with relativism but a separate doctrine, is, as you say, empathy with values which we may or may not share but which belong to other cultures. I do not see why this answer takes any wind out of any of your sails. You are right to say that I believe relativism to be false on both grounds; on the other hand, it is also true that without the first ground – i.e. the common ground between the vast majority of systems of values in different cultures or

among different persons – the second ground would not work. Is this confused? I do hope not.

Your diagram is excellent, and I think does represent my views.

As for your queries: there are such things as subjective values, which are not ultimate in any way and may not be capable of being empathised with – e.g. questions of taste, minor preferences and the opposite. I may be totally unable to empathise with people who can't bear music – I merely note that there are such people and this is true of them. So I think that in the case of non-ultimate and sometimes rather trivial differences of taste, you could speak of subjective values in a perfectly valid way – i.e. no common ground presupposed in such cases: total lack of sympathy, or maybe understanding.

In my view you could not empathise with a psychopath, but I may be wrong about this. I think some people claim to be able to do so. If they do, they do. But my conception of a psychopath is somebody with whom there is no communication.

Are there non-ultimate true values? What is meant by 'true'? Values are values – they are true for those for whom they are true. Or what do you mean?

I am not sure that I have dealt with these points as clearly as I should have done – if so, please write to me again, even if it drives Pat off her rocker.

Since I did not immediately reply to these points in substance, let me comment on them briefly now. First, I don't understand why non-ultimate values should be regarded as subjective, as against objective ultimate values. I suppose Berlin may mean that the objectivity of ultimate values consists (at least in part) of the fact that they are widely shared. But so is a taste for sweet things, and a liking of rhythmical music. It seems to me that values are all equally subjective, or equally objective, or both, depending on how these opposed terms are defined, but that they differ, rather, in *importance* and *variability* – aspects of value that are not (fully) captured by the objective/subjective distinction.

Berlin once wrote a piece entitled 'Subjective versus Objective Ethics' (SVOE), which I published as an appendix to PIRA. Here he writes:

the rules of political and social behaviour, and above all of moral action, which are intended to govern men's inner and outer lives, are obviously of supreme importance; and seem to require a more solid basis than the vagaries of individual temperament, or casual whims subject to transient influence. (PIRA2 325)

Quite so. But Berlin does not provide such a basis in the rest of this text, merely observing that 'value statements, for example the statements of politics, are neither subjective nor objective, but wholly different in kind from the kinds of statements which are so'. He does not go on to specify what this difference in kind consists in, though in a letter of 20 July 1993 he wrote: 'that is a theme to which I return much later – non-a-priori generally accepted values, etc.'.

This general acceptance is one of the criteria on the basis of which, against SVOE, he later calls values objective. Objectivity now seems to be a matter of values being widespread and/or important and/or ultimate and/or prescribed by human nature and/or enjoying a status defined by some unspecified combination of these criteria. Berlin nowhere states his position fully and explicitly, which may of course be because it was not clear in his own mind, except perhaps at an intuitive level. However, it seems right to give him the benefit of the doubt, at any rate in the first instance, and to see if we can elicit from his various incomplete statements a position that is both coherent and plausible. This is what I started to attempt in my diagram.

In early 1993 Berlin asked me to draft for the *Philosopher's Index* an abstract of his reply to Ronald H. McKinney's article 'Towards a Postmodern Ethics: Sir Isaiah Berlin and John Caputo'.[8] He amended my draft to read as follows:

> In correcting some misunderstandings of his position, Berlin clarifies his own ethical views. His empirically based conception of common human values sets a minimum standard of tolerable life, and thus a limit to the range of conflicting moral and cultural options open to men and societies. Everyone is entitled to resist whatever falls outside this wide, variegated 'human horizon'. Berlin sharply distinguishes pluralism and relativism, and rejects all a priori views of value. He explains his attitude to those who reject humanity's shared values. He suggests when such dissenters should be regarded as deranged, and when as criminal.

I was stimulated by reading Berlin's text to ask him for further clarification of core and horizon, about which I was badly confused:

Are the common moral core and the human horizon two different things, or the same thing, or different aspects of the same thing? I had previously thought they were two things, as follows. The common core is the minimum moral content of any acceptable morality, culture, way of life: e.g. in general murder is wrong, the truth should be told. Any attitude to life which rejects this core fails to meet the requirements of humanity. The human horizon, on the other hand, sets an outer limit to the variousness of the further moral and cultural components that are added to the core to make the different moralities and cultures the world contains. Human nature is not infinitely variable, and accordingly there are limits to what we should be prepared to count as an intelligible human way of life. You helpfully refer to 'the fence that encloses the plural values' [CTH2 318].

But one or two of your remarks make me suspect that I may be making too clear a distinction between core and horizon. You say that someone who attempts to 'doom human societies to perdition' would be placed 'beyond the horizon of common human values' – both notions in a portmanteau phrase. You also say that 'the notion of one civilisation provoked by and likely to destroy another' seems to you 'not consistent with a world of minimum common human values [i.e. the core], and so beyond what might be called the normal range of choices that are available if human society is to be able to continue [i.e. the horizon]' [CTH2 317].

Can we, then, distinguish a failure to embody the core from a failure to fall within the horizon? As an example of the latter you instance your familiar pin-pusher. You say his behaviour is 'beyond intelligibility, i.e., outside the horizon of available, chooseable, ultimate values' [CTH2 318]. But might one not equally say that it offends against a principle contained in the core, viz. that one should not gratuitously cause pain to others? I suppose anything outside the horizon will also conflict with the core, but not everything that conflicts with the core lies outside the horizon: is that it? In that case, isn't the man who wishes to doom human societies to perdition against the core, but within the horizon?

Your apparent equation of being morally unintelligible with falling beyond the horizon raises my other main difficulty. If the two are the same, there should be no cases which are intelligible but beyond the horizon. You say of sadomasochists, Byronic heroes, amoral outlaws, ultraNietzschean tragi-Romantics that you do understand them, but you also reject their values. Are these cases to be rejected not because they fall outside the horizon, but because they offend against the core?

If so, not all that lies within the horizon is acceptable. Indeed, you say that there may be ultimate values which you recognise as human but which repel you, and which you are prepared to resist with all possible means. (Can you give me an example, so that I can be sure I understand you aright?) But is it not part of the point of pluralism that, while you do not wish to adopt others' values, you accept that they represent equally legitimate choices from among the available options, and should therefore not be rejected? By this account anything that falls within the human horizon is acceptable, though not, unless it also falls within the core, mandatory. Perhaps one can resolve the dilemma by saying that, to be acceptable, a morality must both fall within the horizon and be consistent with the core. In that case the values you wish to resist repel you because they offend against the core. But it sounds as if you may rather be saying that there are values which pass both tests and yet you will fight against them. Or not? [...]

I have one more, unrelated, query. You say that, according to your view of relativism, the values of another society would be 'arbitrary, or, at best, opaque, although not necessarily unintelligible'. I have tried, and failed, to think of examples of values that would be arbitrary but intelligible. Can you help? [...]

I have been trying to find the passage(s) of Weber which are alleged to anticipate your central pluralist ideas. I enclose one candidate:[9] not, I have reason to believe, the best. Do you know it? Do you think it does say the same as you (albeit incomparably more darkly), or not really?

Berlin replied on 2 March 1993:

The common moral core and the human horizon are two different aspects of the same thing, as you suspect. They are not two things. The common core is not so much the content of any morality, culture etc. as the limit of acceptability. The variety of human sets of values, cultures etc. are delimited by the common core or horizon, but are not distinct from it, in the sense that they are the ingredients of all the members of the variety, and without them the structure of the variety itself cannot stand, i.e. be intelligible (which is my criterion for identifying the various values, cultures etc. that enter the plurality, which are, as you rightly say, not infinite in number). I should therefore maintain [that] 'the failure to embody the core' is not distinguishable 'from a failure to fall within the horizon'. I cannot understand the pin-pusher; therefore for me he falls outside the horizon of chooseable ultimate values. I can understand someone who wants to destroy a civilisation, or cares nothing about human life, etc.: that falls within the human horizon, within the common core, but it is unacceptable to anyone who accepts my constellation of values – and that, I would maintain, of a great many other people at a great many times in a great many places.

'A great many' is variable. To be a pluralist is to be able to put oneself in the position of someone pursuing values very different from, and indeed perhaps wholly hostile to, one's own:[10] I can reject the Homeric world (as described by Vico), which is brutal, mean, savage etc., although generative of masterpieces, while understanding it. All I can do is to assert my own conception of what is permissible and what is not, believe or hope that this forms a spectrum true for a great many people in a great many places, etc., though of course nowhere near everybody – in other words, distinguish sharply what is acceptable and what is intelligible. Hume's man who wants to destroy the world to assuage the pain in a little finger is to me literally unintelligible – that goes beyond the core and the horizon. There is a difference between [such a man and?] a savage, Byronic outsider, or the Nazis, or those who think that blacks are not fully human beings, nearer animals than ourselves, etc., [whom we can understand?] while going to war against them without compunction. Why? Because I defend the only civilisation without which I do not think life is worth living – others obviously disagree. I should maintain that it was not just I personally but a great many other people who form my culture – and a good many other people in the past, and one hopes in the future – [who] accept large portions of what I believe, i.e. look on the world in terms of horizons that greatly overlap with mine. But, in the end, I believe what I believe, defend what I defend, what is ultimate for me is ultimate for me – while still understanding the purposes of others which will destroy everything that I regard as minimally valuable – i.e. without which I do not think life in my sense can be lived – and therefore I wish to oppose with all that I have, unto death if need be, in extreme cases. In that sense [...] the man who wishes to doom human societies is within the core and within the horizon – I may be able to understand his Nietzschean motives, but he is an enemy unto death.

I interrupt here to throw up my hands. This reply, as well as being unclear, is plainly quite inconsistent with what Berlin said earlier about my diagrammatic representation of his view, in which core and horizon are clearly concepts with quite different extensions – core values being a subset of values within the human horizon. One cannot accept both accounts. So which (if either) should one prefer?

One reason for preferring the earlier account is that it enables us to distinguish between two boundaries: one enclosing the minimum requirements, the other the maximum variety, of human morality. From this standpoint the core contains the universal components of all moralities, and the horizon circumscribes the additional components some, but not all, of which are also found in any given morality; beyond the horizon lie the inhuman and the insane.

If, however, the two metaphors are alternative ways of referring to the same boundary, we are a boundary and a distinction short. We can now separate only the human from the inhuman, without being able to subdivide the human into the universal and the culturally variable, unless the (different) thin/thick distinction is to stand in for such a subdivision. This represents a regrettable loss of explanatory power.

On the other hand, if Berlin clearly understood the metaphors in the way my diagram suggests – and despite the fact that he said he did – he could not have described their meaning in the way he does in this later letter, which, taken at face value, supports George Crowder's interpretation as described above (232–3), with the important rider that malign as well as benign conduct falls within the horizon. Moreover, the metaphor of a core is not Berlin's, for all that he accepted and adopted it when deployed by me. But the idea that the metaphor attempts to capture is certainly there at the heart of his thought, since he often spoke of a universal moral minimum (like Hart's minimum content of natural law, as we have seen): again, 'that minimum of moral values accepted by all men without which human societies would disintegrate, and from which, for quasi-biological causes, men cannot depart without perishing' (L4 206). And this description of a minimum implies the distinction between core values and peripheral values that is obscured or lost by the Crowderian version. Not that Crowder minds this, since for him all culturally specific human values are thick versions of thin universal values, so that there are no values outside the core but within the horizon.

Can this muddle be eradicated? I think so. The problem lies in the metaphors, not in the reality they attempt to portray. This might be taken to mean that the metaphors are best dispensed with, on the grounds that they obscure rather than clarify. But I am reluctant to discard them too easily, since they do help us – or me, at any rate – to visualise Berlin's understanding of human morality, so long as we recognise their limitations, and do not expect them to march in step at every point with the reality they aim to elucidate.

The main difficulty is that the core has a dual function. First, it specifies the ingredients that must be present in any acceptable moral system; second, it provides criteria according to which we reject certain attitudes as inhuman. These are not two separate functions, but positive and negative aspects of the same principles. Each core value or principle both requires something from every human being (e.g. respect for life) and excludes its negation (e.g. indifference to life) as inhuman. Core values are both a subset of all human values, and also determinants of the inhuman. It is impossible to represent this dual role in a diagram of the kind I proposed, since such a diagram portrays only the relationships of inclusion and exclusion between different sets. This is why I appended to my diagram the rule 'Nothing within the human horizon conflicts with the moral core', in order to express the second function of the core – its determination of where the horizon falls. I might also have expressed this, perhaps more clearly, by saying 'Anything that conflicts with the core values falls outside the human horizon.'[11] The diagram portrays the first (set-theoretic) aspect of the core, and the letter I am currently quoting emphasises the second (criterial) function. We cannot say that one interpretation is right, the other wrong, since they attend to different aspects of the situation under examination. Let me try to clarify this by suggesting an analogy.

Consider the class of structurally sound buildings. All of these must satisfy certain core requirements, for example that they have adequate foundations, specified in terms of depth, width, location, materials used and so forth. Provided these requirements are met, an indefinitely large range of structurally satisfactory buildings can be erected on the foundations. This could be illustrated by a Euler diagram showing that good foundations are part of a subset of essential architectural properties within a larger set of all possible properties of sound buildings. But there is also a limit to this larger set, a horizon of architectural possibility such that buildings with properties beyond this horizon will sooner or later collapse. This limit is fixed by the essential properties in the diagrammatic subset, but this fact cannot be illustrated in the same diagrammatic fashion, unless one invents some ad hoc symbol such as a cancelled arrow linking the essential subset to the region outside the larger set.

In any event, so long as one keeps the two functions of the core clearly distinct, it ought to be possible to avoid confusion. From the point of view of the first function, we can say that adequate foundations are a positively necessary condition of a sound building, whereas a pitched roof is not. We can divide the features of sound buildings into those that we expect to find in every case and those that can and do vary. Seen in this way, the Euler diagram maps the relationship of essential and additional features: the features of any given building must include both those that are essential to any building, and also some further features that, while not essential, make it possible to complete the building, since one cannot construct a building out of essential features alone (one might even say that it is essential that that a building incorporates some inessential features).

From the point of view of the core's second function, however, the core requirements negatively determine the limits of structural soundness. So, for example, they will entail that a building erected without proper foundations is liable to collapse. In this sense the core and the horizon are two aspects of the same phenomenon, viz. the limits of structural soundness. The core determines where the horizon is to be drawn. And yet they are not identical, because there is an area outside the core but within the horizon, containing possible but inessential architectural features.

Even though we have elicited a way of making sense of the assimilation of core and horizon, it strikes me as unhelpful and unnatural to equate the two notions, for all that both are markers of boundaries. The concept of a core does not comfortably fit a distinction between the human and the inhuman, for it normally separates the more and less central ingredients of a single category. The core of an apple is part of the apple. When we speak of 'core values', we mean the most essential values of a morality; the values outside the core are still values, though they have a less critical role to play. Taken together, all human values are circumscribed by a further boundary (the apple's skin?) beyond which empathy fails. What lies outside this boundary is 'beyond the pale', beyond the fence of the human horizon.

Berlin's pin-pusher is beyond the horizon because he does not understand or accept the core principle that gratuitous pain should not be caused to others, or the principle that others should be treated as ends in themselves and not merely as means to our own ends. In this way, to repeat, the contents of the core define the location of the horizon. This is the source of the temptation to assimilate core and horizon. But it is a temptation that should be resisted, because it falsely identifies rules and what they require or exclude, as if we said that a speed limit is identical to exceeding such a limit.

Berlin did not himself address these questions independently of our correspondence. He may well not have been inclined to visualise the human moral terrain in diagrammatic terms: indeed, given the difficulty of explaining my diagram, perhaps this was just as well. Nor was he in search of a comprehensive, systematic account of human morality. He used different analogies for different purposes, and they may not be successfully combinable into a super-analogy that fits all the points he wishes to make at different times and in different contexts. When he was thinking of the universal moral minimum, it was natural to assent to talk of a core. But when he was thinking of the outer limits of human morality – the boundary beyond which we can no longer empathise with a person's attitudes, behaviour and beliefs – the image of a horizon or fence suggested itself: a point beyond which we cannot see.

I now return to the letter I interrupted. Berlin continues:

> I do not think that anything that is intelligible is beyond the horizon – beyond the horizon, yes, but not beyond the horizon that embraces all the possible (but not infinite) ultimate values.

Unless this is a garbled transcription of what he dictated, I assume the second occurrence of 'horizon' is a reference to the geographical horizon. Anyway, his meaning is clear: the human horizon delimits the intelligible.

> My reason for rejecting the Byronic heroes, the tragic Romantics, etc. [...] is not because they fall outside *the* horizon or *the* core – they fall within it if I understand them – but because they make life in my section of the woods, my variant of all the possible sets of ultimate values, [here he must have omitted the word 'impossible', or 'unacceptable' – PU] – and that is enough. Of course, not all that lies within the horizon is acceptable, at least to me – I do not think that the values of others always constitute equally legitimate choices from among the available options, to use your phrase. But these are human choices: they do not make those who choose

them inhuman; but they are certainly not all legitimate – legitimacy is conferred in the first place by the core, the horizon, i.e. that without which societies cannot go on, situations which one could not conceive as human – but in the second place, against my particular set of convictions. Those two are not the same – the second is a subclass of the first.

I wonder if that makes anything clearer? Perhaps it isn't what you thought I thought – at least, that is what it seems to me at the moment that I think. In other words, there are values which are parts of the core and the horizon, but against which I fight.

There must be further garbling in the penultimate sentence of the penultimate paragraph. Here Berlin is enumerating two sources of moral legitimacy. The first is clear enough: compatibility with the core/horizon. But something has dropped out before 'against my particular set of convictions'. The thought seems to be that moral legitimacy (from my viewpoint) also requires that the values in question do not conflict with my own convictions. Without further argument this seems to amount to a form of relativism: why, after all, should I prefer my convictions to those of someone else ranged against me? This difficulty recurs again and again in these discussions, and represents for me the most serious unresolved crux in understanding Berlin's view. We shall return to it in what follows. Here, though, let me draw attention to one or two unclarities.

Berlin speaks of values that are within the horizon but unacceptable to him, and calls them 'human choices', but not 'equally legitimate' with his own choices. What can he have in mind? It cannot be values that offend against the core, because he has said that the values he is considering are *within* the core. He says that the choices are 'against my particular set of convictions'. Perhaps an example would be belligerency in pursuit of the value of martial glory. If I am a pacifist, martial values will indeed be 'against my particular set of convictions', but they are nevertheless intelligibly human. If this is right, what can Berlin mean when he says 'the second is a subclass of the first'? He appears to be saying that values that offend against my convictions are a subclass of values that offend against the core. But *ex hypothesi* all the values under examination are within the core. I am stuck, unless we posit a deeper muddle than I have noticed. Let us return once more to Berlin's letter:

[...] you ask about 'arbitrary' etc. All I mean by 'arbitrary' is something for which no reasons are, or apparently can be, given. What would be arbitrary but intelligible? The desire to collect large paintings but not small ones, not because you find them more attractive but for their own sake, no reason given. The man who does that is not mad, though he is eccentric. He has goals different from mine; he is fanatical, maybe; it just happens that that fulfils some deep desire of his, which psychoanalysis may or may not liberate him from – irrational, certainly; arbitrary, certainly; but unintelligible? No – I would know how to live with such a man, how to talk to him, how to ask him for his reasons, how to realise that he doesn't bother to give any because he doesn't think it necessary. I wonder if that makes things clearer, I do hope so.

Weber: I am ashamed to say that I have never read him, and now I feel it is too late. But I think you are right; I think where we agree is that he thinks that Hume is right and Kant and Plato are wrong – that statements of fact which are the sphere of science [are] different from the sphere of values; that factual statements cannot entail value statements, although there are ambivalent areas in which one is not sure whether the symbols one uses are those of fact or of values. ('He is virtuous' – is that a term of praise, or a mere report on what he does in accordance with rules prescribed by somebody or other, which one need not accept, in which case it is a purely factual statement about someone's behaviour?) Then all the stuff by him about the conflict of values – true versus beautiful, holy versus good, etc. – that does speak to me. In other words, he accepts that ultimate values are what they are, that people simply proceed in their light, and that they can conflict and still remain ultimate values – polytheism, he calls it, now one god, now another. Some of the gods are against each other, maybe, in which case one has to choose. In the end, though it is a terrible thing to say, in the very end, one has to plump – one can give reasons, but the reasons in the end will only proceed from some larger, wider, deeper plumping. So Weber is certainly an ally – but I had no idea he said anything of this when I invented my views, such as they are.

There are interesting observations in these final paragraphs of the letter that might be discussed, but to do so here would take us too far away from our theme. One point, though, is worth highlighting: when Berlin writes 'one can give reasons, but the reasons in the end will only proceed from some larger, wider, deeper plumping', he confirms my view that to rationalise choices in terms of the form of life to which we are already committed is not really an answer to the sceptic who asks why we have chosen in the way that we have. The sceptic can go on to say: 'Very well, but how do you justify your commitment to that form of life and not another?' If the answer is only 'Because it is mine', the sceptic has won, because he has revealed that my values and choices ultimately proceed from a groundless commitment, or from an inherited tradition that is followed just because it is inherited. So long as this tradition does not offend against the core, this may be enough: I have the right to follow the tradition into which I was born, and to defend it from rival traditions that would destroy it. This is where Berlin's views about the rights of dominant cultures come in.

As may be imagined, I was very thrown by Berlin's letter, writing on 3 March 1993:

> What you say does rather shake me, I admit, as it certainly conflicts with the understanding of your views I had derived from your published work. I must digest your letter further, and look again at the places where you discuss such things in print, and see whether the muddle disappears.

I also responded to what he said about his acquaintance with Weber, a topic of interest to those who are concerned to establish the degree of his originality in espousing value pluralism:

> I am interested that you say that you didn't know about Weber's views when you invented your views (I wonder when that was?!). I had thought that your reference [at L 48/1] to Weber's 'Politics as a Vocation', one of the essays where he touches on such matters, showed that you had Weber early under your belt. You refer to the same translation I consulted [283/9]. More explicit remarks come in another essay, 'Science as a Vocation', in particular this on p. 152: 'the ultimately possible attitudes to life are irreconcilable, and hence their struggle can never be brought to a final conclusion. Thus it is necessary to make a decisive choice.' Isn't that a pretty good shot at a short summary of your kind of pluralism?

I should add that the point Berlin is illustrating in citing Weber here has nothing directly to do with pluralism; and that the reference comes in the introduction to *Four Essays on Liberty*, which was written in the late 1960s.

There is now a gap in the record that may or may not conceal further discussion of the main issues. During this gap I read a draft of John Gray's study of Berlin's thought for the Modern Masters series, edited by Frank Kermode. I had suggested some years before that such a book should be commissioned, but Kermode had dismissed the idea, saying that Berlin was very far from being a significant enough figure. That was before 'my' volumes had appeared. Evidently the attention given to Berlin as a result of these volumes changed Kermode's mind.

I wrote to Berlin about Gray's draft on 29 April 1993:

> I have read the first, rough, draft of John Gray's book on you, and he certainly does you proud. [...] There are only a couple of things in the book that worry me. One is his view (not attributed to you, but not said to be at odds with you either) that the truth of pluralism means that liberalism is only one of a number of different ways of approaching life, and has no special priority. I cannot believe that you would accept this, if only because you speak [at L 216] of 'Pluralism, with the measure of "negative" liberty that it entails'. Perhaps John would reply that this measure of negative liberty falls short of full-blown liberalism. [...]
>
> The other thing concerns the nature and extent of the moral unity of mankind – that chestnut which we have discussed more than once. It may be that your remarks on this topic over the years aren't entirely consistent, if only because your views have developed. However this may be, John's account of it wobbles a bit: sometimes he speaks as if we have only certain basic categories in common (I'm not sure which), sometimes as if there are certain definite norms which can be said to be, so to speak, anthropologically universal. I favour the second, broader account, if only because it seems to me necessary if relativism is to be resisted.

Both these worries seem to me important. The first one, initially voiced publicly by George Crowder in a 1994 article entitled 'Pluralism and Liberalism',[12] has since generated a vast secondary literature on the relationship between pluralism and liberalism. No consensus has emerged, but Crowder himself, having in that initial article rejected the claim that pluralism entails liberalism, later changed his mind, and has now argued in many places for such a connection, though on grounds that go beyond what Berlin explicitly argued. The phrase I quote from 'Two Concepts of Liberty' has created much puzzlement, especially because

Berlin appears to say something opposed to it at CIB 44: 'Pluralism and liberalism are not the same or even overlapping concepts. There are liberal theories which are not pluralistic. I believe in both liberalism and pluralism, but they are not logically connected.' (Note that he does not say that there are pluralistic theories which are not liberal, though there are.) To make matters worse, he then immediately appears to go back on what he has just said, arguing that, given pluralism, 'a minimum degree of toleration, however reluctant, becomes indispensable'. This too falls short of full-blown liberalism, maybe, but it is a step on the road in that direction. It cannot be denied that Berlin's position on this issue is unclear, though his assertion of a link between pluralism and *choice* is beyond doubt:

> The world that we encounter in ordinary experience is one in which we are faced with choices between ends equally ultimate, and claims equally absolute, the realisation of some of which must inevitably involve the sacrifice of others. Indeed, it is because this is their situation that men place such immense value upon the freedom to choose; for if they had an assurance that in some perfect state, realisable by men on earth, no ends pursued by them would ever be in conflict, the necessity and agony of choice would disappear, and with it the central importance of the freedom to choose. (L 213–14)

And again:

> If, as I believe, the ends of men are many, and not all of them are in principle compatible with each other, then the possibility of conflict – and of tragedy – can never wholly be eliminated from human life, either personal or social. The necessity of choosing between absolute claims is then an inescapable characteristic of the human condition. (L 214)

The second worry has not attracted so much attention, so far as I am aware. But it arises at certain points in Berlin's own writings. Here is a passage from his 'Does Political Theory Still Exist?':

> The basic categories (with their corresponding concepts) in terms of which we define men – such notions as society, freedom, sense of time and change, suffering, happiness, productivity, good and bad, right and

wrong, choice, effort, truth, illusion (to take them wholly at random) – are not matters of induction and hypothesis. To think of someone as a human being is *ipso facto* to bring all these notions into play; so that to say of someone that he is a man, but that choice, or the notion of truth, mean nothing to him, would be eccentric: it would clash with what we mean by 'man' not as a matter of verbal definition (which is alterable at will), but as intrinsic to the way in which we think, and (as a matter of 'brute' fact) evidently cannot but think. (CC2 217)

Here Berlin seems to be saying that we cannot help thinking of human beings in terms of certain central concepts and categories such as those he lists. But there are no specific moral norms here, unless we are meant to deduce, for example, an injunction to do what is right rather than what is wrong, or to tell the truth rather than to lie. To say that we cannot help viewing the world through certain spectacles is not the same as insisting that all normal persons agree on certain moral principles. Talk of good and bad, right and wrong, begs the question of *what it is that is good, bad etc*. It is a further step to specify what falls under these concepts. It is this ambiguity which I noticed in Gray's draft, and which seemed to leave the door open to relativism, since different views can be taken by different people of what is right and wrong. In the words Shakespeare gives to Hamlet, 'there is nothing either good or bad, but thinking makes it so' (*Hamlet* 2.2.269–70): Hamlet thinks Denmark a prison, but Rosencrantz and Guildenstern don't. In order to achieve the maximum possible universal moral agreement – surely a worthy aim – we need to extract from an examination of human nature not only a conceptual structure but specific moral judgements. It may be that these judgements are somehow implicit in moral language. Wittgenstein observed: 'If language is to be a means of communication there must be agreement not only in definitions but also (queer as this may sound) in judgements.'[13] But how this is so needs to be spelled out, not merely taken as read.

Berlin's answer is dated 3 May 1993. Although he (properly) did not wish to interfere with Gray's text, he did respond to the two points I had raised:

That pluralism means liberalism is only one of the possibilities .... You are right, I do not think I do believe this. I concede that there are other ways of looking at life, just as that liberty is only one of the values we pursue; but just as there is a sense of liberty[14] in which without it you cannot pursue the values that we do pursue (at any rate, out of choice, as authors of our acts), so liberalism seems to me the only doctrine which actually preaches, if not the desirability of these points of view, at any rate the desirability of the toleration of them, of their variety – provided, of course, that none of them destroys the framework in which they operate, or endangers it in any serious sense.

As for the point about the measure of negative liberty that pluralism, according to me, entails, I think that does not fall short of full-blown liberalism – unless John Gray defines it in some special fashion. If he does, then he may be right, but his notion of liberalism must be even wider than mine. [...]

The moral unity of mankind. Indeed, we have talked about this, off and on, for a long time. I agree with you: even if I may have been vague or inconsistent on the subject, 'basic categories in common' is not enough, that simply means that everybody means something not dissimilar by 'good', 'bad', 'right', 'wrong' etc. But if there is no common ground, no acceptance of particular values recognised as such by a sufficient number of people over a sufficiently long time, then you are right, the danger of relativism rears its hideous head. The question is: is understanding other people's outlooks, cultures etc. the same as sharing norms? I think it is: I think that if you say 'I see how I might live in the light of this or that culture, believe in this or that as dominant values', this is not to accept this culture, these values, but mere understanding seems to me to create a community of shared ground. Is this (*a*) intelligible, (*b*) true? I am not sure – I hope so.

What is 'a community of shared ground'? This phrase seems to me to have a weaker and a stronger sense. In the weaker sense we share only the same conceptual repertoire, so to speak: the same toolbox for analysing and understanding moral problems and predicaments. In the stronger sense we share specific moral principles. As should be clear by now, understanding without agreement needs more explanation than Berlin provides: if we understand both moral attitudes that we share and those we don't share, what distinguishes the two? Sometimes it is empirical error: those we disagree with are mistaken about the facts. But does this cover all cases? Are unshared and shared attitudes distinguished only by rationally arbitrary choice, or can there be coherent argument about where the boundary lies? Is the boundary that between good and evil?

In my reply of 5 May 1993 I wrote:

> I have had a long session with John Gray, and persuaded him to think again about the two issues I drew to your attention: your remarks were most helpful, and I am glad that, on the whole, you backed my judgement. I hope that, when you read the finished book, you will agree that it is reasonably fair and accurate as well as undoubtedly favourable.

I cannot remember what changes, if any, Gray made as a result of our discussion, but a copy of the finished book exists in which Berlin has made occasional marginal comments indicating agreement or disagreement.

A month later (7 June 1993) I returned to the fray, writing to Berlin when he was hospitalised after a fall:

> You have said to me more than once that the important thing about your understanding of pluralism, by contrast with relativism, is that it allows understanding between people who belong to different cultures or whatever, whereas relativism pictures them as inhabiting hermetically sealed worlds, incommunicado as far as other worlds are concerned. This, if I have it right, I understand: intercommunication across cultural boundaries could hardly be more important, both at a practical level, and theoretically, if humanity is to have any moral or metaphysical unity (as I devoutly wish it to have).
>
> What puzzles me, though, is one of the examples you use to characterise relativism: 'I like coffee, you like champagne' – i.e. a difference of taste. The reason this puzzles me is that it seems to me easy for someone who prefers coffee to empathise with someone who prefers champagne, and vice versa. We all know what preferences of taste are like, and can easily imagine what it would be like to have other ones; indeed, our tastes can change over time, and this makes empathy in this area all the easier. I would go further and say that empathy across tastes is much easier than empathy between, say, an eighteenth-century Scot and a Homeric peasant, or any of the other similar types of empathy you discuss.
>
> If I am right about this, then *either* the coffee/champagne example isn't a good example of relativism (but I don't see why it shouldn't be), *or* the important difference between pluralism and relativism isn't a matter of whether empathy is possible.

If we take the latter alternative, then what *is* the crucial distinguishing feature between pluralism and relativism? Could it be, perhaps, that, according to relativism, 'anything goes' – that is, there are no restrictions on what is to count as a value or a morality – whereas pluralism insists that human nature sets limits (your 'human horizon') to what can count under this heading? That is to say, relativism portrays our allegiances and principles as radically *arbitrary*, whereas pluralism sees them as exfoliations of a shared human nature, and holds that their common source binds them together in a relationship of mutual intelligibility.

Even if I am wrong about this (at least as an understanding of your views), I am left with the problem that the coffee/champagne example seems plainly not to illustrate a failure of intelligibility. Do you agree?

If Berlin replied to this, I have not found his letter. I visited him in hospital soon after writing, and my next letter suggests that we discussed my questions viva voce. I do remember once asking him in person about the inadequacy of the coffee/champagne example, mentioning that pregnant women can develop quite uncharacteristic tastes, which seemed to me a clear case of how empathy across tastes might occur within a single consciousness. It was one of the rare occasions when he became cross with me. Whether this was because I had somehow hit home, or just because he was irritated by my persistence, I cannot be sure.

When I heard that he was recovering well, I wrote again:

This news emboldens me to take up the offer you (perhaps rashly) made when I visited you in the Acland – to press you further on our recurrent topic, pluralism and the moral unity of man.

You have often said, following Russell and James,[15] that the key to understanding a thinker is to identify the guiding perception that underlies all his detailed arguments and makes sense of them. There is no reason why this should not also apply to my attempt to understand you, and I wonder whether, if I could properly grasp the driving force behind your observations, I should be less troubled by the fact that, in some respects, they don't still all the questions that arise from *my* underlying preoccupations. (And why should they? There's no reason why your agenda should match mine. The trouble is that I find so much of what you say so satisfying that I want to extract the maximum of enlightenment before concluding that there may be avenues that lead off from your garden but down which you are reluctant to stroll!) I come to my point.

I dare not attempt a complete identification of your *idée(s) maîtresse(s)* [master idea(s)], but part of the wellspring of your interest in pluralism, it seems safe to say, is that it provides a bulwark for liberalism (as against the totalitarianism that has always repelled you); and another part of it is that it provides a more realistic and satisfying account of cultural diversity than does that kind of relativism which despairs of mutual understanding between members of different cultural worlds, or between individuals whose values differ.

These interests I share with you, but there is another which I would stress equally. (In the light of your writings, I think of it as typically Russian, though that's not where *I* got it from.) It is the 'accursed questions' of what we should do, how we should live, what are the limits of the range of acceptable actions, and so on. It seems to me that if one finds this sort of question central, then one naturally looks, in any picture of the workings of morality, for a way of drawing the line between acceptable and unacceptable, and a justification for preventing the unacceptable.

You do of course say a good deal about all this, and naturally I don't for a moment deny that this sort of question engages you: that would be absurd! But what you have to say about understanding unacceptable behaviour on the part of others (e.g. Jew-murdering Nazis – and Muslim-murdering Serbs?) has always worried me a little, and I should like to try to explain why.

I am reminded of John Major's remark about understanding less and condemning more (though I don't wish not to understand, nor am I anxious to condemn for its own sake, certainly not uncomprehendingly); and Roger [Hausheer] once said to me that he felt your account of morality 'doesn't exclude enough'. When you explain untoward behaviour in terms of empirically false beliefs, you appear to assume that such an explanation, where possible, is likely to be the right one. But there is another alternative, which is that the people concerned are not interested in any rational justification of their behaviour, but just want to do whatever it is they are doing: in old-fashioned terminology, they are evil, or at least bad. It may well be, for example, that Nazi activities were indeed underpinned in the minds of some Nazis by the kinds of false beliefs you mention, but I bet that many of them simply hated Jews on no rational grounds, and didn't have qualms about acting accordingly; and, even if they did have false beliefs, would not have been impressed if their error had been pointed out to their satisfaction. Why should we assume that, other things being equal, men will act rationally or beneficently? It isn't true to experience, unfortunately. Good will, rather, sometimes seems to be a fragile flower of special circumstances.

But whatever the true explanation of wrong behaviour, one of the things we look for in a moral outlook is a way of drawing boundaries between right and wrong. To a pluralist, right is multiple and in a state of internal conflict, but it still has limits. The way in which you give priority to drawing the boundaries of understanding sometimes seems to eclipse the need to identify the (different?) boundaries of acceptability. For example, you say that you can understand the extreme Nietzschean Romantic, and the Nazi (given certain false beliefs), but not the person who pushes pins into flesh, or the youths who rape old ladies and steal their trifling savings. The first two fall within the 'human horizon', the last two, presumably, outside it. So far, so good. But the question of which of the four should be accepted or tolerated (or, alternatively, restrained) is, surely, an additional question? Something can be comprehensible but evil. This is why I feel that the 'common core' – the basic minimum of required common moral ground to which we appeal when rejecting certain forms of behaviour – is not the same as the human horizon (the limits of comprehensibility), and why I am concerned that you sometimes appear to assimilate the two.

In a word, what I miss (perhaps wrongly?) is acknowledgement of sheer nastiness as a part of human nature just as much as (if not more than) beneficence; and a clear separation of the question of comprehensibility from the question of acceptability. I hope you will be able to show me that this is a monstrous misunderstanding.

Of course, if I am right that the domains of comprehensibility and acceptability don't entirely overlap, the identification of the limits set by the core and the horizon posited by some interpreters of Berlin, and discussed above, cannot stand. Berlin replied on 5 July 1993:

You are, of course, quite right in saying that probably the wellspring of my interest in pluralism is that it provides a bulwark for liberalism – but not entirely. In the first place, liberalism can occur without pluralism, as in the case of, say, Benjamin Constant, or even J. S. Mill, who approved of freedom of thought and expression, but not for pluralist reasons. But it is true that if pluralism, then some kind of liberalism necessarily follows. But my interest in it is, I think, intrinsic – simply deep devotion to the idea of variety, and delight in the diversity of human experience, which is no doubt a purely psychological fact about me. But then, William James rightly said that people's philosophy is to do with their temperament and character. It is not quite the same as what Russell says, but equally true: some people like unity, tidiness, everything to proceed from a single centre – in fact, hedgehogs; others prefer diversity, untidiness, multiplicity and occasional miracles to interrupt the rigorous flow of causal continuities. I can't deny that I belong to the second group.

Now, about the 'accursed questions'. You are right that I probably was influenced by my Russian favourites about this and your central question. Evil people and evil acts: you are perfectly right – it is not only false empirical propositions which can lead to horrible behaviour; I merely said that [*sc.* said that merely in order] to deny that the Nazis were literally mad, as people sometimes thought, and to explain the conduct of ordinary non-evil Germans who participated in this vast ghastly operation because they thought it right, for the sake of the country, for the sake of winning the war, and ultimately because the Jews were termites and undermined all possibilities of the good life for Germans, for which they saw themselves as working. But that leaves out the question of your category: criminals who commit crimes because they are crimes, evil people who do evil because it is evil, etc. – Milton's Satan, Byronic heroes [etc. To understand][16] is not to forgive. That I have always firmly believed. I remember Austin saying to me: 'If we do not forgive ourselves, as we often don't, why should we forgive others?' Very typical of him. And of course one has to condemn, fight against, evil; whether one understands it or not does not make it in any way more tolerable. Then why does one do it [*sc.* evil/fight against evil?]?

Certainly the common core is not the same as the human horizon – that is your central question, and I am happy to be able to answer it as best I can. The common horizon is entirely to do with intelligibility – you are right. Whereas the common core is central human values – with some variety, it has to be admitted, but at any rate in one's own case simply the values which (*a*) can be regarded as among the central human values, historically speaking: a great many places, a great many periods, etc., though by no means all of them – not exhaustive; and (*b*) what one is prepared to fight for, in some cases die for, whether or not they may alter, or were rejected by others, and so on. So in the end it boils down to one's own personal horizon, which is necessarily part of some social horizon of not only the contemporary culture to which one belongs but something extended into the past as well. But in the final analysis, simply what one is committed to, and prepared to argue for, and prepared to explain in terms of the common beliefs, the common core. That is the only alternative, for me, to objective morality – Kant, Mill, the Churches etc. – which I do not accept.

But when Stuart Hampshire talks about 'absolute evil', I am not sure that I understand that either. I know perfectly well what he means. It cannot do any harm to try and understand the most horrible acts and the most horrible people and the most horrible human characteristics – original sin, in which, like Freud, I certainly believe. Although that is not one's reason for rejecting, or denouncing, or fighting against, or making war upon, those who seem to one destructive of all that one believes in, because one believes in it not just subjectively but as part of some ongoing human outlook – or, at any rate, a particular path in it with which one feels oneself identified. I mean that, even when one says 'I can understand why Torquemada murdered people – given his circumstances, his beliefs, the general outlook of Spanish Catholics, the desire to save souls, etc. etc. etc. – one need not condemn it as totally irrational or unintelligible ...' – the kind of thing that Bishop Creighton argued against Lord Acton – this does not mean that one is not allowed to regard it as wholly evil, not just because of the bad character of the Inquisitors, but because of its intrinsic badness, even if the motives can be explained in human terms: in other words, to be condemned in the name of values which are as absolute as anything one can make in a non-absolute, empirical world, i.e. again many places, many times, many people. In other words, I am with Acton against Creighton: understand whatever you can, but this is no reason for not condemning, even if you can imagine yourself as perpetrating these evils if you were a different person in a different place under different influences, etc.

I am not sure if this is much more coherent than what I have said to you in the past – does it help at all?

The long penultimate paragraph here is certainly not as clear or coherent as I should like. This is partly due to the helter-skelter syntax of Berlin's dictated prose, but I don't think that this is the only problem. Some things are clear, certainly. There is a central set of values (or principles? the two may be different aspects of the same phenomenon) that have as a matter of empirical observation been accepted by most people at most times and in most places. One might add, though Berlin does not do so here, that this is because they derive from human nature: from the basic needs of persons who wish to survive and prosper. At any rate, these shared values are Berlin's empirical substitute for the absolute, a priori values of some other moralists. This is the best that empiricists can do if they are looking for values that all normal human beings can be said to have in common. We defend them because they are, we suppose, intrinsic to our very humanity.

But now a grey area gets tacked on: values 'one is prepared to fight for, in some cases die for, whether or not they may alter, or were rejected by others'. What exactly is the status of these values? Are they here put in a separate category, or is Berlin talking of a second criterion of the same values? If the former, why are they differentiated from the shared values of the other category? Is it because 'they may alter'? But nothing empirical, Berlin tirelessly repeats, can be guaranteed against change. Perhaps we are speaking of values that are more likely to change than the really central ones? This seems more promising. There are values that are crucial for us, but which may not be or have been so crucial for other people, at other times, in other places. So there is an empirically near-universal set of human values, and in a specific context further values that are treated as equally vital, even if they are not so regarded outside that context. This makes sense of what Berlin calls 'one's own personal horizon', though it might be clearer to call it one's own personal moral core, a customised version, so to speak, of the universal core of human morality. In terms of my Euler diagram, they are values that form part of my culture, that fall within the horizon but not within the common core. This fits with the possibility that they 'were rejected by others'. That is to say, they do not form part of the non-negotiable content of other cultures in the way that they do of mine.

The trouble with this interpretation is that, if it is right, Berlin could easily have stated his position in a way that made this clear. The fact that he doesn't suggests to me either that the interpretation isn't in fact right, or that Berlin was deploying an intuitively understood picture which he never quite thought through and spelled out explicitly – or, of course, both. At times his words seem to point in one direction, at times in another. Let us park this issue and move on.

If Berlin is indeed speaking of values that are additional to those contained in the common core, how can we defend them? What do we say to someone who espouses additional values that differ from ours, and may be incompatible with them? Can we appeal only to toleration? If so, is this the kind of toleration that regards the tolerated values as mistaken, or the kind that regards them as options that are perfectly valid though at odds with the options we ourselves favour? In any event, toleration cannot handle all such clashes. In specific situations decisions have to be made, some values sacrificed to others.

Berlin goes on to say that the 'personal horizon [...] is necessarily part of some social horizon of not only the contemporary culture to which one belongs but something extended into the past as well'. This is presumably to say that our personal principles and commitments are not (cannot be) conceived in isolation, but have a social dimension, and form part of a historically continuous process of cultural formation. But then he switches back to the first category again: 'in the final analysis, simply what one is committed to, and prepared to argue for, and prepared to explain in terms of the common beliefs, the common core'.

What is Berlin saying here? Once again I am unable quite to pin it down. Let us return once again to the first principles depicted in the Euler diagram. There is a central core of moral attitudes shared by all normal persons; a wider set of comprehensible values that fall within the sphere of cultural variation rather than belonging to all humanity as such; and beyond these the inhuman and the insane. For me the central problem, to repeat, is to explain how it is possible simultaneously to understand and to condemn. Berlin gives the example of Torquemada, whose conduct we can understand 'given his circumstances, his beliefs, the general outlook of Spanish Catholics, the desire to save souls, etc.'. This explanation is like what he says about Nazism, in that it relies on the ascription of false beliefs to the understood but condemned actor. But now he adds further factors: 'the bad character of the Inquisitors' and the 'intrinsic badness' of what they did, 'even if the motives can be explained in human terms'. He also accepts the idea of 'original sin', namely that humans have a natural propensity to do wrong.

Does this provide the answer to my problem? We understand but condemn evil behaviour because we ourselves are flawed and know what it is to do wrong, to be greedy, selfish, brutal and so on. This is certainly one factor in understanding evil behaviour. So we now have two ways of interpreting actions we wish to condemn: mistaken beliefs on the part of the actors, and the natural propensity to do wrong. Evil acts that spring from normal but malign human impulses are comprehensible in a way that the actions of Berlin's pin-pusher are not. When we explain the Nazis and Torquemada, it seems, we need to deploy both interpretations together. What we see in their actions is evil behaviour reinforced and rationalised by false beliefs, and vice versa. The false beliefs make the evil acts easier to perpetrate and excuse, but original sin makes the false beliefs more seductive.

If we reread Berlin's paragraph in the light of these clarifications, it makes better sense. There are still some wobbles, though, which may suggest that the picture is not yet quite complete. First, he speaks of 'some variety' in the common core. This appears to be a way of reiterating that an empirical category of this kind cannot be expected to be timelessly watertight, with definite boundaries valid in all possible worlds. Human nature is contingent, not necessary; it was not ordained by a divine fiat, but has evolved historically, perhaps in different ways in different places (even if there is some biological criterion of species-membership that links all humans), and all nature teems with variety. The moral world of the earliest humans, let alone their ancestors, must have been very different from ours; indeed, we don't need to go back more than a generation, or very far afield in the contemporary world, to find differences in core moral beliefs. Some really basic principles, closely related to the need for survival and a chance of prosperity, may be more nearly universal by now. But even among basic principles some, at any rate, are of comparatively recent origin. Unprovoked military aggression and empire-building have been regarded as natural and justified for much of human history; indeed, they are still alive and well today. Slavery was abolished only a moment ago *sub specie aeternitatis*, and belief in the divine right of kings is similarly recent. Even Berlin's degree of generalisation – 'a great many places, a great many periods, etc., though by no means all of them' – perhaps goes too far. So the claim of variety in the core, at any rate when this is based on what people actually value as opposed to what human nature requires, is easy to accept.

Next, there is some equivocation about individual variation. Berlin speaks of 'one's own personal horizon' (better, 'core'?) as if each individual has a bespoke set of values that differs to some degree from those common to humanity as a whole. Admittedly, this core is in part socially and historically formed – no man is a moral island – but all the same there is room for variety, between individuals, between groups, between cultures, between historical periods. One's own personal core, as Berlin puts it, is a matter of 'what one is committed to, and prepared to argue for'. But then he pulls back and adds that it is what one is 'prepared to explain in terms of the common beliefs, the common core'. Now we seem to be concerned once more with beliefs shared across all humanity. There does seem to be a muddle of some kind here: a muddled explanation to me, if not a muddled picture in Berlin's mind.

The best I can do at this point is to refer once again to my diagram, which provides not only for a shared core of 'values which are as absolute as anything one can make in a non-absolute, empirical world', but also for variation within the confines of a shared human horizon – 'a particular path in [some ongoing human outlook] with which one feels oneself identified'. Among the core principles is to be found the rejection of malign human tendencies. There may be cases of doubt about whether a tendency is benign or malign. The Homeric value of military prowess may have been regarded positively in ancient times, but today we have serious reservations about some of its manifestations. There should be room for the development over time – the lifetime whether of an individual or of a culture – of greater moral sophistication and understanding. In any case, an answer to my question about how to combine understanding and rejection can be given, as already suggested, in terms of natural human propensities that conflict with our shared moral principles. This seems consistent with what Berlin says in the letter under consideration, for all its unclarity.

I returned to this topic once more, in a letter of 22 February 1995, in which I refer to a recent meeting, returning to the old marrowbone of the explanation of malign behaviour:

> I learnt (but not enough, as usual!) from our last conversation about pluralism etc. We must talk about it further next time, if you can bear it. I was left with the impression that there is nothing more, in your view, to wicked but sane behaviour than that the ends it serves are anti-social: some activities serve the minimum requirements men share better than do others, and for the former we are justified in having a moral preference. This would leave concepts such as 'evil' and perhaps 'wicked' with no work to do of the kind that theologians and others assign to them: they would just be intensified versions of 'anti-social' or somesuch. I wonder if this is really what you think.

It also seemed to follow from what you said that among the ends that men sanely pursue are ends that they would do better not to pursue: i.e. among your objective plurality of ends are not only many which are good, but also some which are bad. Among the bad ones, perhaps, may be some which come into your category of ends shared by most people in most places at most times – perhaps, for instance, selfishness – in which case such sharedness can't be a basis for moral approval? There have been times when there has been general acceptance of practices – e.g. slavery – later regarded as wrong. If general opinion can so change, it cannot be a standard of rightness?

I am as muddled as ever, as you see. Underlying all my difficulties is the feeling that, for you, the only source of wrong behaviour is empirical error, not plain nastiness of character. If you do believe this, it may be a tribute to your purity of character, but it seems over-generous to many of the real people that we know about?

Perhaps we can make another date and pursue this endless discussion, *inter alia*.

Berlin told Pat Utechin: 'I prefer the *alia*.' I don't blame him. Apart from anything else, I seem to have forgotten that he has already conceded that he believed in original sin.

The problem about 'wicked' came up again the following year, when Berlin used the word in his 'My Intellectual Path' (see overleaf), writing 'I do not regard the Nazis, as some people do, as literally pathological or insane, only as wickedly wrong, totally misguided about the facts.' I pressed him on the word, wondering why he used it, and whether the implication that the Nazis' mistaken beliefs were culpable was intended. His explanation of Nazi behaviour in terms of false beliefs sometimes appears to let them off the hook, suggesting that their motives were benevolent even if their beliefs were false. How then are these beliefs wicked? Is one responsible for (all) one's beliefs? If so, is not the conduct they lead to also wicked? If it is, what is gained by attributing wickedness to the beliefs rather than directly to the conduct? My enquiries did not persuade him to alter the text, and I still find the sentence problematic.

Berlin's notes for the last essay he wrote, 'My Intellectual Path' (1995)

12

THE END

On 28 January 1997 I wrote to Berlin asking whether I might publish an expanded second edition of *Personal Impressions*, adding pieces written since the original edition appeared, and perhaps also some earlier pieces that had not been included, especially 'Zionist Politics in Wartime Washington' and 'The Three Strands in My Life' (89). He replied on 1 February 1997: 'Hold your horses.' He agreed to only five further pieces out of the fifteen I had offered him (and in the event one of these was dropped). On what he called the two Jewish pieces he wrote:

> 'Zionist Politics in Washington' produced such attacks on it at the time that the last thing I want is to revive the issue. So for the moment, please, not – after my death, whatever you like. Ditto about the 'Three Strands': I know it's quite a good autobiographical confession, but I think too intimate – I'd rather it didn't appear in my lifetime. Of course, Michael Ignatieff must have read it, and he can take from it what he likes, otherwise not before my death.

Three days later he sent me an early copy of *The Proper Study of Mankind* with an inscription that naturally moved me a good deal: 'for Henry from his coauthor Isaiah with inexpressible feeling'.

On 24 March 1997 I asked him about commentators on and critics of his work:

> I'm becoming increasingly curious about your attitude to the burgeoning industry of secondary literature about your work. We've talked about this in the past, and you've conveyed that you take a pretty detached view, on the whole. But since then the volume of commentary has increased, and it's occurred to me to wonder how you feel about all these chaps arguing about what you mean by such-and-such, whether so-and-so

really follows as you imply it does, and so forth. Don't you feel tempted to stand up and say 'I'll tell you what I mean; I'll tell you whether this follows from that, in my view, and I'll tell you why'?

I have in mind particularly the intense discussions about the relationship between pluralism and liberalism. The last chapter of John Gray's book, of course, set the cat among the pigeons here, though there were also earlier pieces – by Mack and Crowder (the one you and Bernard replied to), for instance. Beata Polanowska-Sygulska has written about this issue, and there are pieces in the pipeline by Graeme Garrard and Jonny Steinberg [...]. What they all want to know in their different ways is whether you believe that the truth of pluralism logically entails that liberalism has pride of place as a political order, or whether, as John Gray avers, the implication of pluralism is precisely the opposite – that liberalism is just one of a number of options in the pluralist bran-tub, and that non-liberal options must be given a fair crack of the whip.

Are you at all inclined to make an authoritative statement on this issue? My guess is that you aren't. Would you have been more tempted to join the fray if all this literature had appeared twenty years ago? Perhaps not: perhaps you don't have a completely clear answer to give? I'd be fascinated to know. But I don't want to make you write a letter about it if you'd rather not, so why don't you come to lunch? It's too long since we met.

I cannot recall whether we met in response to this letter, and I have found no written reply, but I do remember him saying to me once over lunch in the All Souls breakfast room, possibly on this occasion, that it was perfectly normal for ideas to be debated in this way, and that he was entirely relaxed about it, feeling no need to become involved. I admired his Epicurean detachment, but regretted that he would not settle some of the issues that had been raised, especially the question of his own belief about the relationship between pluralism and liberalism. I suspect that he was not entirely clear about this even in his own mind, despite the strong hints that I reported in chapter 11.

In June 1997, members of Wolfson College were asked to suggest a topic for the annual Wolfson College Lectures of 1999. I asked Berlin, by writing on a copy of the College document, if I could propose 'The Ideas of Isaiah Berlin', to mark his ninetieth birthday. He stuck a Post-it note on the sheet, writing thereon: 'leave it till I am gone – then – anything you like. I am sure you expected this I.B.'

On 12 June 1997 I attended a seminar at New College given by Christopher Peacocke, the penultimate item in a series on Oxford philosophers, about Berlin's 1950 article in *Mind*, 'Empirical Propositions and Hypothetical Statements'. The next day I reported to Berlin:

> It was mostly very technical and 'analytic', as one might expect, and I doubt if you will actually wish to read it all through. It was entirely positive, not to say laudatory, about your paper: he thought you were right, and that your ideas could be carried further in various fruitful ways, some of which he explored.
>
> The best bit was the peroration. He referred to your interview with [Jonathan] Glover for *New College News*, in which you tell the Sheffer story,* and give two reasons why you gave up philosophy: (1) that cumulative progress in the subject is not possible; (2) that you were not sufficiently brilliant to do it well. Peacocke asserted that your paper constituted a refutation of both claims. So there!

Peacocke later sent me his text. Here are his actual words:

> After 1945, Berlin's thought moved mainly to matters moral and political, and to the history of ideas. His move away from metaphysics and the theory of meaning was, according to Berlin, extraordinarily influenced by a conversation with Sheffer. Berlin's most striking description of the impact of this conversation is given in an extended interview with Jonathan Glover, for the *New College News* (December 1996).[1] Berlin reports:
>
> > [Sheffer] said that while progress could be made in logic or psychology, or in history, in philosophy the same questions kept being raised, there is no such thing as cumulative progress. I pondered this during my flight back to England. It was dark so I could not read, and too uncomfortable to sleep. After a time I thought,

---

* About how a conversation with H. M. Sheffer at Harvard started, or reinforced, the process of thought that led him to give up philosophy. See CC2 xxvi.

> I don't really want to know the answers to philosophical ques-
> tions – I'll never be first class – not like people like Austin or
> Ayer ... (7)

So here we have two final theses for consideration: that no cumulative
progress is possible in philosophy proper, and that Berlin himself would
in any case never be first class at it. It seems to me that Berlin's paper
'Empirical Propositions and Hypothetical Statements' is a counter-
example to both theses.

Berlin's last letter to me is dated 16 June 1997. I sent it back to him with a
handwritten query, and he returned it to me with his answer, and an additional
note about a piece on his work that I had sent him (I cannot remember which).
He thought this '*quite good* – and a fence against Gray's exaggeration of my
alleged "toss up" idea of which of two incompatible or incommensurable values
to seek?' Finally, a letter from me of 30 June asking some trivial questions came
back with his replies written on it by Pat Utechin. And so our correspondence
ended, with a whimper.

On 22 July Berlin fell ill, and never recovered. I visited him once more, in
October, finding him tired and shrunken, and reported to him on the first of a
series of lectures named after him and given at Corpus Christi College by J. G. A.
Pocock. I had called on Pocock after his first lecture, and he kindly gave me a
copy of his text, which began with a warm encomium to Berlin, to whom I read
it aloud. Berlin listened with closed eyes, observing, when I asked if I should
continue, 'Complete rot so far.' But he did want me to go on, which I did for a
little while, then moving on to other topics. Aline, not wishing me to overtire
her husband, soon cut us short, and as I walked away from the house I passed the
window of the room in which we had met. When I glanced in, Berlin appeared
to be asleep. I thought to myself that I might never see him again.

I was right. Early on 6 November Pat Utechin rang me at home to say he
had died in the Acland Hospital of heart failure just before midnight, having
had a minor operation earlier in the day. She asked me to tell Michael Ignatieff,
which I immediately did: he found the news difficult to take in, as did I. I was
devastated, realising with fuller force than ever before what he meant to me.
The closing words of Plato's *Phaedo* soon came to mind: 'This was the end,
Echecrates, of our friend, a man who, we may affirm, was the best of all the men
of his time whom we have known, and also the surest in wisdom and judgement.'[2]

13

EPILOGUE

The second edition of *Personal Impressions* appeared in 1998, afforced by 'Three Strands in My Life', as Berlin had said it might be once he was gone. I added this postscript to my preface:

> Isaiah Berlin died on 5 November 1997. The book had by then been passed for press, but not actually printed. No changes have been made to the body of the book, but the opportunity has been taken to add, as an epilogue, a slightly shortened version of the address Berlin gave in Jerusalem in May 1979 when he received the Jerusalem Prize for his contribution to the idea of freedom. This moving and perceptive piece [...] has always seemed to me, and to others whom I have consulted, to belong in the book, since it is in effect an autobiographical personal impression. I suggested to Berlin more than once that it should be reprinted in this natural context, but he always gave the characteristic reply that it seemed to him too personal, perhaps too self-regarding, to reappear in a collection in his lifetime; thereafter, however, I should do what I thought best. To my bitter regret, I am now free to add this finishing touch to the volume. (PI2 xiv; PI3 xxxvii)

In the same year *The Proper Study of Mankind* was published in America. I added a postscript to my preface for that edition too, ending with an echo of the words I quote from Plato at the end of the previous chapter:

> Since I am writing this only five weeks after Isaiah Berlin's death, I shall for a moment allow myself to relax an editor's customary, somewhat formal, manner, and express the hope that this retrospective anthology of the work he published in his lifetime may now fittingly take on an extra role: to serve as a tribute to a man I loved, a friend who, of the human beings I have known, was not only the most remarkable and

delightful, but also, in so many ways, the wisest, the surest in judgement, and the best.

I am writing this twenty years after Berlin's death. Throughout these years I continued with my task, publishing seven more volumes of his work posthumously between 1999 and 2006, and then preparing a four-volume edition of his selected letters (published between 2004 and 2015), with the indispensable help of those I acknowledge in my preface, especially my brilliant co-editors Jennifer Holmes and Mark Pottle.

Although my correspondence with Berlin had come to an end, I felt his presence strongly in the texts on which I was working daily. In some cases I was using recordings of his lectures, or handwritten material, and this helped to keep alive the sense that we were still working together on his publications. This feeling was reinforced by the availability and support of his family, especially his widow Aline (until her death in 2014, just short of her one-hundredth birthday) and his stepson the publisher Peter Halban, as well as other fellow trustees.

For much of the period since Berlin died I have struggled with debilitating depression. I believe that this would have afflicted me in any case, since depression runs in my family; but the timing of its onset makes it possible, or even likely, that it was exacerbated, at any rate initially, by the experience of bereavement that followed his death. He was not a father to me – my own wonderful father, who outlived him by two years, needed no substitute – but he was an intellectual and personal lodestar, an inspirational model of truly humane scholarship, an unmatched exemplar of one peculiarly attractive life-affirming form of human excellence and fullness of being.

References and Asides

Letters between Berlin and me are in my possession, and are cited by date, mostly given in the text.

PREFACE

1   *The Journals of Arnold Bennett*, ed. Newman Flower (London etc., 1932–3), ii (1911–21) 62, cited at HF2 9/1.

INTRODUCTION: THE GENIUS AND THE PEDANT

1   Oxford, Bodleian Library, MS. Fisher 147, fol. 60. The remark is about Frank Pakenham (later Lord Longford), a possible author of a Home University Library volume on Karl Marx, later written by IB. Fisher was one of the series editors, and Lever was at Thornton Butterworth, at that time the publishers of the series (later bought by Oxford University Press).
2   MI Tape 4.
3   *Sir Gawain and the Green Knight*, ed. J. R. R. Tolkien and E. V. Gordon (Oxford, 1925), Preface, v: 'a litter of italics, asterisks, and brackets, the trail of the passing editor'.
4   'Fragebogen' (a Proust Questionnaire), *Frankfurter Allgemeine Magazin*, 22 January 1993, 27.
5   'An Introduction to Philosophy', interview with Bryan Magee (the first of the fifteen interviews in the series *Men of Ideas*), recorded 23 May 1976, broadcast 18 January 1978, on BBC2 TV, published with revisions as 'Sir Isaiah Berlin on Men of Ideas and Children's Puzzles', *Listener*, 26 January 1978, 111–13 at 112, and with further revisions as 'An Introduction to Philosophy: Dialogue with Isaiah Berlin' in Bryan Magee (ed.), *Men of Ideas: Some Creators of Contemporary Philosophy* (London, 1978), 14–41 at 28–9. The version given here is a direct transcript of Berlin's spoken words.
6   'Menschen sind meine Landschaft', cited by Alfred Schuler, *Fragmente und Vorträge aus dem Nachlass* (Leipzig, 1940), 51. Cf. letter of 16 August 1968 to Marietta Tree, B 359.
7   Email to Henry Hardy, 28 May 2003. Cf. Nicholas Henderson, 'A Philosopher's Stroll', in BI.

I. THE BEGINNING

1 The last sentence (later discarded by Berlin) of the first draft of 'Meetings with Russian Writers in 1945 and 1956' (in PI).

2 The first issue appeared in 1973; the title was changed to *Romulus* in 1988, when the magazine was relaunched.

3 The evensong occurred on the nearest Sunday, 21 October. Another amateur performance of the anthem may be heard at http://bit.ly/2KqT2PZ.

4 Schenk (a Roman Catholic) and I (a non-believer) became churchwardens of St Frideswide's. When the Archdeacon of Oxford, Carl(yle) Witton-Davies, heard of this, he had us removed.

5 Reported by P. A. Sergeenko in his book on Tolstoy, *Tolstoy i ego sovremenniki* (Moscow, 1911), 13.

6 P. V. Annenkov, 'Zamechatel'noe desyatiletie' (1880), *Literaturnye vospominaniya* (Moscow, 1960), chapter 17, 218; P. V. Annenkov, *The Extraordinary Decade: Literary Memoirs*, ed. Arthur P. Mendel, trans. Irwin R. Titunik (Ann Arbor, 1968), 86.

2. A PROJECT IS BORN

1 Arnold Mallinson, *Quinquagesimo Anno: An Anthology of His Writings Published to Mark His Golden Jubilee Year in the Priesthood*, ed. Henry Hardy (Oxford, 1974: Robert Dugdale). The title is an allusion to Pope Pius XI's 1931 encyclical *Quadragesimo anno*, named, as encyclicals are, after its opening words: 'Quadragesimo anno expleto', 'Now that fifty years have passed' (since the appearance of an earlier encyclical on a similar theme). A second edition, retitled *Under the Blue Hood: A Hotchpotch 1923–1985*, appeared shortly after its author's death in 1985, and remains in print, as does Mallinson's other book, *The Leaning Tower, or Out of the Perpendicular* (Oxford, 1982). The blue hood is that of the author's Oxford BLitt degree.

2 Or 37 on the basis that one item was mistakenly attributed to IB, and a four-part and a two-part item were counted as six items. The letter is at MSB 186/100.

3 Letter of 2 February 1970, MSB 186/168. Berlin does not explicitly exclude material in previously published or forthcoming collections, but would surely have done so in the event.

4 See my preface to TCE.

5 MSB 209/229.

6 MSB 209/317–18.

7 MSB 210/53–4.

8 MSB 210/64.

9 MSB 210/67–8.

10 10 September 1972 to Julian Shuckburgh of Weidenfeld & Nicolson, MSB 368/229.

11 'A Glamorous Salon: Isaiah Berlin's Disparate Gifts', *Encounter* 43 no. 4 (October 1974), 67–72; this article listed many of IB's essays in a long footnote (70 note 6) which concluded suitably: 'if we are not to have Berlin's collected essays for some time still, it would be a useful second best if someone would produce a bibliography instead'.

12 'A Bibliography of Isaiah Berlin', *Lycidas* no. 3 (1975), 41–5 (and subsequent additions and recensions), now continually updated online at http://bit.ly/2OKdVbZ.

13 Berlin wrote to Philip Wiener of the *Journal of the History of Ideas* (11 October 1960) that 'it was written somewhere in the 1940s'. If this is right, it was written before *The Hedgehog and the Fox* (1951–3), and is thus IB's first substantial essay on the history of ideas after his book on Karl Marx (1939).

14 For example, an unsigned review of *The Collected Poems of G. K. Chesterton* that appeared in the *Pauline* (the magazine of St Paul's School, London) in 1928, identified to me as his by a master who was teaching at the school at the time; and a supplementary obituary note on Chaim Weizmann in *The Times* in 1952. The same thing happened later with some of IB's unpublished works, notably 'The Sense of Reality': when I showed him the typescript, corrected in his own hand, he asked: 'Are you sure it is by me?'

15 Though on 6 March I observed that 'there are two or three ways of classifying most items, and correspondingly many ways of subdividing the material for separate publication' – i.e. publication in separate volumes.

16 I cannot recall at what point we agreed that there would be introductions. But IB's letter of 21 November 1977 (58) provides a *terminus ante quem*.

17 Undated MS postcard, probably August 1979, apropos AC.

18 A later performance (18 May 2004), with a different soprano (Alison Eden) and a different accompanist (Matthew Gardner) may be heard at http://bit.ly/2AIZ9iU.

19 Source mislaid.

20 For more of this letter see A 12–14.

21 'Viewpoint', TLS, 26 December 1980, 1464.

3. PHILOSOPHICAL LETTERS, OR, COLD FEET

1 As originally published 'The Concept of Scientific History' consisted (apparently pointlessly) of 26 paragraphs, each preceded by a letter of the alphabet.

2 'Verification' was reprinted in G. H. R. Parkinson (ed.), *The Theory of Meaning* (London, 1968); 'Empirical Propositions and Hypothetical Statements' in Robert J. Swartz (ed.), *Perceiving, Sensing, and Knowing* (New York, 1965); 'The Concept of Scientific History' in Alexander V. Riasanovsky and Barnes Riznik (eds), *Generalizations in Historical Writing* (Philadelphia, 1963), and in William H. Dray (ed.), *Philosophical Analysis and History* (New York, 1966).

3 The essays on romanticism were 'European Unity and Its Vicissitudes' (1959) and 'The Apotheosis of the Romantic Will: The Revolt against the Myth of an Ideal World' (1975), both later included in CTH; I did not mention 'The Romantic Revolution: A Crisis in the History of Modern Thought' (1960), which had not by then been published, but I included this in SR in 1996. Some of the most important Jewish pieces were included in 2000 in *The Power of Ideas*; and the articles on Soviet Russia appeared in 2004 as *The Soviet Mind* (SM).

4 The second of two epigraphs at the head of 'What Do Sensation Terms Mean?', chapter 3 of my DPhil thesis on *Subjective Experience* (Oxford, 1976), is taken from 'Empirical Propositions and Hypothetical Statements': 'the meanings of words *are* affected, and often very deeply affected, by our explicit or implicit causal beliefs, and the analysis of what is meant by an expression may very well reveal all kinds of physical or social or psychological beliefs or assumptions prevalent in a given society, a change in which could affect the meaning of words' (CC2 70; see http://bit.ly/2zAH2eo, 120).

5 Cf. the remark once made, so IB related, by W. A. Spooner to Roy Harrod: 'Mr Harrod, you must not think you aren't the man you once used to think you were' (B 235).

6 Michael Dummett, 'What is a Theory of Meaning? II', in Gareth Evans and John McDowell (eds), *Truth and Meaning: Essays on Semantics* (Oxford, 1976).

4. SELECTED WRITINGS

1 R; the volumes were of course initially published in hardback.

2 R; a comment on E. R. Dodds's choice of IB to present his Duff Cooper prize for *Missing Persons: An Autobiography* (Oxford, 1977) in the year of its publication.

3 Letter to HH, 19 December 1980.

4 The serialisation appeared on 3–6 and 8–11 October 1972; Yellin-Mor's riposte on 18–20 October.

5 I know of fourteen English-language reviews. Had the book been published as a hardback as well as a paperback there may well have been more coverage. In 1969, paperbacks (then mostly reissues of earlier hardbacks) were regarded as poor relations in reviewing terms.

6 'Crescat pecunia Wolfsoniensis!' ('May Wolfson's money grow!') IB, MS note on letter from HH to IB, 9 June 1979. IB had retired from the Presidency of Wolfson on the Ides of March (15 March) 1975, my twenty-sixth birthday.

7 The last two paragraphs of this extract also appear at A 60–1.

8 'Editing Isaiah Berlin's Writings', *British Book News*, January 1978, 3, 5; reprinted in *Lycidas*, 34–5; also available at http://bit.ly/2Objj6T.

9 The quotation is slightly inaccurate, in true Berlinian fashion. In his *Something Ventured* (London etc., 1982), 2, C. M. ('Monty') Woodhouse had referred to IB as 'the only man in Oxford who could pronounce "epistemological" as one syllable'.

10 Noel Annan, 'A Man I Loved', in Hugh Lloyd-Jones (ed.), *Maurice Bowra: A Celebration* (London, 1974), 53.

11 FEL and VH. He had published only one 'proper' book, an intellectual biography of Karl Marx, but that had appeared long ago, in 1939, though it was still in print in its third (soon to be fourth, now fifth) edition. There were also some separately published essays (some of them mentioned in the next paragraph), and *The Age of Enlightenment*, an anthology drawn from the writings of Enlightenment philosophers, with an introduction and commentary (now available in a new edition at http://bit.ly/2NMukfy).

12 The title was chosen by IB after a dinner at King's College, Cambridge, in the room, if I remember, of the anthropologist Meyer Fortes. I had suggested that the anti-orthodoxy of its subjects should be referred to. Present were Fortes, IB, myself, Aileen Kelly and the economist Wynne Godley. I had driven IB to Cambridge for the occasion.

13 I should not have implied that IB knew Roosevelt, whom he never met.

14 Source mislaid.

15 Letter of 8 December 1977.

16 OUP held 'proposal files', of which this was one, on possible books that had been discussed but not yet taken under contract.

17 6 February 1978. The finished essay ran to 25,000 words, and was published in full (in English) only in the volume in question (hardly 'tucked away').

18 'Sir Isaiah's Brand of History', *Sunday Telegraph*, 15 January 1978, 14.

19 Undated MS note on the back of an envelope.

20 'The Men Between', *New Society*, 19 January 1978, 142.

21 2 February 1978.

22 Reviewing PSM in the TLS, 22 August 1997, 3.

23 PU to HH, 12 December 1997.

24 RR2 182. Seventeen years earlier, in a letter of 9 December 1980, IB had described Collini's review of PI (in 'Dream of the Seventh Dominion', *London Review of Books*, 4–17 December 1980, 19–20) as 'pretty empty – I don't know who Collini is, but what he said about Namier wasn't right, and while he was perfectly polite to me it was somehow patronising – in fact, I didn't like it', and later in the same letter as 'Collini's to me somewhat specious lucubrations'.

25 *Worldview*, October 1978, 52–3 at 52 and 53.

26 Apparently a typically 'improved' story: see B 506/2. (IB regularly used " ' for quotations.)

27 Letter of unknown date (the first page is missing). Zeldin's piece is in *Russian Review* 38 no. 3 (July 1979), 364–5.

28 Sophocles, *Antigone* 523: a discarded epigraph for Noel Annan's introduction to PI.

29 Some of IB's letters to Annan are included in the last volume of IB's correspondence, at A 86–90, 95–7, 98–100, 104–5.

30　Why hadn't I? Possibly because Hampshire had been my supervisor, and had not impressed me in that role. Nor had I been able to make much of his *Thought and Action* (London, 1959). Later I read his *Innocence and Experience* (London and Cambridge, Mass., 1989) and revised my ill-informed assessment. It is a wonderful book.

31　In 1986 IB described Peter Burke's *Vico* as (among other things) 'conscientious, painstaking', and Pat asked me 'what is the diff?' (PU to HH, 28 August [1986]).

32　In the same letter he commented drily on the blurb for *Against the Current* in the publisher's list, 'I think the reader may feel some slight astonishment at the fact that I should have written an essay on Moses as a thinker – still, let that be.' Moses was a copywriter's error for Moses Hess.

33　I have not (yet) found the letter in which IB made the observation referred to here.

34　I must have tactlessly and insensitively suggested that his caution about allowing me to include a piece on a Jewish subject might stem from some general embarrassment about being publicly identified as a Jewish author.

35　For example, Williams was strongly against the publication of PIRA, telling me that he found parts of it boring (I believe he also thought mistaken my publication of some of Berlin's extempore lectures). The same negative recommendation was made by a reader for Princeton University Press. Nevertheless, PIRA was published in 2006 with the welcome support of one of the other Berlin trustees, Alan Ryan.

36　In June 2018 my fellow trustees turned down a proposal from me for a new volume of essays, which would have included, inter alia, Berlin's writings on music.

37　I should perhaps make clear that I mostly made checks only when a reference was required for an explicit or implicit quotation. Had I tried to check every factual assertion, nothing would ever have reached publication. Inevitably this meant that I missed some errors, some of which have been subsequently pointed out, and corrected in later editions.

38　Anthony Arblaster, 'Vision and Revision: A Note on the Text of Isaiah Berlin's *Four Essays on Liberty*', *Political Studies* 19 no. 1 (1971), 81–6. This article does indeed include a discussion of IB's views on Marx, but only as evidenced in FEL: there is no reference to KM.

39　Source mislaid.

40　When Pat Utechin wrote to inform me of his change of heart she observed that her note was 'No doubt reqd. for the Collected Corres. of a Young Publisher and an Old Philosopher [...] PS Change title of Coll. Corres. to "of a Y. P. and old Ditherer" (or poss. "Dear Old Fool".)'

41　'Idee zu einer allgemeinen Geschichte in weltbürgerlicher Absicht' ['Idea for a Universal History with a Cosmopolitan Purpose'], *Kant's gesammelte Schriften* (Berlin, 1900–), viii 23.22.

42　I shall not rehearse his specific concerns here, but interested readers can read his letter to me of 9 June 1980, posted in the IBVL in http://bit.ly/2MkGRFU.

43　L. Kopylov, T. Pozdnyakova and N. Popova, '*I eto bylo tak*': *Anna Akhmatova i Isaiya*

Berlin ['*That's How It Was': Anna Akhmatova and Isaiah Berlin*] (St Petersburg, 2009). Cf. Josephine von Zitzewitz, 'That's How It Was: New Theories on Anna Akhmatova and Isaiah Berlin, Her "Guest from the Future"', 'Commentary', TLS, 9 September 2011, 14–15, and PI3 398/1.

44 The initial print run was 5,000, and the reprint 2,000. Hogarth Press Archive, Reading University, MS 2750/A/94, 163.

45 THES, 9 January 1981, 22.

46 'Countries of the Mind', TLS, 26 December 1980, 1459.

47 Later published as 'The Liberal Mind', *Encounter*, May 1981, 83–6.

5. AN UNREMARKABLE DECADE

1 For some of the background see http://bit.ly/2KqVxSn.

2 By a pleasing irony, I recently suggested writing a volume on Berlin himself for the series, now absorbed into Very Short Introductions, but the idea was turned down.

3 Nicola Badaloni, *Introduzione a G. B. Vico* (Milan, 1961).

4 First in a Spanish translation and then in English in *New Vico Studies* 17 (1999), 1–5 (with a reply by Burke, 7–10), and in TCE2.

5 In the former version it appeared first in the NYRB, 14 May 1998, 52–3, then in FL; the latter version was included in L in 2002.

6 Mislaid letter quoted in HH to IB, 16 September 1988.

7 The date he gave in 1960 is probably more accurate than the one he gave in 1988, though because of the war any work done in the 1940s must have been in the concluding years of the decade, so that the two dates aren't that far apart.

8 http://bit.ly/2ObhS8t.

6. THE CROOKED TIMBER OF HUMANITY

1 I did later find this (much massaged) quotation (CC2 293, CTH2 20, L 20, B 106/2, PSM2 16).

2 Berlin took Pass Moderations (an easier version of Honour Moderations, the first public exam) in Classics in December 1928, moving on to Greats, the second part of the Classics course, in Hilary Term 1929.

3 Oxford, Bodleian Library, Dep. Collingwood 12/6 fol. 3.

4 Attachment to letter of 18 April 1989.

5 28 April 1989. The biography was Richard A. Lebrun's *Joseph de Maistre: An Intellectual Militant* (Kingston and Montreal, 1988). On 21 April he had written: 'Reluctantly I agree to omit the fifty or so biographies of him which have appeared in the last thirty-five [*sc.* fifty] years since I began working on him.'

6   *Politiques et moralistes du dix-neuvième siècle*, 1st series (Paris, 1899), 41.

7   *Du Pape*, book 3, chapter 2, 'Liberté civile des hommes', *Oeuvres complètes de J. de Maistre* (Lyon/Paris, 1884–7) ii 338.

8   *Étude sur la souveraineté*, chapter 2, 'Origine de la société', ibid. i 318.

9   A. I. Gertsen, 'S togo berega', chapter 5, 'Consolatio', *Sobranie sochinenii v tridsati tomakh* (Moscow, 1954–66) vi 94; Alexander Herzen, *From the Other Shore*, trans. Moura Budberg, and *The Russian People and Socialism*, trans. Richard Wollheim, introduction by Isaiah Berlin (London, 1956), 108.

10 Even though, in the event, I worked on it full time, it took me twenty-five years to complete the job.

11 Howard Carter, diary, Sunday 26 November 1922. The Griffith Institute, Oxford, TAA Archive i.2.1. Available at http://bit.ly/2vA2omU.

12 See CTH2 149/4 (on 150).

13 Roger Scruton, 'Freedom's Cautious Defender', *The Times*, 3 June 1989, 10.

14 For the source of this phrase see RR2 151–2 and http://bit.ly/2vgQM8U s.v. 'bent twig, the'.

7. *THE MAGUS OF THE NORTH*

1   'Coolidge, William Augustus Brevoort (1850–1926)', in J. R. H. Weaver (ed.), *The Dictionary of National Biography, 1922–1930* (London, 1937), 211–12. Sent by HH to IB, 31 August 1990, with a note saying: 'In different ways, it reminds me of us both!'

2   CTH 157/1; in CTH2 (159/2, on 160), more informatively, she becomes Hélène Kuragin.

3   I have forgotten to whom he said or wrote this, but it burned itself into my memory when I heard of it from Pat Utechin.

4   IB's translation of a phrase in chapter 7 of Turgenev's *First Love*: see *First Love* [and] *A Fire at Sea* (London, 1982; New York, 1983), 40, and E 85/4.

5   Wittgenstein was not explicitly named, but evidently referred to. This similarity is also touched on at AE 275.

6   'The First Romantic? J. G. Hamann's Passionate Critique of the Enlightenment', TLS, 8 October 1993, 3–4; 'The Trouble with the Enlightenment', LRB, 6 January 1994, 12–13.

7   See esp. Oswald Bayer, *Zeitgenosse im Widerspruch: Johann Georg Hamann als radikaler Aufklärer* (Munich and Zurich, 1988).

8   *Der Magus in Norden: J. G. Hamann und der Ursprung des modernen Irrationalismus*, trans. Jens Hagestedt (Berlin, 1995). Berlin wrote a new foreword for this edition, resisting the new German view of Hamann.

9   In FIB2 and at http://bit.ly/2mg7xMF; see also the delivery text of the lecture in PIRA2.

8. *THE SENSE OF REALITY*

1   Berlin's family emigrated to England in 1921; in 1919 they were living in Petrograd.

2   On 30 October 1990 in the House of Commons, rejecting greater centralisation of power in Europe. Hansard, HC (series 6), vol. 178, col. 873: 'No. No. No.'

3   'The Artificial Dialectic' appeared as 'Generalissimo Stalin and the Art of Government' in *Foreign Affairs* in 1952; two pieces by IB published there in 1957, 'The Silence in Russian Culture' and 'The 'Soviet Intelligentsia' (the latter under the pseudonym 'L.'), written as a single essay, were reunited in SM as 'Soviet Russian Culture'.

4   Letter of 7 October 1991, A 429–30 at 429.

5   The first two are now in SR, the third in POI2.

6   I believe she issued the invitation on her own recognisance, only to discover that it was not thought suitable by her superiors. Was this an example of anti-Semitism at the BBC?

7   From the title page of the Authorised Version of the Bible.

8   In the event I added the extra quotations in the references section (with the help of Gunnar Beck), so that they should be available but undisruptive of the lecture text.

9   *Weltgeschichte* (Leipzig, 1881–8).

10 Berlin's own intended title, though it isn't the one that appears at the head of his text: letter to Anna Kallin, 12 February 1954, BBC Written Archives.

11 First in the *Oxford Magazine* in 2004, later in the appendix to POI2 in 2013.

12 In the end Gardiner wrote an introduction, and the volume was dedicated to Berlin's intimate friends Alfred and Irene Brendel.

13 This lecture appeared as 'La rivoluzione romantica: una crisi nella storia del pensiero moderno' in Isaiah Berlin, *Tra la filosofia e la storia delle idee: intervista autobiografica*, ed. Steven Lukes (Florence, 1994: Ponte alle Grazie), 97–122, and as 'Revolution der Romantik: eine grundlegende Krise in der neuzeitlichen Geistesgeschichte', *Lettre international* 34 (Autumn 1996), 76–83. It also appeared in Dutch as 'De romantische revolutie: een crisis in de geschiedenis van het moderne denken', *Nexus* 12 (1995), 16–42.

14 An earlier version of this talk was given at Robert F. Kennedy's Hickory Hill discussion group in 1962; on this occasion the group met, exceptionally, at the White House, at the request of the President, John F. Kennedy.

15 Those listed were eventually published in, respectively, the IBVL, PIRA, POI, SM, POI and SR (titled 'Kant as an Unfamiliar Source of Nationalism', and complementary to the essay on Tagore rather than an alternative to it).

16 Not true, Charles Wilson told me in 2018.

17 'The Wisdom of Isaiah', *Observer*, 15 June 1969, 29. The drawing is due to appear on a new edition of SR in 2019.

18 *Hamlet* 1.3.85.

19 This was the piece eventually published by the NYRB.

20 Blum wrote: 'je me sens partagé entre un lâche soulagement et la honte'. *Le Populaire*, 20 September 1938, 1.

21 In the edition by Stuart D. Warner (Indianapolis, 1993), see 93 ff., 118, 169, 172, 174, 180, 206, 225 and passim.

22 See also 136 above.

23 Of which a further example was his unprompted suggestion that we might print as a foreword what Noel Annan had written about him in his *Our Age: Portrait of a Generation* (London, 1990). After the saga of the PI introduction, this took my breath away, but it was a good idea, and Annan made some changes so that the piece fitted its new context better. Was Berlin trying to compensate Annan for his earlier intransigence?

24 This is a reference to 'The Concept of Scientific History', originally published in 1960 in the journal *History and Theory* (mistakenly importing into the title of the essay, it seems, the title of the journal) as 'History and Theory: The Concept of Scientific History'.

25 Claudina and Casimiro Botelho, the Portuguese couple who looked after them, were visiting their home in Torres Vedras in Portugal.

26 HH annotated at the time 'Actually finished before Italy'.

27 I duly said of this essay in my preface to the book: 'some of the matters it deals with have been touched on by Berlin in other essays, for example "The Hedgehog and the Fox" and "The Concept of Scientific History", but this is his most sustained treatment, and clearly merits a place in this collection' (SR1 x).

28 He insisted on seeing the proof, and of course made further corrections, after the book had gone to the publishers, which as usual maddened me. He wrote a note to Pat after marking these corrections: 'Please send this to Henry quickly. He will *moan* – can't be helped.'

29 In a letter of 7 May Berlin added: 'This is one of several articles which denounce me for inserting myself into Akhmatova's dedications. I don't mind whether Naiman does anything or not. Anyway, I propose to display lofty indifference to all this. Let them all dispute with each other: it makes no difference in the long run.' Annotating a letter from me of 3 April 1997, he made a similar point: 'my identity in this regard has been foolishly (& maliciously) disputed by Soviet writers – to be ignored'.

30 Viktor Esipov, '"Kak vremena Vespasiyana ..." (K probleme geroya v tvorchestve Anny Akhmatovoi 40–60-kh godov)' ['"In the Days of Vespasian ..." (On the Problem of the Hero in the Work of Anna Akhmatova from Her Forties to Her Sixties)'], *Voprosy literatury* 1995 no. 6, 57–85, argues that the poems by Anna Akhmatova normally regarded as dedicated to IB (see PI) are not in fact so dedicated, and that IB does not in fact have a role as 'the guest from the future' in *Poem Without a Hero*.

31 1965 is right: that is the year in which Akhmatova came to England to receive her honorary Oxford degree.

32 AN, friend and amanuensis of Akhmatova, replied to a similar attempt to deny that IB was the 'guest from the future' in 'Vot s kakoi tochki nuzhno smotret' na predmet!

Leonid Zykov, "Nikolay Punin – adresat i geroi liriki Anny Akhmatovoi", *Zvezda* [1995] no. 1' ['What a Way to Look at It! Leonid Zykov, "Nikolay Punin – the addressee and hero of Anna Akhmatova's poems", *Zvezda* [1995] no. 1'], *Segodnya*, 10 March 1995, 10.

33 Kralin, Mikhail, 'Ser Isaiya Berlin i "Gost' iz Budushchego"' ['Sir Isaiah Berlin and "the Guest from the Future"'], in his *Pobedivshee smert' slovo: stati ob Anne Akhmatovoi i vospominaniya o ee sovremennikakh* [*The Word That Has Vanquished Death: Essays on Anna Akhmatova and Memoirs on Her Contemporaries*] (Tomsk, 2000), 190–221. This article, drafted in 1990, was due to appear alongside a Russian translation of IB's 'Meetings with Russian Writers in 1945 and 1956' (in PI) – 'Vstrechi s russkimi pisatelyami v 1945 i 1956 godakh', trans. N. I. Tolstoy, *Zvezda*, 1990 no. 2 (February), 129–57 – but in the event the translation appeared without it. Kralin anticipates some of what is said in *I eto bylo tak*' (274/42).

9. NOT ANGELS OR LUNATICS: BERLIN ON HUMAN NATURE

1 I once told Hardie that I believed (mistakenly, I now think) that the mind and the brain were the same. 'The same what?' he shot back.

2 Cf. 'everything is ultimately psychological' (UD 99; cf. UD 101).

3 Does this phrase not let in some of the items banished by the Enlightenment?

4 '[C]apacity for choosing is intrinsic to rationality' (L 44); 'the notion of action would have to be reconsidered' (L 28).

5 It is not clear what makes a value or goal ultimate. Why is a plate of egg and chips not an ultimate goal? It seems artificial to say that it is (only) a means to satisfying hunger, as it may be preferred to other means of attaining this end, and desired for its own sake, irrespective of its hunger-satisfying properties. I leave this issue on one side, as its resolution is not required for the present exposition.

6 Why is the loss of value incurred by a pluralist choice more tragic than the loss of value that occurs when a (monist) utilitarian computes the best possible action in certain circumstances? Even if no more utility can be squeezed out of the situation, the loss of the further utility that has to be forgone may equally be regarded as tragic. This question too I leave aside.

7 In a fuller discussion one might address the tension between needs and desires, which of course do not necessarily coincide, and ask which, if either, should take priority in an account of basic humanity. My money is on the needs (cf. 189).

8 The whole letter from which this quotation is drawn is highly recommended as one of the fullest and clearest statements of Berlin's view.

9 First published as A. H. Maslow, 'A Theory of Human Motivation', *Psychological Review* 50 no. 4 (1943), 370–96.

10 See, e.g., Martha Nussbaum, *Women and Human Development: The Capabilities Approach* (Cambridge, 2000).

11 Tastes too arise from human nature: why then should they be regarded differently from values? Cf. 251–2.

10. PLURALISM AND RELIGION

1 *Ainsi soit-il, ou, Les jeux sont faits* (Paris, 1952), 174.

2 *De rerum natura* [*On the Nature of Things*] 1. 101.

3 In 2016 a Vietnamese publisher, under government pressure, unilaterally and without notice cut a number of items from their translation of Berlin's *Liberty*. As Berlin wrote, 'the first people totalitarians destroy or silence are men of ideas & free minds' (L 346).

4 17 April 1991. Here we need, of course, to take 'universalist beliefs' as a reference to religious universalism, not to universal values.

5 This exact phrase is not used by IB in his writings, but he does speak in the relevant sense of 'common values' – L 21 ('the common values of men'), 24; RR2 167–8; CTH2 317; POI2 14 – as he does in his reply to this letter (190 below and A 407) and in letters to Hendrik Hoetink, 15 June 1983 (A 205–10), and Beata Polanowska-Sygulska, 28 June 1987 (UD 100). He also uses the phrase 'central core' (AC2 1, UD 222) and writes of 'central human needs and purposes' and 'a nucleus of needs and goals' (L 54).

6 'England's Isaiah', *London Review of Books* 20 December 1990, 3–7, at 7 col. 1.

7 An allusion to the famous quotation from Joseph Schumpeter in the last paragraph of TCL: 'To realise the relative validity of one's convictions and yet stand for them unflinchingly is what distinguishes a civilised man from a barbarian.' Joseph A. Schumpeter, *Capitalism, Socialism and Democracy* (London, 1943), 243.

8 He also deployed another railway metaphor for Berlin's long, complex sentences, saying that they were like transcontinental trains that began life at a normal length but had additional sets of wagons coupled to them at stations along the route.

9 In *The Concept of Law* (Oxford, 1961) Hart argued that there was an empirical foundation to natural law, arising from the need of the individual, and group, to survive: 'our concern is with social arrangements for continued existence' (188); 'there are certain rules of conduct which any social organisation must contain if it is to be viable' (ibid.); 'Such universally recognised principles of conduct which have a basis in elementary truths concerning human beings, their natural environment, and aims, may be considered the *minimum content* of Natural Law' (189). The last quotation suggests adding *aims* to needs and interests as basic to morality.

10 Quentin Skinner's 'historical contextualism' holds that ideas have to be understood in their historical setting, not anachronistically: we cannot have a conversation with Plato as if he were in the same room, sharing our cultural and intellectual baggage. Works of political theory written in the past cannot be treated as if they were contemporary contributions to perennial debates. This view IB substantially rejects. Cf. 97–8, 191.

11 And yet he himself professed 'objective pluralism' (A 210, TCE2 245/1, PSM 390/1). However, his kind of objectivity was empirical, Hampshire's presumably metaphysical.

12 There is a problem about defining this moment, and relating claims of a constant human nature to it, but I do not explore this here.

13 Berlin captures this point well in describing J. G. Hamann's rejection of all necessary truth: 'No bridge is needed between necessary and contingent truths because the laws of the world in which man lives are as contingent as the "facts" in it. All that exists could have been otherwise if God had so chosen, and can be so still. God's creative powers are unlimited, man's are limited; nothing is eternally fixed, at least nothing in the human world – outside it we know nothing, at any rate in this life. The "necessary" is relatively stable, the "contingent" is relatively changing, but this is a matter of degree, not kind' (TCE2 363).

14 *The Persistence of Faith: Religion, Morality and Society in a Secular Age* (London, 1991). I cannot now find such a passage in the published text.

15 Sterling Lamprecht, 'The Need for a Pluralistic Emphasis in Ethics', *Journal of Philosophy, Psychology and Scientific Methods* 17 no. 21 (7 October 1920), 561–72 at 571.

16 Here Berlin seems to backtrack, regrettably, on what he had said before about the worldwide reach of the core (191).

17 Are we perhaps once again concerned here with an ambiguity between the universal values of the core ('the universal validity of one's own views') and the belief that a given value system is universally true ('Certainly a universalist cannot be a pluralist')? If so we need a distinction between, respectively, *universal values* and *universalist morality*. Otherwise why isn't Berlin contradicting himself here? Moreover, there is no reason why a universalist should not be a *value* pluralist, which makes the first part of Berlin's sentence false unless he is thinking of *cultural* pluralism, as perhaps he is. Finally, there is a sense in which the last part of the sentence can be true, if it amounts to the claim that the doctrine of pluralism is universally true. The sentence as a whole is a clear example of the need for more clarity.

18 The title (derived from a remark by Martin Hollis) of an article by Steven Lukes: *Critical Review of International Social and Political Philosophy* 4 no. 4 (2001), 35–54. For Hollis's remark see his 'Is Universalism Ethnocentric?' in Christian Joppke and Steven Lukes (eds), *Multicultural Questions* (Oxford, 1999), 36.

19 I think it is, as I have said (201): but I did not grasp this at the time.

20 But in fact he doesn't (quite) say this?

21 TCE2 403; Johann Georg Hamann, *Briefwechsel*, ed. Walther Ziesemer and Arthur Henkel (Wiesbaden and Frankfurt, 1955–79), v 177.18.

22 *Herders Sämmtliche Werke*, ed. Bernhard Suphan (Berlin, 1877–1913), v 509.

23 'The Assault on the French Enlightenment: 1. Herder and Historical Criticism' (the first of IB's John Danz Lectures, University of Washington, 22 February 1971), http://bit.ly/2uzaPPo.

24 I owe this description of religion to Alan Ryan.

25 'The Tangled Roots of Nazism', *Dimensions: A Journal of Holocaust Studies* 62 (1991), 26–8.

26 The issue in Algeria was whether a Muslim majority might properly vote for an undemocratic Islamic government. On 12 January 1992 Algeria cancelled the second round of its parliamentary elections, the first free elections that the country had seen, to prevent the fundamentalist Islamic Salvation Front (FIS) party, the clear victor in the first round of voting, from coming to power, and the FIS was officially dissolved on 4 March by the military government that had assumed power as Algeria descended into civil war.

27 'I should positively and deliberately refuse to allow myself to be interrogated on any subject whatever of purely religious opinion. I do this on principle. I conceive that no one has any right to question another on his religious opinions.' Letter of 21 June 1865 to Charles Westerton, published in Charles Westerton, 'Mr John Stuart Mill and Westminster', letter of 23 June 1865, *Times*, 24 June 1865, 5e.

28 'When Lord Melbourne had accidentally found himself the unwilling hearer of a rousing Evangelical sermon about sin and its consequences, he exclaimed in much disgust as he left the church: "Things have come to a pretty pass when religion is allowed to invade the sphere of private life!"' One Who Has Kept a Diary [George W(illiam) E(rskine) Russell], *Collections and Recollections* (London, 1898), 79.

29 'God or nature', Spinoza's equivocal characterisation of the universe, sometimes thought atheistic or pantheistic.

30 It was Novalis, not Arnold, who first so described Spinoza, on 11 February 1800: 'Spinoza ist ein Gott-trunkener Mensch.' Novalis, *Schriften*, ed. Ludwig Tieck and Fr[iedrich] Schlegel, 5th ed. (Berlin, 1837), [ii, comprising] part 2 [Zweiter Theil], Fragmente vermischten Inhalts, III. Moralische Ansichten, 261.

31 'Het ware pluralisme', *Nexus* 1995 no. 13, 74–86. It is also available in English in OM and online at http://bit.ly/2LRa13w.

11. THE MORAL CORE AND THE HUMAN HORIZON

1 Oxford, 1996; reissued with revisions as *The Penguin Dictionary of Philosophy* (London etc., 1997). IB's article is at 51–2 and 67–9 in the successive editions. His original text appears as 'My Philosophical Views' at CC2 277–83.

2 'Quod ubique, quod semper, quod ab omnibus creditum est.' *The Commonitorium of Vincentius of Lérins* (434 CE), ed. Reginald Stewart Moxon (Cambridge, 1915), 2. 3 (p. 10, lines 6–7).

3 'Isaiah Berlin in Conversation with Steven Lukes' (1991), *Salmagundi* no. 120 (Fall 1998), 52–134 at 104–5.

4 A slight exaggeration of Vico's 'a gran pena' ('with great difficulty'), *New Science*, book 1, section 4, 'Method', end of first paragraph.

5 See OM 296–7, recapitulated in what follows here.

6 This seems to Crowder to be the general thrust of Berlin's 'Alleged Relativism in Eighteenth-Century European Thought' (in CTH). There Berlin argues that pluralists, such as Vico and Herder, should be distinguished from relativists. While relativists are confined within the 'windowless boxes' of particular perspectives, pluralists 'insist on our need and ability to transcend the values of our own culture or nation or class' (CTH 85), and to evaluate other cultures – presumably by reference to non-relative, i.e. universal, values. What makes this possible is the ability to '"feel oneself into" the mentality of remote societies' (CTH 82). The capacity for cross-cultural empathy is thus evidence, for Crowder, of the universality of value that underwrites that capacity, and points to the truth of pluralism rather than relativism.

7 Edward Westermarck, *Ethical Relativity* (London, 1932), 188–9.

8 Ronald H. McKinney, 'Towards a Postmodern Ethics: Sir Isaiah Berlin and John Caputo', *Journal of Value Inquiry* 26 (1992) no. 3, 395–407. Berlin's reply appears ibid. no. 4, 557–60, and is reprinted in CTH2 as 'Reply to Ronald H. McKinney'.

9 I don't know which passage this was, but it will have been (part of) one of the following: *From Max Weber: Essays in Sociology*, trans. and ed. H. H. Gerth and C. Wright Mills (New York, 1946), 'Politics as a Vocation' (1918), 77–128 at 117, 126, and 'Science as a Vocation' (1918), 129–56 at 147–8, 151–3; 'The Meaning of "Ethical Neutrality" in Sociology and Economics', in Max Weber, *The Methodology of the Social Sciences*, trans. and ed. Edward A. Shils and Henry A. Finch (Glencoe, Illinois, 1949), esp. 17–18. At least the last of these passages was brought to my attention by Roger Hausheer. Even more strikingly Berlinian passages in articles by Sterling Lamprecht in 1920–1, and by A. P. Brogan in 1931, came to my notice only after Berlin's death. I long to know whether he read them; if not, the similarities, in wording as well as in content, are hard to credit. See http://bit.ly/2NPlxcQ.

10 Another example that seems not to fit Crowder's interpretation.

11 But neither version of this principle is compatible with Berlin's inclusion of malignity within the horizon, still less within the core. On this basis the whole diagram might need to be abandoned or radically reconsidered.

12 *Political Studies* 42 (1994), 293–303. Berlin wrote a reply with Bernard Williams, ibid., 306–9 (repr. in CC2).

13 Ludwig Wittgenstein, *Philosophical Investigations*, trans. G. E. M. Anscombe (Oxford, 1953), part 1, § 242. This characteristically gnomic utterance may not be intended to mean what I here take it to mean; but it expresses it quite well.

14 I take this to be a reference to 'basic liberty', free will, a necessary condition of all choice and free action, and of all pursuit of value.

15 Russell, following Santayana, speaks of a non-rational 'animal faith' underlying any claims to knowledge; James of 'temperaments' that determine our philosophical views. Bertrand Russell, *History of Western Philosophy* (New York, 1945; London, 1946), chapter 23, 2nd paragraph. William James, *Pragmatism: A New Name for Some*

Old Ways of Thinking: Popular Lectures on Philosophy (New York, 1907), lecture 1 ('temperaments' introduced at 6). For 'animal faith' see George Santayana, *Scepticism and Animal Faith: Introduction to a System of Philosophy* (London, 1923).

16 There was a discontinuity in Berlin's dictation here. My minimal conjecture may be less than he said.

12. THE END

1 Peacocke was unaware of the even more striking account of this episode in an interview with Frans Boenders: see CC2 294–6.

2 'ἥδε ἡ τελευτή, ὦ Ἐχέκρατες, τοῦ ἑταίρου ἡμῖν ἐγένετο, ἀνδρός, ὡς ἡμεῖς φαῖμεν ἄν, τῶν τότε ὧν ἐπειράθημεν ἀρίστου καὶ ἄλλως φρονιμωτάτου καὶ δικαιοτάτου.' Plato, *Phaedo* 118a.

Biographical Glossary

J. L. AUSTIN
(1911–60)

White's Professor of Moral Philosophy and Fellow of Corpus Christi College, Oxford, 1952–60.

A. J. AYER
(1910–89)

Wykeham Professor of Logic and Fellow of New College, Oxford, 1959–78.

HUGO BRUNNER
(b. 1935)

Publisher; sales director, Chatto and Windus, 1966–76; Deputy General Publisher, OUP, 1977–9; managing director, Chatto and Windus, 1979–83, chair 1983–5; Lord Lieutenant of Oxfordshire 1996–2008.

R. H. S. CROSSMAN
(1907–74)

Academic, journalist and Labour politician; Fellow and Tutor in Philosophy, New College, 1930–7; gave IB his first academic post as a lecturer in philosophy at New College in 1932.

DONALD DAVIDSON
(1917–2003)

Leading US philosopher, moved from Rockefeller to Chicago in 1976.

CECILIA DICK
(1927–95)

Domestic Bursar of Wolfson; her husband Marcus Dick had helped IB compile *The Age of Enlightenment*, and her daughter Cressida is at the time of writing Commissioner of the Metropolitan Police Service.

MICHAEL DUMMETT
(1925–2011)

Fellow of All Souls College, Oxford, 1950–79; later (1979–92) Wykeham Professor of Logic.

MARTIN GREEN
(1932–2015)

Poet and publisher.

STUART HAMPSHIRE
(1914–2004)

Philosopher, Warden of Wadham College 1970–84; one of my doctoral supervisors.

ROGER HAUSHEER
(b. 1945)

Germanist and historian of ideas; Wolfson graduate student 1969–80; friend, admirer and peerless interpreter of IB, on whom he has written several pieces, including introductions to AC, CTH (lost) and PSM (co-editing the latter volume with HH).

AILEEN KELLY (b. 1942) — Russianist, co-editor with HH of RT; Fellow, King's, Cambridge, since 1975. She writes that IB 'inspired my interest in Russian thinkers' and that his 'moral vision has been the constant standard by which I have measured their failings and their strengths': *Toward Another Shore: Russian Thinkers between Necessity and Chance* (New Haven and London, [1998]), ix.

WILLIAM KNEALE (1906–90) — White's Professor of Moral Philosophy, Oxford, 1960–6.

MARGARET MACDONALD (1907–56) — Research fellow, Girton College, Cambridge, 1934–37; librarian, St Hilda's College, Oxford, 1937–46.

DAVID PEARS (1921–2009) — Student (i.e. Fellow), Christ Church, Oxford, 1960–1988; one of my doctoral supervisors.

ANTHONY ('TONY') QUINTON (1925–2010) — Philosopher; President, Trinity College, Oxford, 1978–87.

GILBERT RYLE (1900–76) — Waynflete Professor of Metaphysical Philosophy and Fellow of Magdalen College, Oxford, 1945–68; editor of Mind 1947–71. His *The Concept of Mind* appeared, like the author of the present work, in 1949.

CHRISTOPHER SCHENK (b. 1949) — A fellow philosophical graduate student at Wolfson College, and nephew of Hans Schenk, one of the College's original Fellows. He had been a PPE undergraduate at Jesus, and Treasurer of the Junior Common Room there while a goldfish held the presidency.

J. O. URMSON (1915–2012) — Fellow and Tutor in Philosophy, Corpus Christi College, Oxford, 1959–78; one of my undergraduate tutors.

GEOFFREY WARNOCK (1923–95) — Philosopher; Principal of Hertford College, Oxford, 1971–88.

MARY-BARBARA ZELDIN (1922–81) — Professor of Philosophy and Religion, Hollins College, Virginia, 1970–81.

Index

Douglas Matthews

An asterisk indicates an entry in the biographical glossary on pages 285–6

room at All Souls to HH, 109; on own reputation and character, 131–3; Oxford degree (1928–9), 105, 275 n2 (ch. 6); and philosophical definition, 6; portrait, 33; publication of collected essays proposed, 24–5, 62–3; rejects Hausheer's introduction to *The Crooked Timber of Humanity*, 107–9; as religious non-believer, 184–5, 217–22; on religious practice, 186; retires from Presidency of Wolfson College, 33, 272 n6 (ch. 4); revises will, 101; royalties income, 110, 114, 165; self-portrait for Mautner's *Dictionary of Philosophy*, 228; on variety of moral values, 230–4; writes introductions to Herzen's works, 80; writing style, 15–16, 20; writings on music, 274 n36

Best, Andrew Hall Montagu, 27, 35, 38, 50, 118

Blum, (André) Léon, 158

Bodleian Library: IB's papers deposited at, 113, 134

Book of Isaiah, The (IB), 114

Bookseller (magazine), 39

Botelho, Claudina and Casimiro, 278 n25

Bowra, (Cecil) Maurice: conversation and writing, 16; Edmund Wilson on, 142; IB writes on, 61; on IB's award of OM, 60

Bowra Lecture (1980), 65, 78–9

Brandes, Georg (*né* Morris Cohen), 59

Brendel, Alfred and Irene, 277 n12

British Book News, 56, 59

British Broadcasting Corporation (BBC): IB broadcasts on, 29, 137; suspected anti-Semitism, 277 n6

Brock, Michael George, 14, 30, 64, 101

Brodsky, Iosif Aleksandrovich, 166

Brogan, Albert Perley, 283 n9

Bruner, Jerome Seymour ('Jerry'), 63

* Brunner, Hugo Laurence Joseph, 39, 46, 87, 107

Bryn Mawr College *see* Flexner Lectures

Bullock, Adrian Charles Sebastian, 88

Bullock, Alan Louis Charles, Baron, 101, 118, 123, 129

Burke, (Ulick) Peter: on Vico, 96–7

Callil, Carmen Thérèse, 107

Cambridge Companion to Isaiah Berlin, The, 147

Caputo, John D., 236

Carnarvon, George Edward Stanhope Molyneux Herbert, 5th Earl of, 111

Carpenter, Humphrey William Bouverie, 96

Carson, Peter, 56

Carter, Howard, 111

Carver, Terrell Foster, 156

Cecil, Lord (Edward Christian) David, 7, 142

censorship, 221

Chatto & Windus (publishers), 46, 107

Chesterton, Gilbert Keith: *Collected Poems* reviewed by IB, 271 n14

Chichele professorship (Oxford), 137

Chomsky, (Avram) Noam, 35

Christianity, 195, 197–9; and belief, 215

Christie, Agatha Mary Clarissa, Lady Mallowan, 125

Chukovskaya, Lidiya Korneevna, 65

Churchill, Winston Leonard Spencer-, 61, 84, 113

clericalism, 223, 225

Cohen, Gerald Allan ('Jerry'), 143, 146

Collingwood, Robin George: quotes Kant on crooked timber of humanity, 105

Collini, Stefan, 66–7, 273 n24

Columbia Law Review, 88

Journal of the History of Ideas, 30
Jowett, Benjamin, 142

Kallin, Anna Samoilovna ('Niouta'), 135, 137
'Kant as an Unfamiliar Source of Nationalism' (IB), 164, 277 n15
Kant, Immanuel: belief in God, 221, 223; 'crooked timber' quotation, 91, 105, 170; IB lectures on, 164; and objective morality, 256; on treating others with respect, 175; and values, 177; Weber on, 245
Karl Marx (IB), 86, 271 n13, 273 n11
Keats, John, 65
Kee, Robert, 95
* Kelly, Aileen Mary: admiration for IB's work, 57, 59; attends King's College Cambridge meeting, 273 n12; co-edits IB's Russian works, 35; urges IB to publish *Russian Thinkers*, 64; writes introduction to IB's *Russian Thinkers*, 60, 68, 75, 108
Kennan, George Frost, 8
Kennedy, Jacqueline Lee Bouvier (*née* Bouvier; *later* Onassis): correspondence with IB, 113
Kennedy, John Fitzgerald, 277 n14
Kennedy, Robert Fizgerald, 277 n14
Kermode, (John) Frank, 247
Keynes, John Maynard, Baron, 8, 72
King's College, Cambridge, 273 n12
Kinnock, Neil, Baron, 85
* Kneale, William Calvert, 47
Kralin, Mikhail Mikhailovich, 165, 279 n33

Lamprecht, Sterling Power, 283 n9
language: and human naure, 174
Lebrun, Richard Allen, 116
Lee, Hermione, 92

Leo X, Pope (*né* Giovanni di Lorenzo de' Medici), 153
Lessing, Gotthold Ephraim: *Nathan the Wise*, 154
'Lessons of History, The' (IB), 147
Lever, Tresham Joseph Philip, 1, 269 n1
Lewis, Clarence Irving, 104
liberalism: and free will, 174–5; and liberty, 179; and pluralism, 180, 247–9, 253, 254–5, 264
liberty: negative and positive, 174
Liberty Fund conference (Oxford, 1994), 158
'Life and Opinions of Moses Hess, The' (IB), 31
Lilla, Mark: 'The Trouble with the Enlightenment', 129, 276 n6
Lindsay, Alexander Dunlop, 1st Baron, 59
Locke, John, 223; *A Letter concerning Toleration*, 155
'Logical Translation' (IB), 51, 53
Lucretius (Titus Lucretius Carus): *De rerum natura*, 13, 183
Lukes, Steven Michael, 145–6, 161–2, 282 n3
Lycidas (Wolfson College magazine), 14, 29, 63

Macaulay, Thomas Babington, Baron, 142
* MacDonald, Margaret, 51, 53
Machiavelli, Niccolò, 36, 61, 85
Mack, Eric, 264
McKinney, Ronald Harold: 'Towards a Postmodern Ethics: Sir Isaiah Berlin and John Caputo', 236
MacRae, Donald Gunn, 46
Magee, Bryan Edgar, 6, 111; (ed.) *Men of Ideas: Some Creators of Contemporary Philosophy*, 269 n5

This really is the end.
IB to Michael Ignatieff, 30 December 1996 (A555)